Modern
French
Politics

In memory of Nick Robin, 1955–1997

Modern French Politics

Analysing Conflict and Consensus since 1945

Nick Hewlett

Polity Press

First published 1998 by Polity Press
in association with Blackwell Publishers Ltd.

Editorial office:
Polity Press
65 Bridge Street
Cambridge CB2 1UR, UK

Marketing and production:
Blackwell Publishers Ltd
108 Cowley Road
Oxford OX4 1JF, UK

Published in the USA by
Blackwell Publishers Inc.
Commerce Place
350 Main Street
Malden, MA 02148, USA

ISBN 0–7456–1119–2
ISBN 0–7456–1120–6 (pbk)

A catalogue record for this book is available from the British Library and has been applied for from the Library of Congress.

Typeset in 10 on 12.5 pt Times
by Wearset, Boldon, Tyne and Wear
Printed in Great Britain by TJ International, Padstow, Cornwall

This book is printed on acid-free paper.

Contents

List of Tables and Figure   viii

Acknowledgements   ix

Abbreviations   xi

1 Introduction   1

2 A History of Conflict and Revolt   11

France and modernity   13
Domestic conflict and international relations   20
Political ideology and political parties   22
The polarization of the labour movement and the
    patronat   26
Republicanism and manifestations of a more
    moderate history   28
An exceptional history?   33

3 Political Exceptionalism, 1945–1981   36

Consensus politics in Western Europe since 1945   37
    Britain   39
    The Federal Republic of Germany   42
    Sweden   44
French politics in the post-war era   46
The persistence of radicalism and the absence of
    Fordist compromise   56

4 The End of Exceptionalism? The 1980s and 1990s   60

The decline of overt conflict   63
    The Socialist Party in government   63
    The Communist Party   70
    The decline of traditional Gaullism   73
    Class combativeness and industrial action 78
    Limits to the decline of conflict   81
Explaining consensus: the 1980s as a moment of
    tripartite harmony   85
    The labour movement   85
    Government–capital relations   87
Consensus beyond tripartism   90

5 Social Democracy and the Left   92

The history of social democracy   94
The nature of the left in France   98
Characterizing the Socialist Party   103
A crisis of social democracy?   113

6 The Paradoxes of Gaullist Modernization   119

Authoritarian aspects of de Gaulle's rule   121
The progress of political stability and democracy   128
De Gaulle's foreign policy and the uses of *grandeur*   132
De Gaulle and the economy: modernization from
    above   134
The unevenness of socio-economic change   139

7 The Historical Significance of May 1968   146

Régis Debray and Gilles Lipovetsky: the ruse of
    reason   150
The results of May   159
The spirit of May and the Socialist years   166
Locating May historically   168

8 The Waning of Intellectual Commitment   170

The place of intellectuals in post-war political life   172
The decline of the left intellectual   181
The re-emergence of liberal political thought   187

9 Conclusions   193

The end of history   196
Fordism and post-Fordism: the regulation school   200
Theorizing change   207

Appendices   215
A Regimes in France since 1789   215
B Results of national elections in the Fourth
and Fifth Republics   216
    1 Legislative elections in the Fourth Republic   216
    2 Legislative elections in the Fifth Republic   217
    3 Presidential elections in the Fifth Republic   218
C Presidents of the Republic and Prime
Ministers, 1959–1997   219

Bibliography   220

Index   237

Tables and Figure

Tables

Table 2.1 Agricultural workforce as a percentage of the total working population, 1820–1910   17

Table 2.2 Annual rate of growth of total output, 1870–1961, various countries   18

Table 2.3 Coal output per head and industrial output per head, 1913, for the UK, Germany and France   19

Table 3.1 For and against mainstream politics. Votes cast in legislative elections, 1946–1958   48

Table 3.2 The 1956 legislative election   49

Table 4.1 Socialist results at national elections, 1956–1997   69

Table 4.2 Communist Party results at national elections, 1956–1997   71

Table 4.3 Extreme right results at national elections, 1958–1997   81

Table 5.1 Communist and Socialist voting strengths, legislative elections 1924–1997   102

Table 5.2 Correspondence between voters' sectors of work and voting intentions in the French legislative elections of 1988   105

Table 5.3 Correspondence between voters' occupations and voting in the French legislative elections of 1988   105

Table 5.4 Correspondence between voters' occupations and voting in the French legislative elections of 1993   106

Table 5.5 Membership of the Socialist Party, according to party sources, 1971–1994   115

Table 6.1 Percentage of total votes and seats won by Communists and Socialists in legislative elections, 1956–1968   126

Table 6.2 Sociological composition of the Gaullist electorate, legislative elections, 1962, 1967, 1973   131

Table 6.3 Evolution of the geographical structure of French trade, 1949–1973   138

Table 6.4 Average annual rate of growth in various OECD countries, 1958–1969   142

Figure

Figure 6.1 Balance between left and right in national elections, 1958–1978   125

Acknowledgements

As with most books, there are too many people who have influenced or helped in some other way with this one to name them all here. I would nevertheless like to thank Martyn Cornick, David Drake, Jill Forbes, Robert Gildea, Emmanuel Godin, the late Peter Morris and Paul Webb for reading and commenting either on draft chapters of the book or on earlier papers which influenced it. The anonymous reader for Polity Press made some very useful comments on the penultimate version of the manuscript. I would like to thank in particular my editor Tony Giddens, not only for reading the manuscript and commenting helpfully in the last stages, but for having been so encouraging and prompt several years ago when I sent the initial proposal to Polity. I would also like to thank participants at various research seminars and conferences where I presented some of the ideas which appear in the book, for their interesting reflections or criticisms. These took place at the Universities of Sheffield, Reading, Loughborough and New York, at Merton College Oxford, Royal Holloway College London, London Guildhall University and Oxford Brookes University. Needless to say, although many people have made useful comments and therefore influenced the outcome, the final result is my responsibility alone. (Translations from the French, unless otherwise indicated, are also my own.)

An earlier version of chapter 2 appeared in a book edited by Renate Günther and Jan Windebank entitled *Violence and Conflict in the Politics and Society of Modern France* (Mellen Press, 1995) and for parts of chapters 3 and 5 I drew on a paper published by Loughborough University's European Research Centre, entitled 'Consensus, Socialism and Social Democracy in France' (Studies in European Culture and Society, Paper 10, 1993).

I would like to thank my colleagues at Oxford Brookes University for allowing me the time to write.

The day-to-day process of writing this book was an overwhelmingly enjoyable experience for me, although inevitably hard at times. Above all it will always be associated with the happiness of being with my children Emily and Gus in their early years. Special thanks to them and to Julia, for many things.

Nick Hewlett

Abbreviations

CBI	Confederation of British Industry
CDU	Christlich-Demokratische Union
CERES	Centre d'Etudes, de Recherches, et d'Education Socialistes
GDP	Gross domestic product
CFDT	Confédération Française Démocratique du Travail
CGT	Confédération Générale du Travail
CGT-FO	Confédération Générale du Travail–Force Ouvrière
CNPF	Conseil National du Patronat Français
CSU	Christlich-Soziale Union
DATAR	Delégation à l'aménagement du territoire et à l'action régionale
DGB	Deutsche Gewerkschaftsbund
EDF	Electricité de France
EEC	European Economic Community
EU	European Union
FDP	Freie Demokratische Partei
FGDS	Fédération de la Gauche Démocratique et Socialiste
FLN	Front de Libération Nationale
FN	Front National (National Front)
FO	Force Ouvrière
FRG	Federal Republic of Germany
GNP	Gross national product
LO	Landsorganisationen
MRG	Mouvement des Radicaux de Gauche
MRP	Mouvement Républicain Populaire
NATO	North Atlantic Treaty Organization
OAS	Organisation de l'Armée Secrète
OECD	Organization for Economic Cooperation and Development
ORTF	Office de la Radiodiffusion-Télévision Française
PCF	Parti Communiste Français (Communist Party)
PS	Parti Socialiste (Socialist Party)
PSU	Parti Socialiste Unifié
RATP	Régie Autonome des Transports Parisiens
RFA	République fédérale allemande
RGR	Rassemblement des Gauches Républicaines
RMI	*Revenu minimum d'insertion*
RPF	Rassemblement du Peuple Français
RPR	Rassemblement pour la République

SAC	Service d'Action Civique
SAF	Svenska Arbetsgivareföreningen
SAP	Socialdemocratiska Arbetarpartiet
SFIO	Section Française de l'Internationale Ouvrière
SMIC	Salaire Minimum Interprofessionnelle de Croissance
SPD	Sozialdemokratische Partei Deutschlands
TUC	Trades Union Congress
UDF	Union pour la Démocratie Française
UDR	Union des démocrates pour la république
UDSR	Union démocratique et socialiste de la résistance
UGSD	Union de la gauche socialiste et démocrate

1
Introduction

Modern French political history is shot through with discord, conflict, revolt and violence. Since 1789, revolution, *coup d'état*, invasion, foreign occupation, street fighting and strikes have formed the tumultuous backdrop to France's governmental, parliamentary and party political life. Radicalism on both the left and the right has contributed to France's reputation for being exceptionally conflictual, compared with many other countries of Western Europe. When Mitterrand and the Socialists finally came to power in 1981, they came in the spirit of the French tradition with promises to sweep away the old order and replace it with a society which was more just than France had ever seen before; nationalizations, job creation, wealth tax, new rights for individuals and popular democracy were to change ordinary people's lives fundamentally and forever. At home and abroad, the political right and business people watched aghast as France's first ever wholly left government, including Communists, embarked upon the promised programme of popular emancipation. But they need not have feared. Within a few years the left had embraced capitalism with as much fervour as previous governments of the right and had proved itself far more able than its governmental predecessors to introduce changes in the interests of business. Moreover, the Socialists presided over changes which appeared to bring the conditions of lasting political consensus to France for the first time for many years, and perhaps ever, with changes including the decline of the Communist Party and the trade unions, the Socialist Party's own rapid shift to the centre and the increased legitimacy of the Constitution of the Fifth Republic. Paradoxically, it was the left that had achieved a situation where politics in France were apparently no longer exceptionally conflictual compared with politics in other advanced capitalist countries.

I was prompted to write this book because I agree to an extent with various other observers of French politics that since the early 1980s there is indeed a series of significantly different landmarks which define the French political landscape, and which together amount to greater consensus. My primary task is therefore to explore historically the reasons for this change, including conflictual and consensual tendencies before Mitterrand's arrival at the Elysée Palace. But I have major reservations in relation to the way in which many writers approach the question of the 'normalization' of politics in France.

First, I am struck by the virtual absence of any attempt to apply an overarching theoretical framework to developments since the early 1980s and believe that it is necessary to begin to relate the observed facts to a broader, more theoretical view of the development of politics in order to suggest the reasons for and therefore limits to the decline of conflict in recent years. Many contemporary writers on government and politics in industrialized countries enable the reader to understand the mechanisms of the political systems and trends in the evolution of voting behaviour, public opinion, public policy, pressure groups and so on. But to relate this more empirical approach to the study of politics to a historical, analytical framework which highlights certain medium- and longer-term trends in socio-economic and political evolution is more rare. For the particular project of this book, historically defined notions of political conflict and consensus are necessary if any overall conclusions are to be drawn from the events of the last decade or two in France. It is necessary to look at some major historical moments in French political history and to attempt to tease out both their profounder significance and the effect they had on France. As far as I know there is no other systematic attempt to consider the more consensual contemporary political situation in France both in a historical and in a more theoretical context.

Second, other writers tend to exaggerate the extent of change since the early 1980s and seem therefore to imply that the new signs of consensus show that conflict in French politics and society has necessarily been overcome in a profound way, rather than in what is perhaps a rather superficial way. In fact, social and other forms of conflict inform the political life of all advanced capitalist societies and to attempt to explain new-found consensus in the conventional party political realm requires exploring the relationship between political change and social conflict. It involves taking a critical view of 'normalization', rather than an unquestioning one.

Next, this project was prompted by my unwillingness to accept the notion that apparently consensual politics reflect widespread and real satisfaction with political and social developments in France. Even in the mid-1980s, which was probably the most centre-oriented, consensual moment, there were strong signs that protest was alive and well. Although the French now vote in large numbers for the centre-right and centre-left, whose programmes differ relatively little from each other, and although opinion polls suggest that many voters view the centre-left and the centre-right as almost one and the same, the French still vote in large numbers for the protest-oriented parties; in the first round of the Presidential elections of 1995, 37 per cent of the electorate voted for candidates who clearly situated themselves in opposition to the mainstream right and left, falling into the categories of extreme right, Communist, Trotskyist and Green. (In the 1997 legislative elections the total for these groups was 33 per cent, although the Communists were in alliance with the Socialists.) Just as importantly, according to opinion polls in recent years, politicians are widely regarded as both untrustworthy and corrupt, a view which the frequent political scandals of the 1980s and 1990s have served to confirm. This also suggests that the consensus at the end of the twentieth century is not a profound consensus.

Finally, implicit throughout this book is the question as to whether the decline of conflict and radicalism in French politics also implies greater democracy. Does less conflict really imply a more democratic situation than one where conflict is more overt, where conflict and protest permeates political life at all levels? This is certainly an assumption made by many political analysts. Or does the view that less political conflict equates to a more democratic and just society ironically reflect a desire to 'de-politicize' politics in order to maintain a status quo, to help maintain what is in fact the prevailing ideology by proclaiming the 'end of ideology'? (The end of ideology thesis which was elaborated by Daniel Bell (1960) and others in the 1950s and 1960s has been more prevalent than has been acknowledged, and this sort of approach has implicitly underpinned much academic writing about politics in Western Europe and the United States since the 1950s.) Democracy is still one of the most contested, debated and certainly among the most important concepts in the study of politics. It informs discussions about justice, human rights and freedom, but also such apparently value-free and unproblematic discussions as voting behaviour, behaviour of parties in government and public opinion. Consideration of such fundamental notions as democracy should be made more explicit in the study of governmental,

party political and pressure group politics and not left solely to the
attentions of specialists in political theory.

In this book I take a historical approach to the study of contemporary French politics in an attempt to identify some underlying trends
and in order to begin to identify some causes for these trends, as suggested above. This means that as well as looking at the 1980s and
1990s I examine the evolution of French politics since the Second
World War by looking at various themes and significant historical
moments. By contrast with some writers who work within a more postmodern analytical framework, I believe there is a strong and dis-
cernible logic to the course of history, including political history, which
is largely determined, ultimately, by the development of the capitalist
economy. Such an evolution can be usefully described as 'modernization', for there are therefore trends which are common to all advanced
capitalist societies alongside trends which are more peculiar to individual countries. The interplay between these two phenomena is a major
theme of this book, in the context of what has become known as
'French exceptionalism' and now the end of exceptionalism.

Although the term modernization must be used cautiously, it is a
useful way of approaching social, economic and political developments since the Second World War. Care must be taken not to be
teleological or reductionist when using this approach, that is not to
write as if there could be such a thing as a wholly modernized society, which had somehow reached its final stage, or to attribute all
political change to developments in the economic sphere. But to look
in an overarching fashion at patterns of socio-economic and political
development helps greatly in understanding the present. At the heart
of such an approach is a desire to treat party and governmental politics in the context of social, economic and intellectual developments.
In the heyday of the, often rather crude, modernization theories of
the 1950s and 1960s (e.g. Lerner 1958; Organski 1965), changes in
Third World countries were dealt with within the same analytical
framework as changes in advanced capitalist societies. Such a broad
comparison is outside the scope of this book, but to the extent that I
look at the development of France from a largely agricultural society
to a very modern society (chapters 1 and 2 in particular), the sound-
ness of such a comparison in principle is suggested by my analytical
framework in parts of this book. There is too much compartmental-
ization in the minds of many contemporary political scientists
between industrialized and Third World countries, which means that
some similarities are overlooked.

Before describing this book in more detail, I must add a word about the study of West European politics since the Second World War, which has been strongly influenced by a series of assumptions. For example, there was for many years an assumption that economic prosperity would continue to improve rapidly the lot of the population as a whole, thus reinforcing the preconditions for liberal democracy, or what was viewed as a rational way of organizing the process of political decision making. It was thought that any economic downturn would be the exception to the overall rule of increasingly successful, managed capitalism which Anthony Crosland, the Labour politician and advocate of benign capitalism, said in the late 1950s implied 'the declining importance of economic problems' (Crosland 1963: 357). The long boom of the 1950s, 1960s and early 1970s was of course what lay behind this view, which was shared by many. Following on from this, there was a widespread assumption that liberal democracy would be consolidated in the West and would spread from the NATO countries to the Third World, at least in countries where the Soviet Union did not exert substantial influence. Finally, it was taken for granted that if war broke out in Europe it would be between countries which were champions of capitalism on the one hand and those espousing communism on the other; defence cooperation among NATO countries would ensure that this risk was kept to a minimum.

Put together, these assumptions underpinned a view that politics within West European states was increasingly a question of management of rival but basically similar interests within an economic framework of prosperity for the vast majority of the population and full employment. Political analysis of countries in the Western hemisphere thus became increasingly a question of describing and comparing countries' political systems, of attempting to understand party and governmental behaviour, of quantifying and of translating opinion poll data into likely governmental outcomes. Substantial conflict based on ideological and material differences was not considered to be a subject of serious examination for political analysts, for major conflicts of interest, it was implied, were gradually being replaced by only slightly differing views about similar policy positions. Political science, the academic study of politics, was as a result of these factors not only thought to be dispassionate but also the subject of its study was viewed as increasingly about different ways of organizing an essentially commonly-agreed political agenda. Even when the scenario described above became less plausible at the end of the 1960s, analysis of deep-rooted conflict in Western Europe was left largely to other disciplines.

Since the late 1970s and during the 1980s and 1990s in particular, the credibility of these assumptions has been undermined. Economic crisis appears now to be an endemic feature of capitalism, rather than a blip on the graph of inevitably increasing prosperity for all. Profound social divisions have therefore been forced back onto the political agenda. In most countries of Europe there is a sizeable underclass, made up primarily of the long-term unemployed, but also by the lowest-paid, casual and part-time workers, who often believe that their interests and rights are not taken into consideration by mainstream politics. This is one of the challenges to the success of liberal democracy, as it becomes clear that advanced capitalist societies cannot simply be managed according to an apparently value-free political system. The emergence of the neo-liberal right in government in many countries in the West, the virtual disappearance of Keynesianism and the decline of social democracy are testimony to the fragile nature of the post-war consensus. Other challenges have emerged. For example, although Communist government in Eastern Europe has disappeared and been replaced by forms of liberal democracy for the most part, the challenge to this set of assumptions has been reinforced by the rise of regionalism in European countries, by the rise of nationalism, particularly in the former Eastern bloc, and by the rise of the extreme right. However, mainstream political science does not seem to have caught up with developments in politics itself; rather than going back to the theoretical drawing board in order to question some of the underlying concepts of the discipline, many academics have remained working within the framework established in the 30 years after 1945 and which assumes a more managerial form of politics.

There are two immediate implications of the above for what this book sets out to examine. First, we need to take into account the fact that developments in the formal political sphere cannot be properly understood without fully taking into account socio-economic and more broadly ideological developments. Second, the apparent consensus of the 1980s and 1990s in France, although marking the end of one era, is perhaps beginning to give way to a more conflictual era again. Interestingly, new forms of political conflict in France may well be more akin than in the past to conflict in other countries. France might thus be less exceptional, compared with other West European countries, but once again moving into a conflictual stage; France is perhaps at a junction between a situation where it was moving towards patterns of formal politics seen in other West European countries, but at the same time politics in other West European countries are changing significantly, away from the more moderate, liberal democratic situation of the post-war era. There is some evidence that the more consensual politics of the 1980s have given way to a more complex situation, whereby parties of protest are enjoying greater popularity due to a reaction against precisely the moderation of the mainstream parties, which are seen to be unable to implement any solutions to France's substantial social and political ills.

It is probably clear from what is said above that the ideas and approach in this book are part of a longer-term project which attempts to reassess the way in which we analyse politics in advanced capitalist societies today. It is influenced by Marx and other thinkers who believe that the capitalist system itself is fundamentally unjust. But neither do I despair of change within capitalism which would bring far greater justice than is found in any country at the time of writing. Whilst I believe that liberal democracy is incapable of bringing about a profoundly just political system and society (redistribution of wealth and power are two preconditions of any such radical change), I do not despair of liberal democracy constituting a significant step in the right direction and believe that it can bring about more democratic possibilities. Without shunning the analysis of actual politics, including governmental practice, elections, parties, pressure groups and public opinion, writers and teachers of politics should be more willing to question assumptions on which their analytical framework is based. This means reasserting more empirical political analysis as part of the same overall area of study as political philosophy and other related disciplines (sociology, history, social anthropology, economics), rather than behaving as if we can hive it off into a separate place.

Whether in Third World countries or in advanced capitalist countries, the study of politics should also be about the most basic questions relating to human beings: justice and injustice, happiness and unhappiness, health and sickness, summed up by profounder definitions of democracy and related notions. The crucial nature of governmental politics is often clearer in Third World countries, where the change from one regime to another is sometimes quite literally a matter of life and death, but often less so in richer countries. In fact the responsibilities of politicians – and therefore political analysts – are great in advanced capitalist countries. Although these questions have influenced the way this book has turned out, they remain at the level of informing principles at the moment, thus on the whole they are implicit rather than explicit.

A brief description of each chapter will begin to show how the above becomes worked into the main body of this book.

In Chapter 2 I look at France's history between 1789 and 1945 and ask why French political life was so dominated by conflict. To what extent can theories of social, political and economic modernization help throw light on the conflictual nature of French politics? I contend that the process of modernization itself can create as much conflict as stability, contrary to what many political scientists of the 1950s and 1960s might have assumed, for example. France's unique blend of modernizing, democratic characteristics on the one hand and more 'backward' characteristics on the other combined to produce the political conflict which came to be seen as so quintessentially French.

Chapter 3 constitutes another broad overview, this time of the 35 or so years after the Second World War and again I suggest a framework for understanding the relative absence of political consensus in France. Comparing with Britain, Germany and Sweden, I argue that by contrast with these and other countries in Western Europe, socio-economic developments and government in France were not characterized by compromise between various key sectors in society, notably capital and labour, which elsewhere often organized a greater degree of sharing of the fruits of prosperity. Paradoxically, this compromise came in France, to a certain extent, during the 1980s when it was breaking down elsewhere, but significantly under the aegis of a moderate, then increasingly pragmatic, Socialist government.

In Chapter 4 I examine the politics of the 1980s and early 1990s in France in terms of the decline of conflict, dealing with such elements as decreasing support for the Communist Party, the move towards the centre on the part of the Socialists and the decline of Gaullism as a distinct political doctrine. Although this situation has not been as clear cut in the 1990s as it was in the 1980s, centre-oriented politics still dominate the political scene today and left radicalism in particular has been severely weakened. Although the rise of the extreme right National Front was an early indicator that politics were not as moderate as some had suggested, politics in France remain strongly influenced by forces which seek to manage rather than express distinct interests, by contrast with much of French political history between 1789 and 1981. I suggest that this consensus politics came about partly as a result of greater peace and cooperation between the state, trade unions and employers.

In Chapter 5 I look at the Parti socialiste (PS), which played such an important role in managing the transition to more consensual politics in the 1980s and 1990s. I tackle the question as to what type of party the PS is by looking at the nature of social democracy from a historical point of view and then to what extent the French Socialist Party conforms with the social democratic model. I also look at the left more generally in France since the Second World War and attempt to show how the PS fits into this panorama. Increasingly, writers on French socialism are comparing – and often likening – the PS to socialist parties in southern Europe, notably in Spain, Portugal, Greece and Italy, and I consider this comparison. Finally, I examine the problems of the left in the France of the 1990s and the reasons for the wider, international crisis of social democracy.

In Chapter 6 I begin the first of three examinations of modernizing – albeit unevenly modernizing – aspects of post-war politics. I look at de Gaulle's rule between 1958 and 1969 and argue that it is a key period in the modernization of France's political system and its economy, and an important step in the direction of the type of politics operating in other, more consensual countries. But this was modernization carried through in an authoritarian fashion, which meant that the process was still in some ways part of a more obviously conflictual politics, thus very uneven. So although de Gaulle's Presidency brought greater stability to the government of France, an examination of his bonapartist approach to the Presidency helps explain the powerful popular protests which shook the country in May 1968.

Chapter 7 is concerned more closely with the student and workers' revolt of May 1968 and I consider the theories of two of the most coherent proponents of the notion that May 1968 must be seen as a modernizing moment, namely Régis Debray and Gilles Lipovetsky. However, I take issue with many aspects of their theories because of their teleological and sometimes reductionist nature and thus their failure to recognize the openness of the possible results of May. This indeed is one of the main problems with some approaches to modernization, that is the apparent inevitability of outcomes, the linearity of the process, whereas modernization should be seen as a tendency which can change direction or even be reversed. Lipovetsky's theory, although stimulating, is particularly flawed in its defence of May 1968 as the 'first narcissistic revolution'.

Chapter 8 turns to the role of intellectuals in French political life since the Second World War. I begin by reflecting on the role of intellectuals in advanced capitalist societies generally and the role they play in creating a country's political culture. I then consider why intellectuals in France have been so politically committed, often on the Marxist left, before attempting to explain their drift towards the centre since about the mid-1970s; why have so many abandoned Marxism in favour of more liberal and centre-oriented approaches? I suggest that contemporary intellectuals are still largely reacting against Marxism rather than adopting truly distinct ways of interpreting the world.

Chapter 9, finally, draws some conclusions and suggests some ways in which the issues raised in this book impinge on broader questions in politics and the study of politics. I look briefly and critically at Francis Fukuyama's claim that we have, globally, reached the end of history because there is no credible alternative on a global scale to liberal democracy. I also look at the claims of the French regulation school, whose theories I believe are useful in explaining recent developments in capitalist societies. The regulationists are able to argue convincingly that changes from Fordism to post-Fordism significantly alter the political economy of advanced capitalist societies without, however, suggesting that a wholly new period has emerged after the end of the post-war era.

2
A History of Conflict and Revolt

I do not think that there is more hatred in our country today than in the good old days. The civil war here has been intense or less intense at different times, but it has been ever-present.

François Mauriac, 1968 (1971: 69)

The political history of almost all countries is one of conflict and violence. Most have experienced revolution, civil war, *coup d'etat* or war with other nations; bitter class conflict, religious conflict and regional conflict have likewise been expressed in the politics of many states. France is by no means alone in having a conflictual and violent modern history, even compared with other advanced capitalist societies with such mild-mannered reputations as Britain and the USA, whose present political structures were indeed born of violence. However, France is a particularly interesting case because although it has long been associated with the democratic ideals of the 1789 Revolution, ranked among the world's leading political democracies, and has been pioneering in modern cultural and intellectual spheres, its conflict-ridden and often violent modern history is evidence of a quite different political development from that of the liberal democratic models. The point about France is that, although many aspects of everyday life were probably no more and no less violent or conflictual than in many other countries, profound conflict became an essential element in national politics, an element that many political actors and ideologues over the years took for granted and whose history they re-enacted.

Between the Revolution of 1789 and today, every political regime has ended in *coup d'état*, revolution or war and there have been 15 different constitutions. Every generation, except for the most recent, has witnessed profound political crises provoked by domestic or external events or a combination of the two. France's revolutionary (and therefore violent) past has itself become an enduring subject of national political pride and very often a symbol of progress, an integral and fundamental part of France's political identity. This mystique has come to have a dynamic and an influence of its own, particularly as far as the 1789 Revolution is concerned; for example, at the point when the extreme right Poujadist movement was most popular, in the mid-1950s, 51 Poujadist *députés* were elected on a programme whose main proposal was the summoning of the Estates General, referring directly back to 1789, and on 13 May 1958, in Algiers, insurgents against the French state and in defence of French Algeria formed a Committee of Public Safety and sang the Marseillaise, again referring directly back to the period of the Revolution (Tilly 1975: 27). For the left, the Revolution of 1848, the 1871 Paris Commune, the Popular Front of 1936, Liberation in 1944 and the events of May 1968 all have a particular significance in terms of struggle for justice, popular resistance and the importance of collective action. Each time a barricade was built in the streets of Paris it evoked previous barricades, previous uprisings. The mythology of the revolutionary past has long been expressed in the Marseillaise, *Hymne national* of the First Republic, the Third Republic, the Fourth Republic and the Fifth Republic, with such combative phrases as *aux armes citoyens* and *l'étendard sanglant et levé*. The triad of the 1789 revolution on coins and public buildings, *liberté, égalité, fraternité*, is another reminder of the legitimacy and lasting preoccupation with the great revolution. The annual celebration of the storming of the Bastille on 14 July, the predominance of revolutionary scenes in some of France's best-known visual art and literature and the official nature of the momentous bicentennial celebrations of 1989 are further reminders of both fascination with and pride in this past.

A brief mention of the more significant violent and conflictual moments between 1789 and the present illustrates just how tumultuous French history has been. The 1789 Revolution of course became a national and international landmark of colossal proportions and profoundly altered the political, economic and social history of France. The Terror came in 1793–4 and notably the execution of tens of thousands of alleged enemies of the Revolution. Napoleon Bonaparte's *coup d'état* in 1799 was followed by 15 years of dictatorship. For much of the nineteenth century France led the way in a generally insurgent Europe; the Revolution of 1830 was followed by further revolts in 1831, 1832, 1834 and 1839, accompanied by ever more intense state control. Next came the Revolution of February 1848 followed by the workers' uprising and its quelling in June the same year and the *coup d'état* by Louis Napoleon in 1851, to which there was armed resistance in many parts of France. The revolution of September 1870 was swiftly followed by the 1871 Paris Commune and Thiers' ruthless and bloody crushing of the Commune. There was an attempted *coup d'état* by Marshal MacMahon on 16 May 1877. The rest of the Third Republic, up to 1940, was somewhat calmer, but was nevertheless punctuated by the threat of Boulangist seizure of power in 1888–9, the deeply divisive Dreyfus Affair of 1898–9, the significant strikes of 1919–20, violent demonstration by the extreme right on 6 February 1934 (followed by counter-demonstrations by the left) and the end of the Third Republic due to the collapse of the Maginot Line defences on the German border and thus German invasion in 1940. Four years of often violent occupation, the details of which the French are still attempting to come to terms with, brought profound bitterness as many French people overtly or covertly collaborated with the occupiers whilst others, especially Jews and Communists, suffered terribly. Liberation came in 1944 and was quickly followed by widespread summary executions of suspected collaborators, as well as many other less drastic punishments. Finally, there was the threatened *coup d'état* by French army officers in Algiers on 13 May 1958 and the student and workers' uprising in May 1968, which were the last conflictual political events of substantial proportions.

France and modernity

In many parts of Europe, much of the period we are considering in this chapter was characterized by tremendous social, economic and political upheaval. The nineteenth century was a time of great scientific discoveries in the physical sciences, of engineering revolutions and profound changes in techniques of production, all of which brought changes to people's lives of a magnitude and at a pace that had never been seen before. The new demands of widespread capitalist production meant sea changes in the nature of work and living conditions, both in the countryside and in towns, with large-scale movement of labour not only from country to town but also from one nation to another. The rapidly expanding cities teemed with people often living and working in the most miserable conditions, with greater comfort for only the privileged few. Railways shrank the size of countries and continents in terms of both transport and communications and the press was revolutionized. In short, with the rapid development of industrial capitalism, centuries-old ways of life suddenly disappeared and quite new ones emerged, creating volatile social relations and often revolutionary moments. As Marx and Engels put it in 1848:

> Constant revolutionizing of production, uninterrupted disturbance of all social conditions, everlasting uncertainty and agitation, distinguish the bourgeois epoch from all earlier ones. All fixed, fast-frozen relations, with their train of ancient and venerable prejudices and opinions, are swept away, all new-formed ones become antiquated before they can ossify. All that is solid melts into air, all that is holy is profaned, and man is at last compelled to face with sober senses, his real conditions of life, and his relations with his kind. (Marx and Engels 1968: 38)

This passage to modernity was in all cases fraught, and often bloody. It brought with it profound ideological and political changes and popular revolt, which meant that the nineteenth century in Europe was a particularly intense period of social conflict, revolution, counter-revolution and war. But France had a special place in this history and was often the very home of revolution and counter-revolution, a country whose popular uprisings were a source of inspiration to popular groups in other countries struggling for change as part of the emerging socialist movement, and as time went on a source of dread for the bourgeoisie. In order to understand why this reputation has endured and indeed why the tradition of conflict and revolt has lasted into the twentieth century, we need to explore the reasons why France stood out among other nations and gained a position of revolutionary leader among European countries.

The process of socio-economic modernization was in any case one of turmoil, as I have said, but in addition to this the development of France's economy and social structure was highly uneven, with tremendous counter-tendencies clashing with those of the development of a modern industrial economy and the social and political trappings of a modern capitalist society. Certainly, France was among the richest European nations and by the beginning of the twentieth century belonged to the still small group of industrialized countries; in 1900 the United States, Germany, the United Kingdom and France together represented one-fifth of the world's population and produced four-fifths of its total economic production. Together they had 70 per cent of the world's steam engines. It was the French who dug the Suez Canal, started the Panama Canal and built half the world's ports and railways in the nineteenth century (E. Weber 1977: 277; Zolberg 1986: 397). The Revolution of 1789 enabled capitalism to develop, notably by the way in which it destroyed the power and influence of the aristocracy, thus abolishing many aspects of birth-related hierarchy and privilege, and apparently paving the way for a society where free enterprise could flourish. It also replaced corporate rights with individual ones and thus made the labour market more suitable for free enterprise. Likewise, France was a pioneer in terms of the modernization of the political system. The administrative characteristics of the French state were already radically reformed before the Revolution of 1789 by Richelieu and others, but administrative reform was taken further by Napoleon I after the revolution. Ideologically, the revolution itself promoted loud and clear the ideals which were to become the guiding principles of many a country's political system: economic and political rights based on notions of individual liberty, alongside a commitment to equality before the law. Although 1789 and other revolutions had a violent influence on subsequent French and international history, another important legacy was the legitimacy of parliament, and when France introduced universal male suffrage in 1848 it was the first European country to do so in modern times. Intellectually and culturally France has long had a substantial international influence and widespread access to education was established early. Militarily and diplomatically France was powerful and had one of the world's largest empires.

But despite these trappings of what is often associated with modernity, France's economic and social modernization was distinctly uneven and developments in its political life reflected this. Industry was relatively slow to develop in nineteenth-century France and although it was among the leading industrial nations, by 1900 it was lagging well behind that of Britain, Germany and the United States. Clapham (1923: 53) comments that

> in the course of the nineteenth century most French industries were re-modelled, but it might be said that France never went through an industrial revolution. There was a gradual transformation, a slow shifting of her economic centre of gravity from the side of agriculture to that of industry, and a slow change in the methods of organisation ... In the first half of the century the movement ... is barely perceptible, in spite of the noise and controversy which accompanied it.

By the end of the nineteenth century, French agriculture was behind that of other Western economies as far as mechanization and crop yield were concerned, slowing the population shift to the towns and the overall growth of the economy (Kuisel 1987: 27). France still remained a largely rural country and units of industrial production tended to be small. There was much good farm land, but few natural resources which were conducive to industrialization, like iron and coal. Population growth was slow. Meanwhile entrepreneurial spirit was relatively undeveloped, even among the bourgeoisie, partly because of the dominance of the Catholic church and its disapproval of capital accumulation, the dominance and interventionist orientation of the state (trends which were established well before 1789) and the radicalism of the French working class.

Most importantly of all, perhaps, the state did not substantially push industrial development, largely because of the size and influence of the peasantry. In the mid-nineteenth century 50 per cent of French men were working the land and over a third were still doing so in the 1930s. A strong peasantry implies a population which is on the whole individualistic, divided, which takes little active part in politics and which clings to the predominance of agriculture in the national economy. The 1789 Revolution had made many peasants owners of the land they worked, which meant they were particularly defensive of the traditional way of things. The substantial size of the peasantry and its key position in the economy meant that all political parties with governmental ambitions looked to peasants for support, and this was an important reason for governments not pushing for faster and more widespread industrialization, as such a position would have represented a threat to a significant section of any party of government's electorate.

The obvious counterpart to the substantial size and political importance of the peasantry was the relative smallness of the industrial working class, which played an important part in achieving a more stable situation elsewhere, most notably in Britain. In countries where the industrial working class was already or was becoming the main productive class, representatives of this class compromised to an extent with capital through emerging trade union or pre-trade union organizations and, later, through political parties, and thus brought a degree of stability through the representation of the interests of a large section of society. At the very least, there was an established focus for militancy, which is not to deny the violence and conflict associated with struggles on the part of the early trade union

Table 2.1 Agricultural workforce as % of the total working population 1820–1910

	UK	France	Germany	USA
1820	46	75	80	75
1850	22	64	65	65
1870	15	49	49	50
1910	6	42	18	33

Source: Rioux 1971: 192. © Editions du Seuil, 1971.

movement in Britain, for example. In France there was little channelling of industrial conflict, partly because the working class was not viewed as numerically or politically important enough to compromise with; the working class was not only small but also tended to work in very small groups, whose employment was very unstable anyway (Huard et al. 1982: 265). Also, other classes feared the radicalism of the working class, a radicalism which was demonstrated repeatedly in the course of the nineteenth century. The result was that the marginalized working class, which was placated little, was frequently in open conflict with the capitalist class and its very smallness and relative isolation pushed it further towards the desire for total change, for the overthrow of the existing order. Stanley Hoffmann (1966: 7) comments that 'the French working class was in a most unhappy position; there was a much celebrated community of values between peasants and bourgeois, but all that the bourgeois offered the workers was the prospect of individual ascent through hard work and thrift.' It suffered the turmoil which modernization brought, but often without the advantages enjoyed in other countries.

Capitalism tends to bring workers together in large groups, not only at work but also in the towns and cities where they live. It improves communications and transportation and makes literacy more widespread. This brings improved organizational capacity and political confidence for a large industrial working class and thus improves the conditions for democracy (Rueschemeyer et al. 1992: 6). It is thus significant that Britain, whose industrial revolution was thorough and industrial working class soon a significant proportion of the total population, also had a more stable political life. In a broader context, democracy and political stability tend also to go hand in hand with what Antonio Gramsci described as 'dense civil society'. By civil society Gramsci meant the sum total of social

Table 2.2 Annual rate of growth of total output, 1870–1961, various countries (%)

	1870–1913	1913–50	1950–60	1956–61
Belgium	2.7	1.0	2.9	2.5
Denmark	3.2	2.1	3.3	5.0
France	1.6	0.7	4.4	4.2
Germany	2.9[a]	1.2	7.6	5.9
Italy	1.4	1.3	5.9	6.7
The Netherlands	2.2[b]	2.1	4.9	3.9
Norway	2.2[a]	2.7	3.5	3.4
Sweden	3.0	2.2	3.3	4.0
Switzerland	2.4[c]	2.0	5.1	5.2
UK	2.2	1.7	2.6	2.1
Canada	3.8	2.8	3.9	1.8
USA	4.3[a]	2.9	3.2	2.3
Average	2.7	1.9	4.2	3.9

[a] 1871–1913.
[b] 1900–13.
[c] 1890–1913.
Source: Maddison 1964: 28

organizations and groups that are not directly related to production, government or the family, including informal gatherings of people to play games or sport, pursue hobbies, and so on, but also including trade unions and political parties (Rueschemeyer et al. 1992: 49–50). A dense civil society brings more contact between people of both an informal and formal nature and a higher level of organization in defence of various groups' interests, which tends to foster participative democracy and act as a counter-weight to state power. A developed urban, industrialized society will have a more dense civil society than a society such as France's which was still largely rural, and where even industry bore the hallmarks of rural patterns of organization and behaviour. Until the beginning of the twentieth century there were few areas which were completely industrialized in France, like Lancashire in Britain or the Ruhr in Germany (Thomson 1989: 49). Such a society is likely to be less straightforward to rule and keep control of than one where civil society is more dense, and dense civil society is likely to contribute to the ease with which the ruling class rules, for it means a more stable population and a population whose actions are more predictable. So in France after the Revolution of 1789 the absence of such a society did not ultimately work to the benefit of the ruling class; although a low level of

Table 2.3 Coal output per head and industrial output per head, 1913, for the UK, Germany and France (France = 100)

	Coal	Industry
UK	674	180
Germany	281	157
France	100	100

Source: Kemp 1971: 298

social organization perhaps meant a smaller, less organized counter-force to France's rulers than might otherwise have been the case, it also meant a less predictable population in terms of social and political actions. Certainly in Paris and other larger towns there were at times many political clubs and other organizations which were of a primarily social nature but which soon became political in times of crisis, but these *cercles*, *chambrées* and clubs tended to be small, atomized and vulnerable to closure by the authorities if they began to question the status quo in any serious fashion (Huard et al. 1982: 433). There was a distinct lack of dialogue between the mass of the population and the ruling class, a point which Tocqueville pointed out when he said that already under the *ancien régime* there was an opposition between a 'huge, centralized political power' and socially, by contrast, 'little groups which are unknown or indifferent to one another'. It seemed, he said, 'that the French population is like these elemental bodies in which modern chemistry discovers ever more divisions the closer it looks' (quoted in Winock 1986: 406–7).

In a now classic essay on modern French history Stanley Hoffmann (1966: 3) sums up the peculiarities of French society by talking of a 'stalemate society'. He explores the 'unique mixture of socio-economic systems' and also the 'poor associational life', noting that 'the actors were individuals rather than organizations'. I too have dealt with these aspects of French history, albeit in somewhat different ways from Hoffmann. However, Hoffmann adds a third, related element to his description of 'stalemate society' which is what he describes as 'a peculiarly French style of authority' and is also a useful way of explaining aspects of French history. The development of France's society and politics after the Revolution, he says, meant that the French came to fear face-to-face relations, and instead sought rules administered from above, often by a strong central bureaucracy. This was in part a legacy of the *ancien régime* which had destroyed autonomous sources of power, making groups dependent on the state. France was thus halfway between what Hoffmann regards as a fully democratic model of society, where conflicts are resolved by cooperation, discussion and compromise, and a fully-fledged authoritarian society where decisions are simply imposed from above and where tensions in society abound. Slow economic growth after the Revolution perpetuated this, with its attendant fragmentation and individualism. However, one of the legacies of the Revolution was precisely to contest authoritarianism, which explains the subsequent tendency to revolt against it from time to time. This 'peculiar style of authority', Hoffmann says, is 'not so much the blend as the coexistence of *limited* authoritarianism and *potential* insurrection' (1966: 8).

Domestic conflict and international relations

France's tumultuous history is also bound up with its geopolitical position in a continent which was for long the stage of inter-state battles for superiority. Pre-revolutionary France was for many years the most powerful nation in Europe but was for most of the period between the mid-seventeenth and mid-eighteenth centuries at war with neighbouring states. The major domestic upheavals of the nineteenth and the first half of the twentieth century were often linked either to war or to the foreign invasions which took place in 1814–15, 1870–1, 1914–18 and 1940–5; the defeat of Napoleon at Waterloo and the consequent Restoration was of course a direct result of foreign intervention, as was the Paris Commune, as were the lasting domestic divisions and conflicts caused by German occupation during the Second World War. Almost all international conflicts in which France became involved resulted in changes of constitution (Ehrmann 1968: 15). Thus geographical location and France's position as a key actor on the international scene, factors which had been partially responsible for putting France in such a dominant position in earlier times, later contributed to political instability. As Charles de Gaulle put it in 1946:

> During a period no longer than twice a man's life, France was invaded seven times and had thirteen different regimes ... So many upheavals have put poison in our public life, which has compounded our old Gallic propensity towards divisions and quarrels. (De Gaulle 1970a: 649)

When a country loses a war and in particular when it is invaded by a foreign power, this of course has a demoralizing effect on the population. But such events also have the effect of weakening the ideological hold of the ruling class, because to lose a war or to be invaded by another nation shows the ruling class to be unable to defend its country and this also, more generally, sows seeds of doubt as to the desirability and the legitimacy of the political status quo. It is no accident that at the end of the Franco-Prussian War, at the end of the Second World War and at a moment of profound crisis over Algerian policy in May 1958, there was on each occasion a serious challenge to the legitimacy of the established political order, and in the case of the first two examples serious challenges to the established social order. This is a phenomenon which is by no means confined to France, and Theda Skocpol (1979: 23) has gone as far as saying that modern social revolutions have taken place only in countries which are in 'disadvantaged positions within international arenas'. Examples outside France of war profoundly changing the political state of mind of a population include such momentous upheavals as the 1917 Russian Revolution during the First World War, the German Revolution of 1918, at the end of the First World War, and more generally the struggle for independence on the part of colonized countries in the wake of the Second World War.

The repeated invasions of France, as well as the vulnerable nature of the ruling class, also help explain why France has long had both a highly centralized and an authoritarian state, characteristics which have been prevalent in varying degrees from the *ancien régime* to the present day. Centralization and authoritarianism were in part an attempt to defend the country against encroachment by foreign powers, as well as a way of maintaining control over an unreliable population. However, a strong, unbending and centralized state, with a police force which was often used for directly political ends, meant that opposition groups tended also to be 'total' in orientation, aiming for the overthrow of the political status quo in the absence of the possibility of compromise. The French state developed a predilection for suppression rather than assimilation, repression rather than negotiation, and despite modernizing reforms of the police from time to time, they remained vicious in both reputation and fact, and deeply despised by many political activists, particularly on the left. This was especially the case during the regimes of both Napoleon I and Napoleon III, but the police has been regarded by many governments as an instrument to muzzle opposition and to defend sectarian interests rather than as a defender of law and order *per se*. The key role of the police in the escalation of the events of May 1968 is a relatively recent example of the way in which governments have used the police to attempt to suppress protest brutally (Hewlett: 1988) and as recently as September 1994 Amnesty International concluded that the French police had over the previous few years time after time been guilty of 'reckless and illegal use of force' (*Guardian*, 12 Oct. 1994). Just as importantly, a highly centralized state means that action by groups of protesters is more likely to affect the central state itself as there are fewer devolved entities to absorb the blows which protest groups strike; nascent unrest thus more easily developed into a situation where national political power was threatened. Raymond Tournoux (quoted in H. Weber 1978: 18) describes this as a 'regime without a fuse', where a relatively minor political fault can threaten the whole political system, instead of blowing a fuse at a lower level.

Political ideology and political parties

There was for a long time no more the ideological than the social basis for political compromise in France. Owing in part to the 1789 Revolution but also to the series of authoritarian and dictatorial regimes after the Revolution, political change came to be viewed as being about wiping the slate clean and not simply tinkering with the existing system; there developed an ideological tradition of complete break with the past (and for a few a delving right back into it), where the idea of political change challenged not part but all that went before, where progress implied not reforming the current state of things in order to achieve improvements, but total emancipation. So by contrast with Britain or the United States, where two or three large parties dominated parliamentary life for many years, where political parties tended to represent specific interests, and political programmes different ways of operating within the same system, there was in France a multiplicity of political forces, many of which claimed to represent universal and eternal truths and were often deeply hostile to the founding principles of the regime of the time (Howorth 1987: 106). Political adversaries often did not view each other as legitimate actors, but as candidates for political elimination. The socio-economic and political conditions described above meant that political parties did not begin functioning in anything like the way we accept today as being the democratic norms of political behaviour. This was partly because of the profound nature of social and political conflict, because the frequent revolutions of the nineteenth century had a dynamic of their own, and because of the repression of political activity and political activists. Repression was particularly harsh under the Second Empire, when there was draconian press censorship and severe restrictions on the right of assembly. Ruling political forces felt too insecure in their support, too unstable in their rule to allow more political freedom. Even under the more liberal Third Republic political parties as such were very slow to emerge, with local committees set up temporarily to support a particular candidate in a particular election; even at the end of the Third Republic only the left had anything resembling mass political parties represented by a coherent group of *députés* in parliament.

France thus entered the twentieth century with a legacy which, although tempered by the more moderate period during the last third of the nineteenth century, still meant that on both the right and the left there was a strong tradition of totalism, of creating wholly alternative schemes of things not only in relation to political parties, but to the political system and indeed the overall organization of society. The attachment to universalism, idealism, salvation and unwillingness to compromise was expressed for instance in the success of the Parti Communiste Français (hereafter Communist Party or PCF) from its establishment in 1920 and particularly after 1945, but also in the influence of the extreme right Leagues during the 1930s. The forces of Resistance and Collaboration during the Second World War both drew on and perpetuated this tradition, as did the authoritarianism and idealism of Gaullist ideology.

Constitutions, meanwhile, far from being regarded as neutral charters which set down the rules of the game of the formal political process, were seen as means by which victors ensured power over the vanquished and thus as temporary (Hayward 1983: 1). They tended to reflect either the representative tradition, more commonly associated with liberal democracy, or the more authoritarian, plebiscitary tradition; the constitutions of 1791, 1830, 1875 and 1946 reflected the former tradition and those of 1793, 1848, 1852 and 1958 belong in varying degrees to the latter. The very fact that there were 11 different constitutions between 1789 and 1875 is testimony to political instability, and as Maurice Duverger (1965: 70) has pointed out, during this period France only had a participative, democratic system for a short period and was instead dominated by authoritarian regimes, two monarchies, two empires and several actual dictatorships. In part because of the legacy of 1789, violence was often seen as necessary, or at least acceptable, in order to achieve what the perpetrators of violence viewed as a democratic end, a view which was encouraged by the violence which the state used to counter protest. Again, then, the democratic model of a country whose politics are characterized by discussion, compromise and respect for the opposition (which is nowhere found in perfect form) is far from the case for France.

Intellectuals were deeply concerned with political matters from the eighteenth century onwards and they reinforced this tendency to see much in terms of universal ideas or ideals, a purity of thought, abstraction, idealism and a lack of willingness to compromise. Paris was for long at the forefront of new liberal, democratic and socialist ideas and for example Pierre-Joseph Proudhon and other Utopian socialists had a substantial following. They helped consolidate the tendency towards idealism rather than pragmatism as far as politics were concerned. In many national crises since the end of the nineteenth century in particular, intellectuals have played a leading role, most famously in the Dreyfus Affair. But in the revolts of left and right during the 1930s, Charles Maurras had a profound influence on the extreme right Action Française; in the Resistance and Collaboration of the Second World War, intellectuals were active on both sides: Brasillach and Céline added intellectual credibility to collaboration and Camus did the same for the Resistance, for example. As far as the Algerian War was concerned, for a few years intellectuals and their newspapers, magazines and journals were isolated voices of opposition in a general chorus of approval for France's Algerian policy, but voices which spoke what was to become the majority view. Nor did students enter politics for the first time in May 1968; since 1848 and before, students had taken a keen and active part in political change on both left and right, including riots on the part of Action Française students in the academic year 1908–9 (Zeldin 1979: 119).

A brief look at the Dreyfus Affair at the end of the nineteenth century illustrates the nature of the interplay between intellectuals and politics. Indeed the Dreyfus Affair is often regarded as the moment when the modern, politically committed intellectual was born. The affair began with the apparently uncontroversial conviction for espionage of Captain Alfred Dreyfus, a verdict which was widely accepted not because there was any substantial evidence against Dreyfus, but because few cared about his fate, not least because he was Jewish. The affair became an issue of widespread public interest in January 1898 when the novelist Emile Zola accused the War Office of a judicial crime, in his famous letter, 'J'accuse', published in the newspaper *L'Aurore*. From then on the case was widely and passionately debated, dividing France between the defenders of Dreyfus' innocence, including anticlericals, Protestants, Jews and intellectuals, and his attackers, which included the army, monarchists, Catholics and nationalists. The anti-semitic Catholic writer Charles Maurras was a passionate supporter of the latter camp. The intensity of the dispute was such that the Third Republic itself seemed for a while in danger of collapsing. In the end, Dreyfus was released not as a result of a retrial, which was at last held but which again found him guilty, but after a presidential pardon in 1899. The important point to make here is that the immediate rights and wrongs of the case, the weight of evidence for and against the conviction of the accused, were overshadowed by far broader issues of belief, principle and straightforward prejudice. Ideas, morals and interests played a far more important part in deciding the outcome of the Affair than did the weighing up of evidence regarding guilt and innocence in relation to an alleged offence. This is characteristic of French political history, where matters of disputed fact easily become matters of principle, right and wrong, even good versus evil, and where the political, ideological and institutional status quo is easily threatened as a result.

Ideas at other significant moments have also been more powerful in terms of informing actions than the law. Well into the twentieth century, those who defied the law in order to fight for their beliefs later became representative of the ideological and institutional status quo, thus showing that to act against the law was not necessarily morally wrong. Placing the role of conscience above the law of the land became a dilemma of national proportions during the Second World War when many of those who acted within the law and co-operated fully with the Vichy regime – thus collaborating with the occupying German forces – were later vilified and often punished. To abide by one's principles, rather than by what the law tells one to do, was given moral credence during the Occupation, as it had been at other times when people acted illegally in order to fight what they perceived to be an unjust regime. Some years later, when elements in the French army were on the verge of attempting a *coup d'état* in 1958, they too believed they were acting for the good of France and the French, despite the fact that they were acting directly against the orders of the government. This type of behaviour is far from the ideal liberal democratic model, where the army is neutral and subservient. For the labour movement, meanwhile, the memories of state-perpetrated violence against the Communards and many other less spectacular instances of harsh repression confirmed the belief that to struggle for what was morally just was likely to involve breaking the law.

The polarization of the labour movement and the *patronat*

The often fraught development of the labour movement is illustrative of the degree of social and political instability in France (Lorwin 1966). Soon after the Revolution, the Constituent Assembly introduced the Le Chapelier law prohibiting associations of workers, a law which was passed in response to strikes by journeymen in favour of higher wages. The Napoleonic penal code of 1810 went further and made any attempt to form a trade union a criminal offence. This remained law well beyond the middle of the nineteenth century; although government sometimes tolerated the organization of workers, just as often it would repress it harshly. By the time of the revolution in February 1848 it was the industrial proletariat as well as artisans who took to the barricades in force and the new government went some way to meeting their demand for work by setting up national workshops (*ateliers nationaux*), although in practice the workshops only provided a tiny wage for what was often unnecessary work. When the government decided to shut down the workshops in June, however, there followed several days of pitched battles on the street in what became known as the 'June days'. Several thousand workers were killed and many more arrested, and both the nascent trade unions and the wider socialist movement were badly damaged, leaving a lasting bitterness. Napoleon III outlawed workers' organizations until 1864 when a new law finally gave workers the right to associate and to strike. For the rest of the 1860s an early form of trade unionism in the form of *chambres syndicales ouvrières* grew up rapidly but was overshadowed by the Franco-Prussian War and the Workers' International was harshly repressed by the government. But it was the assault on the Paris Commune by the Thiers provisional government in May 1871 which left the most lasting scar on the French workers' movement. About 20,000 Communards were killed in the streets or executed by firing squad, more than 4,000 deported to New Caledonia, several thousand imprisoned in France, and many others fled Paris. The effect of the blood spilled during these events has been likened to the crystallizing effect on the working class in Russia of the killings of 1905 and the Kolyma massacre of 1911 (Perrot 1986: 97), and when the first real trade union confederation, the Confédération Générale du Travail, was established in 1895, the radicalism which was to mark the subsequent history of the French workers' movement, still in evidence today, was firmly established. Of the leading industrial countries only France had as its major labour organization one which rejected the idea of pursuing its interests within the framework of established political entities, in the shape of the CGT (Zolberg 1986: 398). The CGT was strongly influenced by revolutionary syndicalism, which often meant a great reluctance to negotiate with employers. The labour movement was also small and at the beginning of the twentieth century trade union membership represented about 15 per cent of the labour force in manufacturing, compared with 20 per cent in the US, 25–30 per cent in Germany and 30–40 per cent in Britain (Zolberg 1986: 398). Nor was there a large party of the working class before the development of the socialist Section Française de l'Internationale Ouvrière (SFIO), built up from the unification of various smaller groups prior to its creation in 1905 and consolidation up to 1914. Relations between the organized working class and the state were very far from those of any liberal democratic model and the labour movement was very far from integrated into the governmental scheme of things.

The attitude of French employers, the *patronat*, likewise, reflects the uneven development of capitalism in France and also helps explain the fate of the often ghettoized workers' movement. Analysts point out that there have long been two quite distinct types of employer in France (e.g. H. Weber 1986: 48). On the one hand, there have been employers whose values are inherited from the *ancien régime*, who act with the prudence of rural elites in the case of smaller companies and like lords in their fief in the larger ones. Bunel and Saglio (1979) argue that the three major characteristics of this particular *patronat* are (1) protectionism, with an extremely wary attitude towards measures which might encourage competition with foreign companies, (2) Malthusianism, implying a very cautious attitude towards growth either of the national economy or the firm, and finally (3) paternalism, where the firm is regarded as a sort of extended family, whose ownership is passed down from generation to generation and whose owner and *patron* is the equivalent of the family patriarch. The head of the company is responsible for the material and moral wellbeing of the employees and might tolerate company unions where they express the wishes of the company's workforce only. But what is anathema to this particular employer culture is the existence of trade unions which are part of a broader movement and which act in the interests of labour as a whole, as any such movement is regarded as being unnecessary given the supposedly enlightened and understanding attitude of the employer. This type of employer culture was predominant up until the beginning of the 1960s and this – alongside a very radical tradition in the labour movement – speaks volumes as to the nature of relations within the firm, characterized by a distinct lack of dialogue between the two sides of industry.

There was on the other hand a more 'modern' *patronat* in France which was in favour of international trade, rapid growth of both the national economy as a whole and the individual firm, and which was somewhat more tolerant of the trade union movement. This second type of culture has been more influential only during two relatively short periods, namely under the Second Empire (1852–70) and since the beginning of the Fifth Republic in 1958, when in both cases for a significant period there has been a favourable economic climate and a strong state which encouraged this approach to the economy and the firm. Whilst the former, paternalistic culture tended to be found in smaller firms and the other in larger ones, this was not always the case. Indeed a paternalistic attitude predominates in some larger companies even today (H. Weber 1986: 51).

Republicanism and manifestations of a more moderate history

It would be wrong to sum up the entire history of France even between 1789 and 1945 as one of unremitting conflict, in terms of either political ideology or political practice, and to ignore more liberal democratic traditions and practices would make the more consensual developments since the early 1980s difficult to understand. Alongside the predilection for revolt in order to achieve total change, another important legacy of the 1789 Revolution was the belief in progress, modernity, rationality and in particular popular democracy, all of which became embodied in the republican tradition, which has been influential in varying degrees since 1789, and has at times had a moderating influence on the course of French political history (Kamenka 1988: 99). Republicanism has taken many forms and was an influence on various political thinkers and actors during the nineteenth century well before it inspired the founding of a political party as such and at the heart of the tradition is a belief in popular sovereignty, representative institutions and political freedom, in the tradition of liberty, equality and fraternity proclaimed in the wake of the Revolution. Inspired by the *Philosophes* of the eighteenth century such as Rousseau and Voltaire, but also the English seventeenth-century philosphers Hobbes and Locke, republicans were firm believers in the importance of individual liberties. Reason and education go hand in hand, a match which expresses a belief in the ability of the people to rule the nation fairly, given the right circumstances, and more general social reform is also important (Hazareesingh 1994: 65–96). In practice, the republican cause suffered many setbacks and did not become established as a lasting influence on government until the last third of the nineteenth century and did not reach its apogee until the first part of the twentieth century. But the adoption of universal male suffrage by the Jacobin constitution of 1793, for instance, was testimony to an early – if short-lived – success of one important politically modernizing aspect of the movement, and this reform, along with the Declaration of the Rights of Man, was to serve as a guiding light for republicans of later generations. Under the First Republic there were also plans to introduce universal primary education, although this project never saw the light of day, and was realized a century later under the Third Republic. The Second Republic reintroduced universal male suffrage in 1848, giving almost ten million Frenchmen the right to vote, compared with less than a quarter of a million before the 1848 Revolution, and less than three-quarters of a million in England at the time (Huard 1992: 76). Again, however, the experiment was short-lived and suffrage was restricted again in 1850.

Certainly, the progressive and liberal democratic aspects of early republicanism should not be overstated. Among the more bloody episodes of republican history are the Terror of 1793–4, which involved 17,000 executions and half a million people put in prison, and the bloody battles of the Vendée in 1793–5, resulting in 200,000 deaths (E. Weber 1988: 174–5). The execution of Louis XVI in January 1793 was also an act of republican fervour. However, the Third Republic (1870–1940), which was arguably the high point of republicanism, was the first prolonged period of relatively stable government in the modern history of France, illustrated by the fact that it still remains by far the longest-lasting political regime since the Revolution, including the Fifth Republic. The Constitution established liberal democratic rules of political organization, giving a key role to both local and national representative institutions, and universal male suffrage was an important part of the success of the republican project. Laws of 1881 established freedom of association and freedom of the press, and the Waldeck–Rousseau law of 1884 legalized trade unions, whilst Jules Ferry's laws of 1881 and 1882 established free, compulsory and secular primary education, a reform which according to Ferry would bring the end of class struggle thanks to 'the fusion which results from the mixing of rich and poor on school benches' (quoted in Berstein 1992: 192).

From the turn of the century the Parti Radical, arguably France's first modern political party, played an important role in national politics, expressing many of the aims the Republic came to stand for. A loosely-organized party, created in 1901, the Radical Party was firmly attached to the institutions of the Third Republic, was in favour of social reform, state intervention in order to correct some of the most extreme social inequalities, limited nationalization of private companies, and had a patriotic foreign policy which sought to regulate international conflict via international law established by negotiations between states (Berstein and Berstein 1987: 257). It was a very broad grouping of different forces, ranging from near socialists to conservatives, albeit republican conservatives, but within the party all groups were faithful to the more liberal democratic aspects of the legacy of the Revolution. Supported by the liberal middle classes, the progressive wing of the Radical Party was concerned in particular with more social justice, whereas the conservative wing was concerned with the importance of private property, law and order and stable government.

Serge Berstein (1991: 4–7) argues that in the entire history of France since the 1789 Revolution there have only been two periods of political consensus. The first period lasted from 1905 to 1929, the Golden Age of republicanism, and the other from 1975 to the present day. The consensus of the first period emerged partly as a result of the victory of liberal democratic principles from the Dreyfus Affair and in particular the idea that the individual needed rights in order to stand up to the power of the state; thus the idea emerged that the political system should be as weak as possible so as to offer this protection. As the Radical philosopher Alain put it:

> Democracy ... is naught else but the continually effective power of deposing kings and specialists the very instant they no longer manage affairs according to the interests of the greatest numbers. That power used to be exercised by revolution or barricade; it is now exercised by questions to ministers and votes of censure. (Quoted in Soltau 1931: 409)

During the initial phase of this consensual period, up to the beginning of the First World War, the economy prospered, the republican model of democracy based on the ownership of property by the petty bourgeoisie was widely appreciated and the institutions of the state were widely respected, all the more so as attention became increasingly focused on defence policy because of the growing threat of war. The influence of organizations hostile to the regime, like revolutionary syndicalism on the left and Action Française on the right, was marginal. After the outbreak of war in 1914 the government, described by President of the Republic Raymond Poincaré as an *Union sacrée*, rallied party leaders from right, centre and left, including two leaders of the socialist Section Française de l'Internationale Ouvrière (SFIO), Jules Guesde and Marcel Sembat, who stayed in government until 1917 (Berstein and Berstein 1987: 322). The government made the war effort an absolute priority and was at pains not to divide the parties which supported it, but it did become increasingly associated with the nationalist right. Finally, from 1919 to 1929, there was consensus to the extent that there was from 1919 to 1923 government which continued in the spirit of the *Union sacrée*, although the Socialists and Communists were excluded and the Radicals remained outside government. (The PCF was established in 1920.) After a period of more familiar left–right head-on confrontation between 1923, when the Radicals moved into the opposition, and 1926, when the *Cartel des Gauches* government fell, Raymond Poincaré came back as Prime Minister and remained in post until 1929, carrying out measures which were broadly acceptable to all parties except the PCF and the SFIO. This government was based on a policy of stabilization of the franc, reconciliation with Germany and strengthening wartime alliances, and strong opposition to Bolshevism and Alsatian autonomism. It also took measures to

democratize the school system, laid the basis of a social housing policy and introduced the first major piece of legislation on social security. With the onset of economic crisis at the end of the 1920s and in
the 1930s, the often violent clashes between fascism and communism
and then war between supporters of the German Occupation and
Resistance fighters, consensus was shattered and was not to return
for several decades. Berstein is largely correct to highlight the consensual nature of much of the first three decades of the twentieth
century, although it should be pointed out that particularly in the
years 1906, 1907 and 1908 government action against strikers was
often brutal, and contributed to consolidating the tradition of repression of trade union activism; Georges Clemenceau, who was Minister
of the Interior then *Président du Conseil* during these years, was particularly associated with the trade union repression, which left at
least six strikers dead and 50 injured at industrial disputes at Draveil
and Villeneuve-Saint-Georges, and he earned himself the names
'France's number one cop' and 'the red beast' (Dreyfus 1982: 19).
Also, the PCF received roughly 10 per cent of the vote in the first 15
years of its existence and was of course often far from accepting the
legitimacy of governments' actions; it was influenced in every detail
of its policies and actions by the newly-formed Soviet Union.

The later period of consensus suggested by Berstein, from 1974 to
the present day, is one to which we return in subsequent chapters,
but suffice it to say here that what Berstein does not emphasize is the
far greater caesura between conflict and consensus in the early 1980s
than in 1974.

It should also be said that the Third Republic was in many ways an
ineffective regime, although as Rémond (1965: 236) points out, it survived the storms of many a political crisis, including the attempted
coup d'état by Marshal MacMahon on 16 May 1877, the Dreyfus
Affair, the First World War, turmoil around the *Cartel des Gauches*,
and the political conflicts of the mid-1930s, where pitched battles
between the extreme right leagues and the left were followed by the
Popular Front government, which was accompanied by a massive
wave of strikes. Governments of the Third Republic did not address
some profound structural socio-economic problems; the electoral
dominance of the small peasant farmer meant that they made only
tentative and limited reforms in favour of the working class and
there was little support for larger industrial concerns, whilst giving
strong support to the small-scale, landowning farmer, who indeed
became the electoral mainstay of the Republic. The emphasis placed

on the sanctity of private property, ideological references back to the principles of 1789, the Declaration of the Rights of Man and cultural *rayonnement* in the new French colonies meant a constant harking back to the past and thus a strong counter-tendency to some of the Republic's more modernizing inclinations, characteristics which were present during the Fourth Republic as well. The clash between modernizing and conservative tendencies, so prevalent in the nineteenth century, was still present, although the consequences were perhaps less dramatic. Weak government meant that there were very frequent changes, with 60 different governments between 1870 and 1914 (Stevens 1992: 17). Thiers, in a famous phrase, described the Third Republic as 'the regime that divides us least'.

The period 1870–1940, and in particular much of the first 30 years of the twentieth century, may thus be seen as a partial hiatus between periods of turbulence. From the 1930s onwards, and particularly after the German invasion in 1940, France returned to a situation where politics were clearly marked by profound conflict and instability. Only after the departure of de Gaulle in 1969 was this to change, and then only slowly.

An exceptional history?

France's modern political history is clearly dominated by revolt and conflict. But is it correct to argue that France should be treated as an exceptional case among West European countries, in that its history is exceptionally violent and conflictual? French history, particularly up to the end of the Second World War, was very far from being characterized by the establishment of a stable, liberal democratic scheme of things. Compared with Britain, the United States, Switzerland or much of Scandinavia, the degree of violence is high and the fragility of political regimes more intense, although as Tilly et al. (1975: 280) point out, even Britain, which has not had a revolution since 1688, and is often held up as a model country in terms of social, economic and political change without violence, has had violent and conflictual moments in the nineteenth and twentieth centuries, associated with Luddism, Temperance, feminism, pacifism and the organization of labour. Nevertheless, compared with the countries with more mild-mannered reputations, France is indeed exceptional. On the other hand, there are greater similarities with Germany and Italy in terms of political conflict in the period we have been dealing with in this chapter, where in both cases political violence has been common in the nineteenth and twentieth centuries. But even so, as Michel Winock (1986: 9) argues, the model of France's historical trajectory is different to that of many other countries of Europe, including others which also have a reputation for being politically turbulent. Winock points out that many countries evolved as follows: (1) abolition or liberalization of the *ancien régime*; (2) counter-revolution followed by dictatorship; (3) establishment of liberal democracy. This was the pattern in Germany, Italy, Austria, Spain, Portugal and Greece. In France, a republican regime and universal suffrage came early, but much of the history of the nineteenth century in particular was one of tremendous tensions between forces of reaction and authoritarianism on the one hand and forces of progress, modernization and democracy on the other, a process which explains in part why there were ten different constitutions between 1789 and 1875. It is the combination of two strong and strongly opposing tendencies – modernizing and reactionary – which sets France apart somewhat from so many other nations and makes its history so spectacularly one of conflict and revolt.

An empirical study by Small and Singer (1982) counts the number of deaths in civil and interstate wars from 1816 to 1980 and shows that France has certainly had a particularly bloody political history. Even discounting the violent period from 1789 to 1816, France had the second highest number of civil wars (three) of all European countries (after Spain, with seven). These civil wars, which occurred in 1830, 1848 and 1871, accounted for a total 24,000 deaths. In terms of the number of interstate wars in which countries took part during the same period, France ranks number one, with 22 wars, although England and Russia come a close second, each with 19 wars, followed by Turkey (18) and Italy (12). Again, this discounts the period 1789–1816. France also spent more actual time at war than any other nation, with an average of 3.71 months per year. Total war deaths during the period amounted to almost two million, or roughly 12,000 per year, a level surpassed only by Germany and Russia. In raw statistical terms, then, France's particularly violent and conflictual reputation is confirmed.

As I have argued, some aspects of French history can be interpreted as the steady development of modernity and the more stable political trappings which often go with it. Barrington Moore, in his famous comparative analysis of social and political development,

Social Origins of Dictatorship and Democracy (1966 [1979]), uses French history as an example of the parliamentary democratic road to political modernity and contrasts this history with that of other countries whose development lead either to fascist dictatorship or to communist dictatorship, exemplified by Germany and Japan in the former case and Russia and China in the latter. However, as may be deduced from the discussion above, I also believe that although Moore is in some ways correct to place France alongside Britain and the United States of America in terms of a more liberal democratic path to modernity than elsewhere, I believe a look at the details of France's political history since 1789 suggests the need for a more refined taxonomy of countries' development, which would at least put France within a subsection of the group of countries with a parliamentary democratic development, if not in an altogether distinct group (Skocpol 1973).

It is partly the fact that violence and conflict became intimately connected with the process of government, constitution, political debate and popular demands for change, with constant references back to the Revolution of 1789 in particular, but also subsequent ones, that sets France apart somewhat from other countries. Whilst all countries diverge from an abstract and ideal model of steady progress to liberal democracy, it would be true to say that France, among the countries deemed to be at the forefront of modernity, diverged to a particularly large degree. But if France is exceptional, which it seems to be, this exceptionalism does not in itself constitute an explanation for conflict and violence, just as the exploration of the notion of 'end of exceptionalism' since the 1970s, or the beginning of the 1980s, does not itself constitute a theory of change. Both approaches simply note what is happening. If one believes that the development of capitalism brought certain social and political characteristics common to many different countries, it is necessary to seek to explain different paths to the present. Not to suggest a pattern of development and a reason for this development either means resigning oneself to simple description, or assuming that developments in individual countries are due to wholly distinct phenomena, both of which approaches are inadequate.

3
Political Exceptionalism, 1945–1981

Two regiments of parachutists from Algeria and two detachments of parachutists stationed in the south-west ... were to meet ... in the Paris region. With the help of – or at least with no hindrance from – the police and CRS riot police, the parachutists were to occupy the Hôtel de Ville, the police headquarters, the regional centre for post and telecommunications, the Eiffel Tower, television and radio studios, the National Assembly, the Foreign Ministry and the President's office.

General Jouhaud, describing Operation Resurrection, planned for 19 May 1958 (quoted in Lacouture 1985: 778)

The political history of France continued to be particularly turbulent after the Second World War and the first 25 years after the war were in some ways more conflictual than the years 1900–39. During the war, of course, the ready collaboration by large numbers of people with the Nazi occupier meant that what historians (e.g. Azéma, Rioux and Rousso 1985) sometimes describe as the 'Franco-French war' had moved from the realm of politics and ideology and become an actual civil war. French Resistance activists identified French collaborators as mortal enemies, and some of those who collaborated condoned and sometimes participated in the torture and killing of resisters, Jews and other perceived enemies of the German Reich and therefore enemies of Vichy France. Rifts which arose or were compounded during this period endured, and indeed still exist in some respects to this day. But in order to explore the unstable and conflictual aspects of modern French history in the period between 1945 and 1981, I continue to put special emphasis on the socio-economic development of France and the way in which uneven socio-economic modernization affected the political situation.

In order to attempt an explanation of France's political 'exceptionalism', in this chapter I compare directly the post-war history of France with that of other countries. After the Second World War, a new situation emerged in many north-west European countries, which combined the task of economic reconstruction with the construction of a new consensus in social relations. This was possible in part because of the degree of consensus which had already developed in social and political life in many advanced capitalist countries, and in part because of the new, favourable conditions for economic growth which emerged from the Second World War. I examine the nature of and the basis for consensus politics in Germany, Britain and Sweden during the post-war period, before going on to examine the very different situation in France.

Consensus politics in Western Europe since 1945

Preliminary qualifications are necessary before exploring the politics of Germany, Britain and Sweden. Ultimately, of course, it is incorrect to speak of widespread consensus when analysing any political situation, because the very existence of distinct political parties and other political forces is an indication of lack of consensus, a word whose dictionary definition is 'agreement in opinion' (*OED* 1973). It is a case of degree, and the extent of agreement between the various parties in some countries, often not acknowledged by the parties themselves, for strategic reasons, justifies the use of the word 'consensus'. Indeed Raymond Williams has an interesting view of consensus, which he defines as 'a policy of avoiding or evading differences or divisions of opinion in an attempt to "secure the centre" or "occupy the middle ground"' (Williams 1976: 77). This perhaps overstates and at the same time oversimplifies – if applied to politics – parties' deliberate intentions, but if we extend this notion a little, we can say that in some countries during the post-war period governments were partially successful in avoiding, or ignoring, differences and divisions in society at large in order to secure the centre, or occupy the middle ground, and thus stay in power. Next, and following on from Williams' points, general agreement between political parties on policies and even superficial agreement between voters (perhaps indicated by common voting habits) does not mean that there is an absence of social discontent and there may well be manifestations of social unrest; in countries known for their political consensus after the war, social divisions and discontent were sometimes clear to see, including for example the widely supported British miners' strike of 1973–4. In the Federal Republic of Germany (FRG), often thought to be a model of moderation and harmony, there were deep social tensions related to various issues including harsh living and working conditions for guest workers and poverty among pensioners (Fulbrook 1992: 93). However, there was broad agreement between dominant parties in both countries on many major policy issues. Thus it is probably correct to say that in these more consensual countries social antagonisms were less obviously represented in the political sphere and that there was thus a less obvious relationship between problems in civil society and party politics. (It might also plausibly be argued that Britain and Germany were actually more just societies, but tackling that question is beyond the scope of this discussion.) In France, by contrast, for many years social injustices and inequalities were reflected in the more formal politics of the country.

The analytical framework which informs the discussion below can be summarized as follows. In many advanced capitalist countries after the Second World War, there emerged agreements between capital, labour and the state which were, in an immediate sense at least, mutually beneficial. During this Golden Age of capitalism, in return for higher wages, welfare protection, basic trade union rights and virtually full employment, labour leaders agreed to limit strike and other protest action and in general accepted that it was the right of employers to make the pursuit of profit their driving principle. This helped governments, in the mean time, to implement programmes of economic reconstruction, often following a Keynesian policy of expanding the public sector, creating jobs, and offering higher wages in order to stimulate demand. During the period of post-war economic prosperity, this approach set the tone for a more consensus-oriented pattern of politics and industrial relations. Britain, West Germany and Sweden are among the countries which clearly exemplify – in slightly different ways – this pattern of development, but it is worth mentioning that there are other countries which could also be used to illustrate the point being made here, such as Austria, Denmark, Norway and the Netherlands, which developed in similar ways. Broadly speaking, this perspective is borrowed from the so-called regulation school, a theory which I discuss further at the end of this chapter, and in chapter 8.

Britain

In Britain, the politics of consensus were particularly striking for the first thirty years after the Second World War. One important reason for this was the substantially increased role for organized labour in shaping policy priorities, which brought the representatives of the working class into the governmental sphere rather than being left on the outside. During the war itself, the working class in general and the trade unions in particular had already gained a status which they had never enjoyed before, including during the First World War. Seen far more as a People's War than the 1914–18 war had been, with much disruption of working-class civilian life, the assumption was that the war would result in substantial gains for the ordinary person (Dutton 1991: 10; Kavanagh and Morris 1989). During the war there was a coalition government of the Labour, Conservative and Liberal parties with Conservative Winston Churchill as Prime Minister and Ernest Bevin, the former leader of Britain's largest trade union, the Transport and General Workers' Union, as Minister of Labour. In the 1945 Labour government under Prime Minister Clement Attlee, Bevin became Foreign Secretary and George Isaacs, the chairman of the Trades Union Congress (TUC), was Minister of Labour. The extent of agreement between the two major parties on both foreign and domestic issues was at that time clearly expressed by Churchill, when in his first speech as leader of the opposition, he said:

> it is evident that not only are we two parties in the House agreed on the main essentials of foreign policy and in our moral outlook on world affairs but we also have an immense programme, prepared by our joint exertions during the Coalition, which requires to be brought into law and made an inherent part of the life of the people. Here and there, there may be differences of emphasis and view, but, in the main, no Parliament has ever assembled with such a mass of agreed legislation as lies before us this afternoon. (Quoted in Sked and Cook 1979: 25)

The first post-war Labour government was responsible for implementing policies which were to set the tone for the next 25 years, policies which achieved economic prosperity and improved the living standards of the vast majority of the population. For the first time the working class was brought into a position of mass consumption.

The preconditions for this state of affairs were a healthy economy and an organized compromise between the interests of labour and the interests of capital, which is sometimes described as the post-war settlement (e.g. Dutton 1991: *passim*). This settlement depended on the economy being healthy enough for employers both to increase profits and at the same time concede some of the demands of labour, such as pay rises, shorter working hours and the nationalization of key sectors of the economy.

As time went by there were, of course, frequent disagreements and arguments between the two major political parties and they by no means systematically agreed on policy details. But they shared a common set of political assumptions which broadly informed their respective programmes and the degree of difference in policy was slight. Dennis Kavanagh and Peter Morris have shown convincingly that there was profound policy consensus between Labour and Conservative parties on the mixed economy, full employment, the welfare state, foreign and defence policy and the role of trade unions, from the Second World War right up to the beginning of the premiership of Margaret Thatcher in 1979 (Kavanagh and Morris 1989: *passim*). Most notably, Labour and Conservative parties (and indeed the Liberals as well) agreed on the need for a comprehensive welfare state and Keynesian-inspired management of a mixed economy which guaranteed as near full employment as possible, low inflation and steady economic growth. Crucially, both parties were committed to implementing policy in close consultation with the main interest groups, notably the TUC and Confederation of British Industry (CBI). As far as foreign policy was concerned, both parties were committed in particular to standing alongside the United States in defending the West against the perceived threat of aggression from the Soviet Union, without sacrificing Britain's independent status as a leading international power both economically and diplomatically. When Churchill became Prime Minister again in 1951 after the Conservative election victory, he said: 'Controversy there must be on some of the issues before us, but this will be a small part of the work and interests we have in common' and the leading Labour politician Richard Crossman commented that the new Conservative cabinet was 'only very slightly to the right of the most recent Attlee government' (quoted in Dutton 1991: 43).

Trade unions were vital political and economic actors during the post-war boom years and almost all were affiliated to the TUC. A key to the politics of consensus of the time was indeed the ability and desire of governments to involve union leaders (and thus union members) in feeling responsible for running the economy, and successive governments, whether Labour or Conservative, remained committed to negotiations with unions over pay and other economic matters; every government from 1945 to 1979, except the Churchill and Eden governments from 1951 to 1957, tried to set up a formal incomes policy (Kavanagh and Morris 1989: 112). The prevailing attitude was clearly spelled out by Edward Heath when in 1972 he told Conservative Party conference that 'the trade unions and the employers [must] share fully with government the benefits and obligations of running the economy' (Kavanagh and Morris 1989: 61). The CBI, meanwhile, was consistently ready to negotiate with trade unions over pay and other matters and the institutionalization of corporatist consultations perhaps reached its apogee after the creation of the tripartite National Economic Development Council in 1962. But even 15 years later, Grant and Marsh (1977: 145) comment that 'the stock phrase – "consultations are taking place with the CBI and the TUC" – is one that is now often heard in Parliament.'

Just as one precondition for this sort of consensus was the good health of the economy, when the economy began to falter at the end of the 1960s, there were already hints that the consensus between the two major parties would do the same. Indeed this was already apparent in the Conservative manifesto for the 1966 General Election, which set out proposals to reduce income tax, increase competition and restrict the provision of welfare benefits. But it took until the election of the Conservatives in 1979 under the leadership of Margaret Thatcher for the post-war consensus to be ideologically and politically challenged head-on, with a commitment to market regulation of the economy, privatizations, a gradual erosion of a fully comprehensive welfare state, and an end to the involvement of the TUC and CBI in policy making.

The population at large, even during the years of economic crisis, apparently approved of the politics of consensus on the whole. Certainly, there were from time to time signs of public dissent from important aspects of government policy, such as during the 1956 Suez crisis and in the early 1970s when strikes eventually brought down the Heath government, in February 1974. However, trade unions were on the whole moderate, to the extent that they saw collective bargaining and defence of their members' immediate material interests as their overriding concern, with an institutional commitment to Labourism. There were few street disturbances of any real significance. There was no large Communist Party, no significant party of the extreme right and no party which was ideologically or strategically located outside of the ambit of the parliamentary system, a system so dominated by the Labour and Conservative parties. In short, there was no significant, widespread protest against the consensual status quo.

A major and enduring exception to the rule of peace and consensus on post-war British territory was the situation in the North of Ireland, where there has been widespread armed conflict for much of the time since 1969, when British troops were sent in. However, for all the conflict, violence and roughly 3,000 deaths of soldiers and civilians in the North of Ireland there were no related crises for governments or political parties in Westminster, little discussion on the Irish question within trade unions and little public protest of any real significance, even from pressure groups such as Troops Out.

The Federal Republic of Germany

There are many parallels to be drawn between Britain after the Second World War and the situation in the Federal Republic of Germany. Within a political framework imposed by the Allies after the Second World War, there was a great deal of inter-party cooperation over the reconstruction of the country and in particular the creation of the conditions for Germany's long-lasting and much-envied post-war economic prosperity. Parties and trade unions worked closely together in the task of reconstruction, with widespread agreement on the need for expansion of the welfare state, a politically regulated market economy and the establishment of structures for capital–labour cooperation which would lay the basis for a lasting climate of political and social peace.

From 1949 until the early 1980s, apart from brief deviations, the closeness of the parties' orientations was demonstrated in the various coalition governments made up of all three possible combinations of what has often been described as a 'two-and-a-half' party system: Christian Democrats (Christlich-Demokratische Union/Christlich-Soziale Union (CDU/CSU)) on the centre-right, the small Freie Demokratische Partei (FDP) in the centre and the Sozialdemokratische Partei Deutschlands (SPD) on the centre-left). From 1949 until 1966 the Christian Democrats were in coalition governments with the FDP, apart from the years 1957–61, when the CDU/CSU had a majority on its own. From 1966 to 1969 the extent of agreement between the two major parties was neatly demonstrated by a Grand Coalition government of Christian Democrats and Social Democrats, during which time there was virtually no opposition. Otto Kirchheimer points to the particularly high level of agreement between the Christian Democrats and Social Democrats at the time and describes this period as one of 'vanishing opposition' (Kirchheimer: 1966). From 1969 to 1982 the SPD and FDP governed together.

The Bundestag election results from 1965 to 1980 show clearly how dominant and stable the three main parties had become: the CDU/CSU's share of the vote ranged from 45 to 47 per cent of the total, the SPD's from 39 to 46 per cent and the FDP's from 6 to 11 per cent. In the 1976 election (in which the SDP's slogan was, significantly, 'Model Deutschland') the three big parties received 99 per cent of the total (Padgett 1989: 126). The size of the real opposition outside this dominant system thus represented a small minority; there was no large Communist Party and no significant force on the extreme right. When Green members of parliament entered the Bundestag in 1983, it was the first time a new party had entered parliament since 1950 (Dalton 1989: 100).

Meanwhile, outside the realm of party politics, trade unions and employers cooperated to achieve what were perceived as common objectives. After the Second World War the Allied powers imposed a new, industry-based system of trade unions to replace the pre-1933 system (banned by the Nazis) which had been based on religious and political differences. Roughly 40 per cent of the working population was in a trade union and, crucially, trade unions were moderate and were virtually all affiliated to the Deutsche Gewerkschaftsbund (DGB) union confederation. As in other countries where post-war political consensus was particularly notable, trade union leaders were thus able to negotiate with employers in the knowledge that they represented a large proportion of the working population. In 1951, the system of *Mitbestimmung*, or co-determination, was created in large firms in the iron and steel industry, which allowed for strong worker and union representation on boards of directors, and in 1976 *Mitbestimmung* was extended to all limited companies with more than 1,000 employees. Corporatism, then, was highly developed in the FRG and government was strongly influenced by representative pressure groups; as Mary Fulbrook puts it, 'major interest groups – the employers' federation, representatives of the farming lobby, trade unionists – came together to work out the details of acceptable policy compromises before any draft legislation was put to parliament for final, almost purely formal, approval' (Fulbrook 1992: 35). This was particularly important during the period of intense tripartite cooperation between 1967 and 1977, known as Concerted Action (*Konzertierte Aktion*), when DGB leaders, the employers' Federation of German Industry and the state met frequently to discuss what were perceived as mutually beneficial policies.

As in Britain, there has been a decline of the post-war consensus in West Germany since the late 1970s, after the period of strong economic growth slowed, although economic decline came later in Germany than in Britain. Already in the mid-1970s the expansion of the welfare state stopped, but real economic problems only arrived at the beginning of the 1980s and Helmut Kohl's becoming Chancellor in 1982 as the leader of the centre-right CDU/CSU-FDP coalition heralded a shift, described by the CDU/CSU as a *Wende* (turn, or reorientation). The emergence of the Greens as a parliamentary force to be reckoned with indicated a break with the harmonious post-war period, as did the rise of the right-wing Republican Party. More significant, however, in terms of finally ending the post-war order of things has been the unification of Germany, bringing with it much increased economic and ecological problems and the continued rise of the extreme right.

Sweden

In Sweden a form of enlightened welfare capitalism became deeply rooted, particularly under the governance of the Social Democratic Party, Socialdemocratiska Arbetarpartiet (SAP), and politics of consensus and compromise became the political *modus operandi*. Social Democratic rule began before the Second World War, in 1932, and lasted, alone or in partnership, without interruption until 1976. During this period there were only three Prime Ministers (Per Albin Hansson, Tage Erlander and Olof Palme), all of them Social Democrats. Then, after six years of non-Social Democratic rule, SAP again became the party of government and remained so until 1991. Between 1943 and 1991 SAP never received less than 41.5 per cent of the vote at parliamentary elections, although it has only twice received more than 50 per cent (in 1940 and 1968) and in the 1991 elections it received only 37.6 per cent (Hancock et al. 1993: 533). The dominant parties of both left and right are moderate, and smaller parties have governed with both centre-left and centre-right. When the Greens entered Parliament in 1988 they were the first new party to do so in seventy years.

The keys to understanding the stability of this centre-oriented system of government are similar to those which explain the post-war settlement in the other countries discussed above. These are economic prosperity and full employment promoted by government, a highly developed welfare state, a large, unified trade movement organizationally and ideologically allied to a centre-left party, a business class willing to compromise, centre-oriented political parties with widespread electoral support, and the absence of significant extremes on the right or the left of the political spectrum in terms of either political parties or pressure groups.

The post-war settlement in Sweden was already anticipated by the Basic Agreement signed by the trade union Landsorganisationen (LO) and the employers' organization Svenska Arbetsgivareföreningen (SAF) in 1938, when they agreed detailed procedures for conducting industrial relations in the firm. In return for employers agreeing to drop demands for legal restrictions on the right to strike, LO conceded that any contract between one of its member unions and employers would recognize the right of employers to hire and fire. This spirit of compromise continued to characterize the situation after the war and indeed is one of the major ingredients for the success of the post-war settlement in Sweden. An example of this spirit of compromise is cooperation between labour and employer representatives on the tripartite National Labour Market Board, which among other things organizes training and retraining of workers and attempts to relocate workers whose firm has closed.

Governmental arrangements promoting cooperation are particularly developed in Sweden and have been described as 'democratic corporatism' (Hancock et al. 1991). For example, governments set up *statsutredningar*, or state commissions, made up of interest group and political parties' representatives, to report on an area of proposed legislation, and their views are often important in influencing the final form legislation takes. Consultation also takes place under what is known as the 'remiss' system, where ministries ask for the official views of interested pressure groups on proposed legislation and report these views to Parliament alongside the government's own views (Castles 1975).

As in Britain and Germany, consensual government and industrial relations arrangements did not of course imply a total absence of conflict. For instance, during the 1970s LO promoted the idea of setting up Wage Earner Funds which would eventually enable some employee groups to obtain a majority stake in their firm's shares. This was fiercely opposed by SAF and played an important part in SAP's defeat at the parliamentary election in 1976. As in many other countries, the 1980s and early 1990s have more generally proved a more testing time for Sweden's consensual model, with more overt friction between employers and employees and even a partial erosion of the welfare state, all of which went hand in hand with SAP's conclusive defeat in 1991.

French politics in the post-war era

In France, the political situation which prevailed during the period of post-war economic reconstruction was markedly different from that in the countries explored above. There was a brief period after the Liberation in 1944 when it seemed as if social peace might prevail, when right, centre and left parties worked together in a coalition government and established as their common task the physical and economic reconstruction of the country, working broadly along Keynesian lines. During this period often described as 'tripartism', which lasted until May 1947, the major forces of the wartime Resistance movement worked together, within the party political framework of the Christian democratic Mouvement Républicain Populaire (MRP), the Communist Party (PCF) and the socialist Section Française de l'Internationale Ouvrière (SFIO). The parties cooperated on the implementation of the immediate post-war programme, including nationalization of key sectors of the economy, raising levels of productivity, ensuring full employment and extending the provisions of the welfare state.

It soon became clear, however, that despite favourable economic conditions, the lasting agreement in other countries between organized labour, the state and business was impossible to achieve in France. During the period of tripartism Communist and other trade union leaders instructed their membership to be moderate in their demands and the pursuit of these demands. But the Communists were excluded from government in May 1947 after they declared their support for a strike at Renault and abandoned their previous policy of not rocking the industrial relations boat. The Communist-oriented CGT was the most influential trade union confederation and from 1947 onwards reverted to the solidly class-against-class positions it had held before the Popular Front of the 1930s, which often meant a refusal even to enter into negotiations with management unless terms seemed particularly favourable to the unions. More generally, the onset of the Cold War meant that forces to the right of the very popular PCF were no longer prepared to share government with it, due in part to pressure from the United States government. There were many political parties in Parliament at the time and none attracted anything like an absolute majority. In the parliamentary elections of November 1946, for example, the three most popular parties were the PCF (which received 28.8 per cent of votes), the MRP (26.3 per cent) and the socialist SFIO (18.1 per cent). The collapse of tripartite government set the tone for the entire period from 1947 to 1968, and many aspects of the subsequent hostility which characterized these years remained well beyond 1968.

We need to identify the most significant characteristics of the post-war period which distinguish France from other, more consensual countries. First, there was no dominant, centre-oriented party on either the left or the right which could in any lasting way steer France towards generally agreed aims in reconstruction. By stark contrast with Britain, West Germany, Sweden and elsewhere in north-west Europe, there was a large and powerful Communist Party which successfully drew support away from the Socialists, and on the right Gaullism and more obviously extreme right parties drew attention away from more moderate currents. The volatility of right wing party politics was demonstrated in the first 15 years after the war by the sudden rise and then decline of the Christian democratic MRP, the rise and fall of the Gaullist Rassemblement du Peuple Français (RPF) and finally the rise and fall of the Poujadists. On the left, volatility was expressed at the end of the 1950s by the fragmentation of the SFIO. A large proportion of the working class voted Communist and for a time many with right-wing sympathies voted Gaullist, despite the fact that both parties were seen as being mainly hostile to governmental politics of the Fourth Republic. Second, trade unions were small compared with those in other West European countries and they did not organize anywhere near a majority of the working population. This meant that in terms of size alone trade unions could not be relied upon to guarantee a low level of militancy in exchange for improved working conditions, for instance. But the trade union movement also had a tradition of militancy and was dominated by

Table 3.1 For and against mainstream politics. Votes cast in legislative elections, 1946–58 (% of total votes)

	June 1946	November 1946	June 1951	January 1956
Parties supporting the regime				
Socialists	21.1	17.8	14.6	15.2
Radicals and allies	11.6	11.1	10.0	15.2
Christian democrats	28.2	25.9	12.6	11.1
Total	60.9	54.8	36.2	41.5
Parties opposing the regime				
Communists	25.9	28.2	26.9	25.9
Gaullists and allies	—	3.0	21.6	3.9[a]
Poujadists				11.6
Extreme right				1.2
Total	25.9	31.2	48.5	42.6
Others	12.9	13.7	14.1	15.7

[a] The Gaullists split their support between a left-wing Republican Front alliance including the Socialist Party and some Radicals, and a more right-wing alliance including Christian Democrats.
Source: Stevens 1992: 257

the Communist orientation of the CGT, which did not lend itself to moderate agreements with employers. Finally, there was no established tradition of negotiation between capital and labour; whilst on the one hand trade unions were steeped in a radical tradition, on the other employers were extremely hostile to the idea of systematic negotiations with unions. Up until 1968 at least, by contrast with the situation in many other countries, employers remained deeply paternalistic. As Henri Weber comments:

> this [paternalistic] approach to industrial relations and to the role of different actors in the firm leaves little room for worker representation and still less for its organized and ongoing form, trade unionism. Trade unions, all trade unions ... are seen as intruders and troublemakers who should be driven out. (1986: 92–3)

Added to all this was, more generally, France's tradition of overt conflict, which was itself to an extent self-perpetuating.

It might be argued that politicians of the Fourth Republic were successful in putting together coalition governments whose composi-

Table 3.2 The 1956 legislative election

Party	Votes	%	Seats	%
Extreme right	335,000	1.6	3	0.6
Poujadists	2,608,000	12.3	52[a]	9.6
Social Republicans	911,000	4.3	16	2.9
Conservatives	3,086,000	14.6	94	17.3
MRP	2,356,000	11.1	71	13.0
Radicals	2,853,000	13.5	71	13.0
SFIO	3,188,000	15.0	88	16.2
PCF	5,492,000	25.9	145	26.7
Other left	355,000	1.7	4	0.7

[a] 10 Poujadist deputies subsequently unseated included in total.
Source: Cole and Campbell 1989: 86

tion and programmes were based on compromise between the various parties. This is partially true, but the extraordinarily unstable nature of government under the Fourth Republic (there were 25 different governments and 15 different Prime Ministers in the short life of the Republic) often reflected attempts to form governments with the participation of parties who had little in common apart from a wish to exclude the extremes of left and right. The most striking instances of this practice occurred during the so-called Third Force period between 1947 and 1951, when centre-left and centre-right joined forces to form governments whose main purpose was to exclude Communists and Gaullists (see e.g. Rioux 1987: 151–63). But Table 3.2 shows how in the 1956 legislative election the extremes were real forces to be reckoned with.

It might also be objected that state economic planning, which was very successful in achieving high rates of economic growth and which was sometimes envied even by more consensus-oriented countries, was an example of successful cooperation of government, labour leaders and employers. But in fact trade unions soon became marginal to the planning process; both the CGT and Force Ouvrière (FO) withdrew from meetings on the Second Plan (1953–7) and stayed almost completely away from the planning process until the Eighth Plan launched by the new Socialist government in 1981 (P. Hall 1986: 158). Hall comments that, because of their organizational weakness, 'there was little the unions could do to prevent the state from using the Plan to forge an alliance with the dynamic sections of capital' (1986: 159). As another writer puts it, the French system of organized industrial growth succeeded not because of the agreement on the necessary strategy between labour and capital, but on the ability of those at the centre of the process to subordinate the interests of labour and other groups in their plans. It was predicated on and required the traditional weakness of wage-earning groups in French politics. It would otherwise never have succeeded. (Herberg 1981: 513)

In order to understand the nature of France's conflictual politics during the post-war era, it is helpful to examine in more detail why there was no dominant socialist party on the one hand and why, on the other, there was no moderate party on the right, like the Christian democratic parties in Italy and West Germany or the Conservative Party in Britain. Turning first to socialism, the twentieth century did not begin auspiciously for the SFIO. By contrast to the situation in Britain, for example, where the Labour Party sprang from a well-established and relatively moderate trade union movement, the French labour movement was small and highly combative. As discussed in chapter 2, the deaths of many Communards in the repression of 1871 had helped remove any possibility of relative peace between the state and the trade unions. Late industrialization meant that the industrial working class and therefore the trade union movement was small and hence unable to defend working-class interests in an effective way through widespread collective bargaining. Entrenched hostility on the part of the *patronat* towards trade unions compounded both the smallness of the movement and its radicalism, and the fact that the French labour movement was steeped in a radical tradition meant that, when the PCF was founded in 1920, a large proportion of SFIO members left the party to join the Communists and the SFIO found itself severely weakened. Although the SFIO built up its membership again during the 1920s and 1930s (reaching the pre-PCF level under the Popular Front in 1936) the PCF was to remain an obstacle to greater Socialist success for very many years. In 1940, Socialists were divided over what attitude to take towards Pétain and the image of partial collaboration was never wholly shaken off. Next, the SFIO sided, as we have seen, with the right and against communism during the Cold War.

In fact in general the SFIO was closely associated with some of the least noble moments of Fourth Republic political history: during the miners' strike of 1948, it was the Socialist Interior Minister, Jules Moch, who sent in troops against striking miners which resulted in at least two deaths; the SFIO was intimately involved in formulating policies which resulted in torture and deaths in French custody of members of the nationalist community in Algeria; and it was the Socialist Prime Minister Guy Mollet who collaborated with the British in sending troops to Egypt in an attempt to impose their will on President Nasser after he had nationalized the Suez Canal. Indeed the general orientation of the SFIO under the Fourth Republic has been described by Michel Winock (1978) as 'le socialisme expéditionnaire'. In 1958 the SFIO was split over the issue of whether de Gaulle should be supported as the only person able to avoid armed conflict in France itself as a result of the Algerian question, and this set the tone for the rest of the decade and much of the 1960s as well. The Republic with which the Socialists had been so much associated had failed miserably and the new constitution was approved by a large majority. The SFIO's behaviour under the Fourth Republic came to be seen by many progressive French people as deeply reactionary, and a significant legacy of politics under the Fourth Republic was that participation in government had earned the Socialist current a very bad reputation whereas the PCF, excluded from power, emerged in far better shape.

Turning to the right, backward socio-economic conditions, collaboration with the Germans on the part of certain elements of the right during the Second World War, strong anti-communism as a result of the success of the PCF and finally the war with Algeria prevented the establishment of a stable, moderate right in the form of a large conservative or Christian democratic party along the lines of developments in Italy and Germany, or something like the Conservative Party in Britain. Attempts to set up a dominant centre-right party after the Second World War at first seemed promising with the formation of the MRP, which received roughly a quarter of all votes at the end of the war. The MRP's leaders were mainly Christian democrats who were keen to defend the legacy of the Resistance and who were also faithful to de Gaulle. But in mid-1947 de Gaulle launched the RPF in order to express mass opposition to the constitution of the Fourth Republic and in support of the ideas expressed in his Discours de Bayeux in June 1946. Supposedly above the petty squabbles of party politics, the RPF soon developed a hard-right image and the appeal for many of its supporters was its virulent anti-communism. The RPF recruited large numbers of militants and in the legislative elections of June 1951 it received 22.5 per cent of the vote. The effect of RPF activity on the MRP was disastrous, with many former MRP voters lending their support to the Gaullists, so in the same legislative elections the MRP received only 13.4 per cent of the vote. (The MRP had already a tarnished reputation because of an influx of former Vichy supporters in 1945 and 1946, quite contrary to the wishes of its leadership.)

France's foreign relations in the 1950s also help explain the lack of political consensus. The Algerian war was a major reason for the sharp divisions and unstable governments of the Fourth Republic, and ultimately killed it off. France sent its army into Algeria in 1954 in order to combat the increasingly well-supported struggle for national liberation, soon after the humiliating defeat for the French in the battle of Dien Bien Phu, which led to withdrawal from Indo-China. Not only did it become increasingly apparent that the French would not win the Algerian war, but the army became maddened by its suspicions that politicians in Paris intended to pull out of Algeria and grant independence. The profound political and social divisions over Algeria came to a head in 1958, amid a growing threat of *coup d'état* and civil war in domestic France, and once again opened the door to Charles de Gaulle, who this time was able to implement his ideas for a new constitution which established a strong executive and a greatly weakened parliament. However, the creation of the European Community was to become an important factor in the gradual stabilization of French politics, despite de Gaulle's ambivalence towards the building of a unified Europe.

The Fifth Republic in its early years imposed a certain stability on formal politics in France, and government certainly no longer seemed weak. But under what Nicos Poulantzas might have described as a 'régime d'exception', stability was not achieved in anything like the way it had been in other countries (Poulantzas 1979). Instead of broad agreement between governmental forces and almost equally strong opposition parties, the influence of de Gaulle and his political allies was – at least at first – overwhelming. De Gaulle ruled with a conviction that he alone could solve France's problems, threatening political, social and economic mayhem if he should lose an election or a referendum, and this was a threat which many French people apparently took seriously. Meanwhile, the weakened opposition parties on the left were strongly opposed to the political principles of de Gaulle's governments, with the PCF light years from the governmental politics of the day, describing Gaullism as 'open dictatorship by big capital' and François Mitterrand (presidential candidate for the left in 1965) insisting that the very constitutional basis for the new regime was a 'coup d'état permanent', an expression he adopted as the title of his book about the new constitution, published in 1964 (Mitterrand 1964). By this time the Socialist current was highly fragmented, and was indeed profoundly divided on whether to support de Gaulle's return to power in 1958.

Despite de Gaulle's declared commitment to financial and organizational *participation* of workers in the affairs of their firms, consistent and thorough cooperation between unions and management remained as remote as ever. Employers continued to act in a high-handed way towards trade unions and their workforce in general, and company-level collective bargaining was particularly weak. When in June 1965 the National Assembly passed a law offering slightly improved trade union representation in the workplace, the employer's Conseil National du Patronat Français (CNPF) issued a statement saying 'we shall never permit union penetration into the firm. It will be necessary to impose this upon us by force' (quoted in Shain 1980: 209). In case of industrial action of any intensity a well-armed riot police was available to physically beat protesters into submission rather than concede any real changes. Thus although the economic modernization of post-war France continued apace, it certainly was not accompanied by the more liberal democratic model of politics and industrial relations in other countries. The situation examined above, in addition to a more general neglect of social reform during the de Gaulle years, helps explain the causes of the events of May 1968, and various writers have interpreted the events of 1968 as both a manifestation of and a catalyst to socio-political modernization (see chapter 7). Indeed, during the 12 years between the departure of de Gaulle and the arrival of Mitterrand in the Elysée Palace, France's politics did become calmer and more akin to the social and political situation in other countries of Western Europe. There was much social reform under Giscard d'Estaing, who oversaw, for example: the reduction of the age of majority from 21 to 18 years; wider availability of contraception; the legalization of abortion; divorce by mutual consent; reform of the social security system; a lowering of the age of retirement, and the passage of a law on equal pay and employment opportunities for women and protection against redundancy. This reforming zeal lasted only two years or so, partly because of the deepening economic crisis, but these were significant reforms and reflected an awareness that the old order had to be changed substantially. Giscard's political philosophy, as expressed in his book *Démocratie française*, was certainly more akin to that of the liberal right elsewhere in Europe (Giscard d'Estaing 1976). A sudden, regime-threatening revolt seemed to have become more remote, but during this period the PCF still attracted one voter in five, and the Socialist current re-emerged as the Socialist Party in a firmly radical guise. The CGT still dominated the trade union movement and the Confédération Française Démocratique du Travail (CFDT) was committed to experimenting with ideas such as *autogestion* (a form of workers' control) which, it was argued, would bring about a transformation from capitalism to socialism.

As far as industrial relations were concerned, both Pompidou and then Giscard d'Estaing at first actively encouraged better relations between the two sides of industry. With Pompidou's election as President of the Republic in June 1969 and his appointment of Jacques Chaban-Delmas as Prime Minister, there began a period of three years of liberal reforms, and in a speech before Parliament outlining his government's intentions in September 1969 Chaban-Delmas described his intentions for what he described as 'New Society' policies. The government would give priority to encouraging 'relations between employers and employees based on negotiation', he said, in order to go beyond the 'archaic and conservative' nature of French industrial relations (in Portelli 1987: 212). In particular, the government encouraged a company-level *contrat de progrès* between nationalized firms and trade unions, which guaranteed improvements in workers' living standards in return for a certain level of productivity. Other changes included pressure on the employers' federation, CNPF, to negotiate systematically over differences with trade unions, a law allowing pay agreements at company level and a law which extended the right to training leave (Bridgford 1982). This particular period of reform was brought to a close by elements of the parliamentary majority to the right of Chaban-Delmas and when Pompidou replaced Chaban-Delmas by Pierre Messmer. But Giscard d'Estaing revived the spirit of social reform and to an extent industrial relations reform, by encouraging negotiations between the two sides of industry.

May 1968 came as a major shock to the CNPF, which had for many years taken for granted the ability of employers to act virtually unilaterally, particularly at local level. The years 1969–74 were characterized by widespread negotiations, resulting in the signature of at least ten major collective agreements, and after May 1968 the French *patronat* became far more open to the idea of collective bargaining. In 1972 the leader of the CNPF, Paul Huvelin, was replaced by

François Ceyrac, supported by a relatively progressive group, Entreprise et Progrès, distinct from the CNPF leadership and made up largely of young employers (H. Weber 1986: 191). However, trade unions were still far from integrated into the governmental process and any form of tripartism was entirely out of the question.

If any one factor can be identified during the 1970s which was later to contribute substantially to guiding France to a situation where it was more similar to other countries, it was the reconstruction of the Socialist current in the form of the PS. Encouraged by Mitterrand's relative success in the presidential elections of 1965, where he received 45.5 per cent of the vote in the second round, and by May 1968, the Socialist Party was founded in 1969. Freed from its associations with colonial entanglement under the Fourth Republic, French Socialism was able to further reconstitute itself around the leadership of François Mitterrand at the crucial Congrès d'Epinay in 1971. In 1972, the PS signed a *Programme commun de gouvernement* with the PCF in a move which was to prove the decisive factor in solving the long-standing problem for French Socialists, namely PCF hegemony over the left. A solidly class-based programme including widespread nationalizations, reduction in working time, pay and benefit rises and some constitutional reform, the *Programme commun* appeared as the acceptable electoral face of what the PCF in particular had hitherto stood for. But it became apparent in the cantonal elections of March 1976 and municipal elections of March 1977 that the PS was reaping most of the benefits from the alliance, which prompted the PCF effectively to withdraw in September 1977. The PS had by now been able to rebuild itself as a credible left alternative to the political parties running the country since 1958 and, despite a setback for the left in the 1978 legislative elections due to PCF withdrawal from the Union of the Left, Mitterrand was able to draw on the popularity of the Union of the Left period to emerge victorious in the presidential elections in 1981. Indeed Mitterrand's 1981 electoral platform was greatly inspired by the 1972 *Programme commun*.

After the signature of the Evian Agreements in 1962 which formally began the process of granting Algerian independence, France's foreign relations became progressively an area upon which the French agreed. Instead of being associated with division and trauma, as had been the case so often in modern history, political parties often had virtually common positions on France's relations with the rest of the world. De Gaulle constantly stressed the importance of a great and independent role for France overseas and won many allies and supporters by so doing. His close relationship with Germany within a Europe where France played an important role likewise was popular among politicians of various hues and with their supporters. One of the main features and successes of Giscard d'Estaing's foreign policy was to continue and to consolidate this relationship. Another of de Gaulle's enduring legacies came in the realm of defence, and even the PS and the PCF came out in favour of the *Force de frappe* independent nuclear deterrent in 1977–8. It can credibly be argued, then, that under de Gaulle, Pompidou and Giscard d'Estaing there existed a large and increasing degree of consensus on foreign policy which was a hint of the broader consensus which came in the 1980s.

The persistence of radicalism and the absence of Fordist compromise

To sum up, the socio-economic and political development of France was profoundly different from that of many north-west European countries, largely as a result of its polarized social structures and political history. In France post-war socio-economic modernization took place in the absence of social or political compromise, by contrast with Britain, West Germany, Sweden and other countries which I have not had the space to examine here. In the realm of politics in France sharp divisions were indicated by such phenomena as governmental instability under the Fourth Republic, political crises in 1958 and 1968, the size and popularity of the PCF, the authoritarian nature of Gaullism and the constitution of the Fifth Republic. By contrast with the other countries I have looked at, there were no large, centre-oriented political parties which could be described as consensual parties. Underpinning the consensual politics of other countries were trade unions which played an active role in tripartite arrangements, something which was not possible in France. Although a gradual move towards more moderate politics and industrial relations was apparent, under Giscard d'Estaing in particular, there were constant reminders of the radicalism which had characterized France's polity for so long; the PCF continued to receive roughly 20 per cent of the vote until 1978, the *Parti socialiste* was greatly influenced by Marxism and was obliged to ally with the PCF in order to have any hope of participating in government, a situation perhaps more reminiscent of the politics of southern European countries than France's north European neighbours. However, it was precisely the fact that France also had much in common with other north-west European countries and practised diplomatic and militarily rapprochement with the NATO countries that made France such an interesting case.

Before going on to look at the situation in the 1980s and 1990s, it is worth pausing to look at notions of Fordism and post-Fordism, which have informed the argument in this chapter and will continue to do so in chapter 4. These notions are borrowed from the regulation school, which I discuss in a more general way in chapter 9. According to those who broadly fall within this school, the post-war boom in industrialized countries is best understood in terms of a 'Fordist technological paradigm', or mode of work organization. Fordism, after the American motor car manufacturer Henry Ford, was characterized by mass production of standardized products based on the principle of repetitivity of minor tasks (Taylorism). This was pioneered on a large scale in the car industry. Crucially, it also meant mass consumption, and a large proportion of the working class was for the first time able to buy consumer goods. Through a shift in the distribution of profits between capital and labour (made possible by higher productivity and therefore higher profits), a virtuous circle was created where mass production stimulated mass consumption, and vice versa. This, broadly speaking, was the road taken by the French economy after the Second World War, as in many other West European countries.

Regulation school analysts also speak in terms of a 'mode of regulation', meaning the way in which the necessary compromise is achieved between various social actors, in particular capital and labour. In other countries, labour was willing to exercise restraint with respect to industrial action because this seemed the best way to ensure a higher standard of living and better working conditions than the working class had known before. For capital, it seemed worth offering higher wages, higher levels of employment, improved working conditions and ongoing collective bargaining in order to persuade labour to keep rocking the productive boat to a minimum. The state, in the mean time, played an important role in economic reconstruction and prosperity, not only through coordinating the national economy in such a way as to foster appropriate conditions for Fordism to work, but also as a key employer of labour. It acted as go-between for capital and labour in tripartite planning and negotiating bodies and set up a welfare infrastructure which helped guarantee a certain degree of material security, which in turn helped stimulate demand as well as creating a climate of greater industrial peace. The state was often controlled by a moderate (social democratic) left or moderate (perhaps Christian democratic) right, or some sort of coalition government of these moderate forces. As we have seen, in France such arrangements failed to materialize properly for many years and came closest to realization, I will argue, when the PS came to power in 1981.

However, according to regulation school analysis, even where Fordism found a firm foothold, Fordist ways of arranging production and consumption began to run into difficulties by the end of the 1960s: domestic markets approached saturation point and competition for markets abroad became increasingly intense. Meanwhile technological innovation meant that production could become more specialized and smaller batches of products easily made, which was particularly important for specialist 'niche' products, for which there was a growing market. 'Flexible specialization' is thus the hallmark of the post-Fordist technological paradigm and the pursuit of the Fordist pattern of the production–consumption dynamic has been progressively abandoned. Typically, the accompanying mode of regulation has changed to the extent that employers rely less on conciliatory arrangements with trade unions, the state has withdrawn somewhat from regulating the economy and even more so from organizing cooperation between capital and labour. Welfare provision has been reduced. The clearest examples of governments following neo-liberal, post-Fordist political programmes were the Thatcher and Reagan governments, but others followed suit, not only in Britain and the USA, but also in West Germany and Sweden, for example. Consensus politics seemed in many countries to be a thing of the past.

I have certain reservations in relation to regulation theory and would not agree that capitalism now works in as different a way as some regulation advocates claim. The theoretical framework does help, however, in the investigation of some social, political and economic developments since the late 1960s, and the relevance of this – highly simplified – account of post-Fordism to my wider argument is clear. Social democratic parties played a crucial role in the post-war consensus. They were ideally placed, as centre-left parties with a predisposition to compromise with capital, to serve as facilitators in the Fordist order of things. In post-Fordist times, however, they were no longer able to organize in such a way as to please their largely working-class electorate and to organize the mode of regulation in such a way that the economy could flourish. When the PS achieved office in 1981 with a left social democratic programme, it was thus seriously out of step with prevailing socio-economic practices.

4
The End of
Exceptionalism?
The 1980s and 1990s

> In a short space of time, nearly all the issues over which elections were fought, majorities in parliament rose and fell, which nourished debates, and gave meaning and colour to our political life, have ceased to evoke any passion, have lost their lustre and have in some cases disappeared altogether.
>
> *René Rémond (1993: 21)*

The Mitterrand years began with tremendous hopes and ended with bitter disappointment for the left. After an initial period of substantial left-wing reform in the first two years of Socialist government, analysts began to suggest that France had at last shed its radical political mantle and was becoming increasingly like politically consensual countries in north-west Europe, and like the United States. According to these writers, the significant indicators of change included party politics becoming more moderate, trade unions less militant, disinclination on the part of the French to take to the streets, and fewer strikes. Differences between long-term political and social adversaries had declined considerably, particularly left versus right and employers versus employees. At the same time, France's intellectuals were departing from an established tradition of radicalism, particularly on the left. In short, the French were embracing uncharacteristically sedate political habits. One of the clearest expressions of this view appeared in 1988, when the prominent 'revisionist' historian of the French Revolution, François Furet, in collaboration with the historian and journalist Jacques Julliard, and the sociologist Pierre Rosanvallon, published *La République du centre*, subtitled 'La fin de l'exception française'. In this the authors argue:

What we are now experiencing is quite simply the end of political exceptionalism. Because of a history which has no parallel, characterized by the early rise of the state and liberally sprinkled with revolutions, France has had until recently a special place among modern nations, and one which she saw as exemplary.

We have a way of organizing our national dramas, of celebrating our conflicting passions, of elevating our idiosyncrasies into political forms which has aroused at the same time admiration and irritation in foreign observers. The elites of the people we once colonized retain an undying nostalgia for our political theatrics. What will become of this? We are losing this genius for politics. If we carry on in this way we will attract far less criticism, but also far less interest. We are falling into line. (Furet, Julliard and Rosanvallon 1988: 11)

Various other leading academics have summed up developments in French politics since the early 1980s in similar terms. For example, the political historians René Rémond (1993) and Serge Berstein (1991), the political scientists Roland Cayrol and Pascal Perrineau (1988) and the philosopher Alain Finkielkraut (1987; 1991) have each in varying degrees adopted as an organizing principle of political development this notion of a significant turn towards moderation and consensus since the beginning of the 1980s. Only two years after Mitterrand's victory as President of the Republic the political journalist Alain Duhamel wrote an article in *Le Monde* analysing opinion poll data, entitled 'Un Consensus hexagonal éclatant' (Duhamel 1983), and on the tenth anniversary of Mitterrand's election Finkielkraut commented that 'it is not [just] the idea that communism is progressive that the left has consigned to the scrap heap, but the notion of emancipation itself' (Finkielkraut 1991: 63); in a short space of time the idea that left politics could help attain a higher state of human freedom had disappeared. Jack Hayward, the British political scientist and leading authority on France, has likewise written of the 'exhaustion of the revolutionary impetus' (1994: 15). For some, like Serge Berstein, this more moderate political condition had already begun to manifest itself during the Presidency of Giscard d'Estaing in the 1970s, and for Henri Mendras in the mid-1960s (Mendras 1988), but for all these writers the Socialist 1980s and early 1990s saw a far more advanced state of consensus.

In this chapter I begin by outlining the major changes which conform to the thesis that politics have become more moderate. I broadly agree that there are developments along the lines suggested by the writers referred to above and that some fundamental and probably enduring changes have taken place, although, as I point out below, the reaction against this more moderate state of affairs has in the 1990s, ironically, meant more electoral support for the extremes. However, unless we are to resort to some variant of the 'end of ideology' thesis expounded by Daniel Bell and others in the late 1950s (D. Bell 1960; Lipset 1959; Shils 1955), or to suggest that the French have simply changed their minds and decided in voluntaristic fashion to adopt a liberal democratic outlook more associated with the countries of north-west Europe and the USA, we need to establish a framework of analysis which helps explain these changes. For despite the fact that according to many academics and other writers this decline of political and social conflict is the major overarching development of the period since 1981, little work has been done to explore the underlying reasons for the apparent decline of revolutionary fervour; the case for viewing French politics as less conflictual is often stated but rarely explained in any depth. In particular we need to explain the decline of any widespread faith in a radical left alternative, as represented for many years most concretely by a sizeable vote for the PCF and strong support for the CGT and CFDT trade union confederations, as well as what Finkielkraut describes as the decline in a more generalized belief in the notion of emancipation. But just as importantly we need to establish a framework which helps to understand the limits of these changes in the direction of moderation, limits which became particularly clear in the early and mid-1990s, when the main vehicle of the more consensual politics of the 1980s, the Socialist Party, began suffering from a severe lack of support and, as a result, an identity crisis. Even in the 1997 legislative elections, which the left won, the Socialists only received about a quarter of all votes in the first round (Table 4.1). This reflects, more generally, the dwindling support for the major political parties.

I suggest that to gain a better understanding of the more consensual period in French politics since the early 1980s it is again helpful to explore the fact that there was a greater degree of agreement between the state, employers and trade unions during certain periods of PS government, which is the approach I take in chapter 3 where I compare France with other European countries in earlier times. Although it does not offer a complete explanation, this paradigm helps one to understand the interplay of various forces which coincided with the highest point of consensual politics France has ever known. It is also intended to compensate for the virtual absence of this sort of approach in most other analyses of France in the 1980s and 1990s.

The decline of overt conflict

In 1988 Cayrol and Perrineau asserted that 'in a society which is moving towards the centre, political elites which are increasingly alike argue over programmes which are also converging!' (Cayrol and Perrineau 1988: 27). A look at political parties and other socio-political forces demonstrates that this is largely true for the period we are considering, but some qualification is necessary, in particular in relation to the early and mid-1990s.

The Socialist Party in government

The most crucial changes in party politics in France since 1981 have been associated with the governmental behaviour and programme of the Socialist Party (PS), which went from being a party with a highly conspicuous anti-capitalist stance in the 1970s and the initial part of the 1980s to being a party which soon went on to make tremendous concessions to the interests of capital, mainly in an attempt to attenuate the effects of France's economic problems and thus to remain in power. It changed very rapidly from being a party which had a programme clearly influenced by Marxism to one which had fully embraced the politics of pragmatism, and in particular neo-liberal economic policy. A brief look at the trajectory followed by the PS as a party of government in the 1980s and early 1990s illustrates the degree to which it changed and the extent to which it converged with the parties of the centre-right in terms of ideology and programme.

After a campaign when François Mitterrand and his colleagues had spoken in the party manifesto, *Projet socialiste*, of the need for a 'break with capitalism' (p. 22), Mitterrand was elected President of the Republic in May 1981 on a platform which drew heavily on the Socialist Party's and Communist Party's Common Programme of Government of 1972. Mitterrand's success was followed by a landslide victory for the Socialists in the legislative elections in June the same year and there began one of the most radical periods of reform the country had ever seen. Between 1981 and 1984, the Socialist government, which included four Communist ministers, achieved three major structural reforms which had been heralded as crucial steps towards the building of a socialist France. First, they nationalized five large industrial groups (Compagnie Générale d'Electricité, Saint-Gobain, Péchiney, Rhône-Poulenc and Thomson-Brandt), 39 banks and two financial institutions. This meant that sales from public firms went from 17 per cent to 30 per cent of total sales, while the proportion of all employees working for the state went from 11 per cent to 25 per cent. Second, they introduced substantial industrial relations reform in the shape of the Auroux laws (named after Minister of Labour Jean Auroux), which sought to strengthen the role of trade unions in the firm and in particular to make annual collective bargaining compulsory. The laws also strengthened the role of the firm's works council and set up forums for discussion on work issues in larger firms (see e.g. Millot and Roulleau 1984). Third, the Socialists undertook the most substantial political and administrative decentralization programme in France's history in an attempt to reduce the political, administrative, economic and cultural stranglehold which Paris had on the provinces, and more generally to reduce the dominance of the state over the individual citizen (Keating and Hainsworth 1986). There were many other subsidiary reforms in the first two years of Socialist government, which included: reduction of the legally-defined working week from 40 to 39 hours, increasing statutory holiday entitlement from four to five weeks per year, the creation of many thousands of jobs in the public sector, reducing the age of retirement from 65 to 60 years for all, creating a ministry for women's rights, substantially increasing welfare benefits and the minimum wage, abolishing the death penalty, regularizing the status of 300,000 previously illegal immigrants and introducing a wealth tax. In short, the PS began implementing a programme which hundreds of thousands of left-wing voters regarded as a massive antidote to over 20 years of government by the right and many people did view these reforms as a first step in the direction of a break with capitalism.

The honeymoon period was short-lived, however, and when the economic crisis began to hit hard the government decided to devalue the franc in October 1981. Unemployment was rising fast and in mid-1982, after just over a year in government, a substantial change of direction became apparent when the government implemented a pay and prices freeze. This was a step which greatly pleased employers but which the right had never dared take. From 1982 onwards, the government concentrated on measures which it hoped would both save the economy from the worst effects of the crisis and in particular appeal to employers, in whom the Socialist government now invested great faith and who were now seen as helping France escape further economic decline and therefore electoral catastrophe for the PS. Indeed one of the most significant economic changes under Mitterrand was to break the tendency for wage settlements to be at or above the rate of inflation. Income differentials increased significantly during Mitterrand's Presidency (Forbes and Hewlett 1994: 206–9). Thus the radicalism of the first period of Socialist government had given way to an unmistakable 'realism' by mid-1983. In 1984 the Communists left government, as did the Prime Minister who had been the symbol of left-wing optimism in 1981, Pierre Mauroy. In his place came the more technocratic, pragmatic Laurent Fabius, who remained in power until the legislative elections of 1986. (See Hoffmann, Ross and Malzacher 1987; Mazey and Newman 1987; Favier and Martin-Roland 1990.)

It was largely economic problems and high levels of unemployment which meant the right won the 1986 legislative elections and Mitterrand, whose presidential term lasted until 1988, was faced with a choice between resigning and therefore almost certainly handing over his post to the right, or staying with a right-wing prime minister and government. That Mitterrand decided he could fruitfully 'cohabit' with a right-wing prime minister and government was another token of his new-found pragmatism, and he was indeed able to share power without major conflict with the right up until his re-election in 1988. As it turned out, *cohabitation*, as it became known, was a godsend as far as Mitterrand's presidential credibility was concerned, for the period between 1986 and the presidential elections of 1988 allowed him to create an image of himself as a president representing national unity, to establish a distance between himself and the right's increasingly unpopular programme of reforms and thus to recover the enormous amount of personal ground lost in the opinion polls in the early to mid-1980s.

Mitterrand won the presidential elections of 1988 on the strength of an election manifesto which contrasted starkly with his *110 propositions pour la France* of 1981 and speaks volumes as to the ideological distance travelled by the President and the PS between 1981 and 1988. Entitled *Lettre à tous les Français* and subtitled, significantly,

La France unie, the 1988 manifesto contained none of the radicalism of 1981 and outlined a bland, centrist set of positions. One of the few real innovations contained in the programme was the promise of a new guaranteed minimum income for all those in dire need (including the long-term unemployed and the young *nouveaux pauvres*), the *Revenu minimum d'insertion* (RMI). But the RMI was, typically, so uncontroversial that it was broadly approved of by the right as well. The value of shares on the Paris Bourse actually rose immediately after the presidential election result was announced, in stark contrast to the situation in 1981, when Mitterrand's election sent the value of shares into free fall and they had to be artificially stopped from falling further.

Mitterrand took his re-election as a mandate to set up government of the centre and this heralded an era of consolidation of the consensus politics he had adopted. The legislative elections which followed Mitterrand's re-election did not result in an absolute majority for the PS, so the new government, led by Michel Rocard, had to juggle with PCF or centre-right support according to which quarter new legislation was likely to attract support from. Mitterrand and Rocard pursued a policy of *ouverture* (openness), which meant promoting participation in government by the centre-right and by people who were not career politicians. Although *ouverture* had limited success, it was another token of the distance travelled by the PS in the space of a few years. Recourse to constitutional devices to force through legislation in the absence of an obvious parliamentary majority became commonplace, so consensus government of the early 1990s was an uneasy business.

In May 1991 Mitterrand announced that Prime Minister Michel Rocard was to be replaced by Edith Cresson, the first woman Prime Minister in France's entire political history. This was designed to improve the PS's tarnished image in the eyes of the electorate, with the local elections of 1992 and legislative elections of 1993 in mind. But Cresson was not a popular Prime Minister and by the end of 1991 both she and President Mitterrand had fallen greatly in public esteem, according to opinion polls. After local elections in spring 1992 in which the Socialists did particularly badly, Cresson was replaced as Prime Minister by Pierre Bérégovoy, who had a reputation for a distinctly unsentimental approach to economics and was seen as the best hope as Prime Minister in the run-up to the spring 1993 legislative elections. The results of the 1993 elections were disastrous for the PS and indeed cast doubt as to the future of the party at all, given that it and its allies received little more than half the number of votes it received in 1988, or 17.6 per cent of the vote (compared with 34.8 per cent in 1988) and only 70 seats in Parliament (compared with 276 in 1988), a decline confirmed by the cantonal elections of March 1993 and the European elections of June 1994. But Mitterrand's willingness to cohabit again with the right, this time far more on the right's terms, was testimony to the distance which the PS had travelled since 1981. In July 1993 Mitterrand made a speech on privatization of industries in which he said glumly, 'we act according to the circumstances' (quoted in Gélédan 1993: 249), a phrase which summed up the pragmatism in many areas of Socialist policy at the end of their period in office and the absence of any real idea of how to capture the imagination of the Socialist electorate. Certainly, the Socialist current in France had a long history of centrist cooperation both before and after the Second World War, but the effect of its substantial change of direction during the Socialist decade of the 1980s was to enable the reduction of political radicalism in other areas as well.

While the PS reeled from the shock of the 1993 legislative election defeat, its various factions desperately sought solutions to its crisis of popularity. Its failure to keep the flame of socialism burning whilst in power had not only been damaging electorally but had meant that the level of activism by PS members was at its lowest since the reunification of the Socialist current at the Congrès d'Epinay in 1971 (Colombani and Portelli 1995: 205). However, renewed hope came at the presidential elections in 1995 when the PS candidate Lionel Jospin unexpectedly became the candidate with the most votes in the first round, with 23.3 per cent. Although this was due partly to the Gaullist vote being split two ways, between Chirac and Balladur, and although Chirac beat Jospin comfortably in the second round, Jospin's success brought new hope to many in the PS after the humiliations of the elections two years before. Relations between Chirac and Jospin remained cordial throughout and beyond the campaign; the political cartoonist Plantu summed up the polite, mild-mannered tenor of the left–right debate in a series of drawings of Jospin and Chirac, who are both depicted as trying to out-compliment the other on the success of their campaigns (*L'Express*, 18 May 1995). Again, this clearly reminds us of the distance travelled by the PS since 1981.

The victory of the left at the 1997 legislative elections was a measure of the unpopularity of Chirac as president and Alain Juppé as prime minister. Elected on a more traditionally social democratic platform than Jospin's 1995 programme, the PS entered the third period of *cohabitation* in a government which included both Communists and Greens. Although the government declared its intention to prioritize tackling social deprivation and unemployment which it claimed the right had made worse, it was more than willing to cohabit with Gaullist Jacques Chirac. The president, meanwhile, had no alternative to *cohabitation*, apart from resignation and political oblivion. The 1990s thus continued with yet another experiment – a right-wing president and left-wing government – without any feeling of real optimism on the part of the electorate; high levels of abstention seemed to point to real disillusionment with both left and right (*Le Monde* 1997: 43).

Turning to France's foreign relations under Mitterrand, here too there was a rapprochement with policy of other industrialized nations, rather than radicalism, which is what many at first expected. The PS document *Projet socialiste* published in 1980 had promised new, post-imperialist relations with Third World countries, and during a trip to Mexico in October 1981 Mitterrand made a famous speech in solidarity with oppressed peoples throughout the world. France even sent 15 million dollars of military aid to the Sandinistas in Nicaragua in 1981. But this approach was soon abandoned in favour of the more traditional French foreign policy which included intervening to defend existing regimes, particularly in Africa, regardless of their respect for liberal democracy or in some cases human rights. Mitterrand was certainly more pro-American than any previous President of the Fifth Republic and his enthusiasm for deployment of Cruise and Pershing missiles in Europe (though not in France) led him to call upon Germans to accept the missiles, in a speech in January 1983 to the West German parliament. In the Middle East, Mitterrand became the first French president to make an official visit to Israel, thus ending the traditional coolness France had shown towards the state. The Socialists maintained close relations with the Arab world, but fell in with other NATO countries in waging war on Iraq and supporting Iran, whereas alliances had been very much the contrary before the 1991 Gulf War.

As far as Europe was concerned, Mitterrand and the PS soon abandoned their characterization of the EEC as an organization which existed mainly to defend multinational firms' interests and became highly pro-European, and particularly in favour of the single market of 1992. The market-oriented Single European Act indeed chimed well with the Socialists' new-found respect for market forces.

Table 4.1 Socialist results at national elections, 1956–97

			Votes	% total
SFIO	1956	Legislative elections	3,247,431	15.2
SFIO	1958	Legislative elections (1st round)	3,171,459	15.5
SFIO	1962	Legislative elections (1st round)	2,279,209	12.4
FGDS	1967	Legislative elections (1st round)	4,231,173	18.9
FGDS	1968	Legislative elections (1st round)	3,662,443	16.5
G. Defferre	1969	Presidential election (1st round)	1,127,733	5.1
UGSD	1973	Legislative elections (1st round)	4,946,082	20.8
PS–MRG	1978	Legislative elections (1st round)	7,009,830	25.0
F. Mitterrand	1979	European elections	4,725,031	23.7
F. Mitterrand	1981	Presidential election (1st round)	7,437,282	26.1
PS–MRG	1981	Legislative elections (1st round)	9,347,185	37.7
L. Jospin	1984	European elections	4,129,202	20.8
F. Mitterrand	1988	Presidential election (1st round)	10,092,985	33.9
Presidential majority	1988	Legislative elections	9,048,268	37.7
L. Fabius	1989	European elections	4,286,354	23.6
PS	1993	Legislative elections (1st round)	4,476,716	17.6
European solidarity	1994	European elections	2,781,028	14.5
L. Jospin	1995	Presidential election (1st round)	7,097,786	23.3
PS–PRS	1997	Legislative elections (1st round)	6,469,766	25.6

Source: Ysmal 1989: 241; *Année politique, économique et sociale* 1989: 225, 1993: 138, 1994: 153, 1995: 179; *Le Monde* 1997: 43

Mitterrand's support for the Maastricht Treaty, which was to bring greater political and economic cooperation, was confirmed by a small majority in favour at the referendum on Maastricht in September 1992. In the realm of defence, the Socialists remained in favour of the independent French *Force de frappe* nuclear strike force, but during the Gulf War in particular it was clear that France's room for manoeuvre outside the sphere of influence of NATO was severely limited (Levy 1987; Cohen 1991).

To sum up, Mitterrand and the PS had significantly moved the locus of *Parti Socialiste* ideology and governmental policy towards the centre, and had thus substantially reduced the distance between the PS and the parties of the centre-right. They had confirmed the move to the right on the part of the PS by the Socialist president successfully 'cohabiting' in both 1986–8 and 1993–5 with governments of the centre-right and by showing that a smooth transition was possible between government of the left and government of the right; this was such a novelty for the Fifth Republic that it was given a special name, '*alternance*', a process which many had doubted was possible. The third period of *cohabitation* from June 1997 was further confirmation of this trend. In fact, the Socialists had consolidated the legitimacy of the Constitution of the Fifth Republic as the organizing text for governmental politics as a whole, a constitution which had until 1981 been regarded by many on the left as an instrument designed for the right and compatible only with right-wing government.

The Communist Party

The fate of the Communist Party (PCF) is another striking illustration of the decline of radicalism in French politics. During the period between the end of the Second World War and 1978 the PCF had been the largest political party in terms of membership, had enjoyed the support of at least one in five voters and had been the single largest obstacle to the emergence of a sizeable centre-left socialist party or overtly social democratic party of the type often found in other West European countries. The fact that France had a large, well-supported communist party which had long been a major obstacle to the PS coming to power and a central factor determining PS strategy in the 1970s (see e.g. D. S. Bell and Criddle 1988), was one important way in which politics had been of a different nature in France from in most other countries in north-west Europe in the post-war period. Indeed the fact that the PCF only flirted briefly with the more moderate, conciliatory politics of Eurocommunism and then reverted to a the more traditional Stalinist variant of European communism meant that the PCF even set itself apart from other large southern European communist parties, in particular the Spanish and Italian parties. These latter parties had made substantial ideological moves towards more consensual politics during the 1970s, accepting that it was more realistic to reform capitalism than to overthrow it and that the Soviet Union was deeply flawed (Carrillo 1977).

It has been argued, with some justification, that the PCF had been in decline for some time before the success of the PS at the elections of 1981 (e.g. Touchard 1977: 325–35). After a period of widespread support during the Fourth Republic, the advent of the Fifth Republic in 1958 had immediately seen a reduction in votes from 25.9 per cent in the legislative elections of 1956 to 18.9 per cent in the legislative elections of 1958 and a dramatic reduction in the parliamentary strength of the PCF, partly due to the change of electoral system. This was a blow from which the PCF never fully recovered. The

Table 4.2 Communist Party results at national elections, 1956–97

		Votes	% total
1956	Legislative elections	5,514,403	25.9
1958	Legislative elections (1st round)	3,870,184	18.9
1962	Legislative elections (1st round)	4,010,463	21.9
1967	Legislative elections (1st round)	5,039,032	22.5
1968	Legislative elections (1st round)	4,434,831	20.0
1969	Presidential election (1st round)	4,779,539	21.5
1973	Legislative elections (1st round)	5,085,356	21.4
1978	Legislative elections	5,791,525	20.6
1979	European elections (1st round)	4,100,261	20.6
1981	Presidential election (1st round)	4,412,949	15.5
1981	Legislative elections	4,003,025	16.1
1984	European elections	2,211,305	11.2
1986	Legislative elections (1st round)	2,663,259	9.7
1988	Presidential election (1st round)	2,043,031	6.9
1988	Legislative elections (1st round)	2,680,120	11.2
1989	European elections	1,401,171	7.7
1993	Legislative elections (1st round)	2,336,254	9.2
1994	European elections	1,334,234	6.9
1995	Presidential election (1st round)	2,632,460	8.6
1997	Legislative elections (1st round)	2,509,357	9.91

Source: Ysmal 1989: 229; Année politique, économique et sociale 1989: 225, 1993: 138, 1994: 153, 1995: 179; Le Monde 1997: 43

events of May 1968 came as a further blow, partly because of the right-wing backlash in the elections of June 1968 which again dented the PCF's electoral fortunes, and partly because participants in the events of May saw the PCF as at best marginal, and at worst opposed to the tremendous fillip to radical left-wing ideas brought by the uprising. The gradual disillusionment with the Soviet Union among its former admirers during the 1950s, 1960s and 1970s likewise contributed to the erosion of the PCF's popularity. Finally, from the mid- to late 1970s the decline in the number of employees in heavy industry such as iron and steel, shipbuilding and chemicals meant that the traditional PCF support base in terms of both membership and voting was undermined. However, despite all these factors, the PCF continued to obtain the support of roughly 20 per cent of voters right up until the legislative elections of 1978 and its membership actually grew in the 1970s, during the period of the Common Programme of Government, although certainly not as much as the party claimed. Colette Ysmal estimates that PCF membership rose from 390,000 in 1972 to 520,000 in 1978, which would mean that it was still by far the largest political party (Ysmal 1989: 163). Thus the PCF continued to be a key player in the politics of the left, a party which attracted roughly the same number of votes as the PS – sometimes more – and which was therefore still an unavoidable factor to be taken into account in the PS's struggle to achieve power.

It was during the 1980s that this situation changed dramatically. The PCF entered government in 1981, although in a very junior capacity (it was given four ministries, which were Transport, Civil Service, Health, and Vocational Training). This period in government, which included the policy U-turn of 1982–3, was most damaging for the PCF in terms of its radical credentials. A party which had consistently represented the interests of the least well off and disempowered and which had only once been in government, from 1944 to 1947, cooperated in implementing policies which were designed to make the working class pay for economic recovery and this during a period of rapidly rising unemployment, which increased from 7.3 per cent of the working population in 1981 to 8.7 per cent in 1984 and 10.3 per cent in 1985. In the 1981 legislative elections the PCF already suffered a substantial drop in electoral support, to 15.3 per cent of the electorate, a situation which was only to deteriorate, albeit unevenly, as the years went by. Membership also fell dramatically during the 1980s and 1990s, although there is little agreement between analysts on actual figures (D. S. Bell and Criddle 1994: 212). Participation in government was an experience from which the PCF was not to recover, despite its resignation in 1984 and its position of semi-opposition to Socialist rule, or at least dubious dependability as far as the PS was concerned, subsequently. But the decline in PCF fortunes was also related to the phenomenon mentioned above, namely the capture by the PS of the moral high ground as far as the left electorate was concerned and the reputation of the PCF as a dyed-in-the-wool Stalinist party. The break-up of Eastern Europe and the PCF's inability to adapt in light of this also played a role in discrediting it, of course. Since Robert Hue became leader of the PCF in 1994, the party has begun to adapt in a more active fashion to the post-Soviet reality of the international order and the apparent lack of prospects for communism world-wide. Hue's 8.6 per cent of the vote at the presidential elections of 1995 was a clear improvement on André Lajoinie's 6.8 per cent in 1988 and was partly a result of this process of change. The party's 9.9 per cent in 1997 was even better. But short of unforeseen and dramatic changes at an international level, the PCF is unlikely to be able to resist increased marginalization in the medium term, and in the longer term its viability as an independent left party is certainly questionable.

The decline of traditional Gaullism

Since the early 1980s the centre-right has come to resemble the right in other north-west European countries far more than before, mainly because of changes associated with the Gaullist party, the Rassemblement pour la République (RPR). This evolution is worth dwelling upon a little, particularly as its significance is often missed. For a long time Gaullist philosophy and party politics reflected an unconventional set of ideas compared with centre-right parties in many north-west European countries, ideas which seemed appropriate to a France in an almost permanent state of emergency, from the end of the Second World War up to 1962. In a general way the time-specific, extraordinary nature of Gaullism – associated with the defence of the French nation in time of crisis on the one hand and the figure of de Gaulle on the other – has necessarily dwindled progressively since the departure and death of de Gaulle. For instance much of the *grandeur* disappeared from Gaullist rhetoric soon after de Gaulle's death. But more recently and more concretely there are two major areas of neo-Gaullist policy which have evolved in a particularly striking way in the direction of centre-right policy in other countries. Well beyond the death of de Gaulle in 1970, Gaullist party doctrine included both a strong belief in a *dirigiste* intervention by the state in the economy and civil society in general, and independence for France in international affairs, including strongly defended independence with regard to the position of France in Europe. These elements of Gaullism were closely associated with the autocratic and authoritarian rule of de Gaulle himself, who had returned to power in 1958 when the political situation was very unstable and when there was a serious threat of *coup d'état* on the part of the army. But these particular characteristics of traditional Gaullism were still to be found as recently as 1978, in the RPR manifesto for the legislative elections of that year, albeit in somewhat diluted form (Ysmal 1989: 131).

Since the beginning of the 1980s, both these policy orientations have virtually disappeared. The RPR has adopted a highly positive attitude towards the market economy and has moved away from advocating strong state intervention. When RPR leader Jacques

Chirac became Prime Minister in 1986, one of the main planks of the new governmental programme was to transfer about 65 companies from the public sector to the private sector, including some nationalized by de Gaulle. These included important banks and financial institutions such as the Société Générale, Paribas and Suez, the largest television channel, TF1 and large industrial groups such as CGE, Matra and Saint-Gobain. Industrial unrest in December 1986 and the formation of another Socialist government after the legislative elections in 1988 temporarily put a stop to such sweeping privatization. But important deregulation of the economy also took place during the period when Jacques Chirac was Prime Minister, including deregulation of exchange controls, deregulation of financial markets (similar to the 'Big Bang' which took place under the Thatcher government in the UK), and ending government price controls of certain key consumer items. The requirement for employers to obtain permission to make workers redundant was abolished, a measure which had been introduced in 1975 when Chirac was Prime Minister for the first time. The government also cut taxes for individuals and abolished the wealth tax introduced by the Socialists. Although the state remained an important influence over the French economy, the first government of *cohabitation* thus fully embraced the market-oriented ethos of many other EU members' economic policies in the 1980s and early 1990s, which was in part a recognition of the importance of the integrated European market and the market-oriented character of EU institutions themselves. When the Gaullist leader Edouard Balladur became Prime Minister in 1993, a policy priority was once again to privatize, including such significant companies as Banque Nationale de Paris, the chemicals group Rhône-Poulenc, Elf Aquitaine, and the post-war state flagship Renault, although Renault's privatization was partial.

In the economic sphere, then, Gaullism has certainly changed greatly and is now far less exceptional in terms of right-wing policy than it was in the days of de Gaulle or the 1970s. But just as importantly, on looking back over the period since the early 1980s the most important turning point for French economic policy is 1983, when the Socialist government embarked on the famous economic U-turn, rather than 1986, 1993 or 1995, when the right won national elections. In other words, right and left economic policy is certainly far closer since 1983 than it had ever been before.

Turning now to shifts in the realm of Gaullist foreign policy, de Gaulle's fierce defence of France's independence in Europe had gone as far as boycotting the meetings of the EU Council of Ministers in Brussels between June 1965 and January 1966, because of proposals to take certain important decisions by majority voting on the Council of Ministers, rather than by discussing and compromising until there was consensus. He also vetoed Britain's entry to the EU, partly because of fears of American influence in Europe if Britain were allowed in. Although Gaullist President Pompidou's attitude towards Europe was less strongly in favour of French independence (he arranged a referendum on British entry, for example, whose outcome was in favour), Gaullists were still extremely wary of what they regarded as encroachment by the European Community in their affairs. By the mid-1980s, however, most Gaullists were in favour of the Single European Act, whose intention was to abolish the remaining barriers to the free movement of goods, services, capital and labour. Combining characteristics of a stronger, more integrated Europe and moves towards a freer market, this was testimony to how far the RPR had moved over a decade or so. Certainly, when it came to taking up a position over the question of the Maastricht Treaty in the 1992 referendum, the RPR was still profoundly divided, and Jacques Chirac's position of voting in favour of Maastricht only narrowly won the day. But the successful future of a stronger and more integrated European Union is now almost universally viewed by Gaullists, as well as other mainstream politicians, as being of key importance to the future of France. Likewise, Gaullist anti-Americanism has now virtually disappeared and is no longer expressed in Gaullist governmental behaviour. But perhaps the most striking change to Gaullist policy has come in the realm of defence, with President Chirac officially taking France back into NATO's integrated command structure in June 1996, 30 years after de Gaulle pulled France out as a gesture of defiance against an organization he saw as threatening French independence. Chirac himself has travelled a long way since 1979, when he warned in traditional Gaullist fashion against 'the passive abandonment of care for our destiny to foreign hands' (quoted in Cayrol and Perrineau 1988: 14).

Strong, charismatic leadership was for a long time a crucial feature of the success of Gaullism and its greatest moment of crisis as a political movement since 1958 came after the death of Georges Pompidou in 1974. It seems, however, that with the 'normalization' of the RPR even this outstanding feature of traditional Gaullism is no longer an indispensable recipe for success. During the second period of *cohabitation*, from 1993 to 1995, the unexpectedly high level of popularity of Gaullist Prime Minister Edouard Balladur was based not on an image of a tough leader staunchly defending traditional Gaullist values, but on an image of someone who was unexceptional, bland and dependable, and certainly not tough dynamism which would be more the style of a leader in the Gaullist tradition. Balladur was popular because of this image, rather than despite it, and the image of the man goes with the nature of the RPR's new political principles, or relative lack of them. Even Chirac has toned down his tough, dynamic image in favour of a more accessible persona who is willing to see his opponent's point of view.

On the question of support for the Gaullists, the proportion of overall votes for the centre-right taken by the Gaullists has dwindled considerably, again endorsing the notion that Gaullism has become just another strand of the centre-right rather than a movement with something really distinct to contribute. In the legislative elections of 1993 the RPR attracted 46.1 per cent of the total vote for the moderate right, which was the lowest proportion since 1958 in legislative elections, apart from those of 1973, when Gaullism was in a very difficult stage (Jaffré 1989: 17; Knapp 1994: 151). Just as significantly, the sociological and geographical profile of the electorate has likewise shifted in a direction which is far more typical of a traditional conservative party, and the RPR no longer enjoys support from anything like the broad cross-section of the population which de Gaulle and his party received in the 1960s. Although there is evidence of a slight movement back towards the RPR on the part of the working class in the mid-1990s, Gaullist support has generally become far more rural, older and Catholic. Indeed the RPR electorate nowadays is often more classically of the right than the UDF's (Knapp 1994: 166–73).

In short, the Gaullist movement today has no credibility as a broad movement which organically expresses the will of the French people, a view which de Gaulle was able to argue more convincingly in the 1960s, and the RPR has become more like conservative, Christian democratic, or other centre-right parties in other countries, and more like its partner in government, the centre-right coalition grouping the Union pour la Démocratie Française (UDF). Indeed the UDF itself has shifted towards the RPR to the extent that it has largely abandoned the politically liberal positions it adopted in the 1970s under the influence of Giscard d'Estaing, which had resulted in progressive reforms on issues which included abortion, contraception and prisons (Frears 1981). Jérome Jaffré has suggested that Gaullism as an

autonomous electoral force has actually disappeared and has been
replaced by a broader 'conservative grouping' in electoral terms,
made up of an amalgam of RPR and UDF (Jaffré 1989: 18). Indeed
an RPR regional councillor and prominent internal party critic published a much-discussed book in 1988, after the defeat of the right, in
which he appealed for the formal unification of RPR and UDF. He
pointed out that policy differences hardly existed:

> There is not a single aspect of political debate over the past two
> years – *cohabitation*, defence, internal security, relations with East-
> ern Europe, the construction of Europe, liberalization of the eco-
> nomy, the future of the welfare state, tax and social security
> contributions, immigration, the legal system, the death penalty, tele-
> vision and radio, relations with the National Front – which gave rise
> to a clear difference between the attitudes of the RPR and the
> UDF. (Bourlanges 1988: 293)

It is also worth mentioning that the positions of the UDF and RPR
on major issues do not now differ substantially from the positions of
the PS, particularly on Europe and the economy. One of the best-
known points of Mitterrand's 1988 presidential election manifesto
was his promise neither to re-nationalize what the right had privatized during 1986–8, nor privatize further, a position which became
know as '*ni, ni*' ('neither, nor'). With the PS becoming very much a
defender of the institutions of the Fifth Republic and the decline of
even half-hearted opposition to the Republic and its constitution,
Gaullism has also lost its distinction as being the political knight
defending de Gaulle's constitution against attacks from the left
(Shain 1991: 68). As far as Europe is concerned, differences among
leading members of the RPR are almost certainly greater than differences between Jacques Chirac, the PS and the UDF. By the time of
the 1993 legislative election campaign, by stark contrast with the situation in the early 1980s, a reading of the manifestos of the mainstream right and the mainstream left showed that they had virtually
the same positions on the major issues of the day, namely the economy, immigration, education and foreign policy (Hanley 1993:
418–19). This was reflected in public opinion, according to the polls,
which consistently pointed to a widespread and growing belief in the
late 1980s and early 1990s that there was little difference between
mainstream left and mainstream right and a belief that it made little
difference to most French people who won elections, left or right
(Rémond 1993: 20). Politicians had great difficulty in asserting what

was distinct about their particular party, how it differed from other centre-oriented parties. The 1995 presidential election campaign also showed that there was continued ideological convergence between the centre-left and centre-right, which was expressed in the pro- grammes and rhetoric of the three major candidates: the PS candi- date Lionel Jospin, and the two Gaullist candidates, Jacques Chirac and Edouard Balladur. Jospin and Chirac in particular both focused on solidarity with and help for the unemployed, the poor, the home- less and indeed all those excluded from mainstream society (*'les exclus'*). In the now traditional televised debate by the two second- round candidates there was a great deal of common ground; there was some divergence of views on economic policy, but for instance the future of Europe was not a point of contention and the National Front was not even mentioned by name (*Le Monde*, 4 May 1995). In the 1997 legislative elections differences between centre-left and centre-right were somewhat greater, but nothing like the chasm of the early 1980s and before.

It must be said that the popularity of the National Front (FN) has certainly been a substantial problem for the more mainstream right since the early 1980s and has caused the RPR and UDF to examine their tactics and programmes carefully in order to attempt to mini- mize the FN's influence. This has at times meant a departure from centre-oriented behaviour, and even some electoral alliances at local level between the RPR and the FN. Some policy changes have been strongly influenced by the success of the FN, such as great emphasis on 'law and order' during both periods of *cohabitation* and changes to the nationality laws in 1993. In this way the right's tendency towards becoming a more moderate bloc has been tempered, but not to a considerable degree. As Andrew Knapp comments, the domi- nant trend for the RPR has been towards an 'amalgam of social con- servatism and economic "liberalism" that resembles the baggage of any other right-wing party' (Knapp 1994: 395).

Class combativeness and industrial action

The level of traditional forms of working-class militancy has dropped since the beginning of the 1980s. Although this has been a character- istic of most West European countries during the 1980s and 1990s, it was particularly acute in France. One indicator of this decline is the sharp fall in the number of days lost in strike activity, partly because of the economic problems, including high unemployment, since the early 1980s, and partly because trade union leaders discouraged strike activity during the honeymoon period between government and trade unions in the early 1980s (a point which I explore more fully below). Another indicator of the same general phenomenon is the drop in union membership from roughly 20 per cent of the working population in the late 1970s to roughly 10 per cent in the mid-1980s and well under 10 per cent in the early 1990s, according to most estimates, which was the lowest figure for all OECD countries. Part of this same trend is the relative increase in support for the more moderate union candidates in works council elections since the early 1980s (notably those representing the anti-Communist Force Ouvrière), and also for non-union candidates. (OECD 1991: 104; Dreyfus 1995: 330)

It was also noticeable that there was relatively little popular mobilization in the streets during the Socialist 1980s and early to mid-1990s and in the wake of 1981 certainly nothing like the mass demonstrations and strike activity which took place in the aftermath of the formation of the Popular Front government in 1936 or the huge wave of strikes in 1947 which put an end to the tripartite government of reconstruction with the dismissal of the Communist ministers in May that year. On each of these previous occasions there was mass organization in order to exert pressure on the progressive government of the day to implement more radical reforms. By contrast, the most significant – indeed huge – street demonstration of the 1980s was organized in June 1984 not by the left but by the conservative forces who turned out in protest against increased incorporation of private schools into the state system.

It was under a Socialist government that the erstwhile bastion of the CGT Renault Billancourt was closed without major dispute with the unions, and in 1994 Renault was partially privatized without the left and the trade unions fighting it with any success. The privatization of Renault ten years before would have been unthinkable and impossible. Certainly, there have been significant strikes since the beginning of the 1980s. At the beginning of 1984 there was a widespread strike at Citroën Aulnay, and Talbot Poissy, and by steel workers in Longwy, Lorraine, in each case in protest against industrial restructuring encouraged by the Socialist government. In December 1986–January 1987 there was a public sector strike which helped convince the right-wing government to modify or drop some of its more extreme policies, following close on the heels of widespread (and successful) school and university student mobilization against a new education bill which sought to make entry to higher education more selective. The early 1990s saw strike activity by the employees of Air France, large demonstrations against a government proposal to create a special, reduced minimum wage for young people (dubbed '*le SMIC jeunes*'), and large demonstrations against increased state aid for private education, not to mention sometimes dramatic demonstrations by fishermen and farmers over falling prices. Most significant of all disputes, perhaps, was the huge public sector strike in December 1995 over various issues including proposed reform of the social security system, a strike which paralysed the Paris public transport system for several weeks. But although these are reminders that popular mobilization is far from dead, they do not constitute a re-emergence of regular and powerful strikes and other related activities.

Where there were strikes, they tended to be limited to particular sectors, rather than being widespread and intersectorial of the type which were common in the 1960s and 1970s. Also, there was greater contrast than in the past between the private sector, which was very badly affected by unemployment and where workers were reluctant to strike, and the public sector, where employees' jobs were more protected. Teachers, nurses, postal workers and workers in public transport were all involved in disputes in the 1980s and the first half of the 1990s. But the only substantial private sector strike of the first six years of the 1990s was at the electronics firm Alsthom in Belfort, in December 1994.

In keeping with the decline of class combativeness in more visible forms, the influence of Marxism generally has also declined markedly. Various interpretations of Marxism enjoyed great authority for much of the post-war period, but by the end of the 1980s it was viewed by many as a thing of the past. Within political parties, trade unions and among the intelligentsia, including in universities, Marxism went from being an accepted starting point for the analysis of many aspects of history, philosophy, economics and (albeit less often) politics, to being the preoccupation of a tiny minority. Instead, ideas originating from the liberal right and the centre became more popular, although there were no ideologues from this intellectual arena of any comparable weight to Sartre in the 1950s and 1960s, or Althusser and Merleau-Ponty in the 1970s (see chapter 7).

Table 4.3 Extreme right results at national elections, 1958–97

		Votes	% total
1958	Legislative elections (1st round)	526,644	2.6
1962	Referendum April 1962	1,809,074	9.3
1962	Legislative elections (1st round)	139,200	0.8
1965	Presidential election (1st round)	1,253,958	5.3
1967	Legislative elections (1st round)	124,862	0.6
1968	Legislative elections (1st round)	18,933	0.1
1973	Legislative elections (1st round)	122,498	0.5
1974	Presidential election (1st round)	189,304	0.8
1978	Legislative elections (1st round)	210,761	0.8
1979	European elections	265,289	1.3
1981	Presidential election		
1981	Legislative elections (1st round)	90,422	0.4
1984	European elections	2,193,777	11.1
1986	Legislative elections	2,760,880	9.9
1988	Presidential election (1st round)	4,350,260	14.6
1988	Legislative elections (1st round)	2,371,157	9.9
1989	European elections	2,129,668	11.7
1993	Legislative elections (1st round)	3,159,477	12.4
1994	European elections[a]	4,428,408	23.0
1995	Presidential election (1st round)[a]	6,014,024	19.5
1997	Legislative elections (1st round)	3,822,519	15.1

[a]Le Pen plus de Villiers.
Source: Ysmal 1989: 270; *Année politique, économique et sociale* 1989: 225, 1993: 138, 1994: 153, 1995: 179; *Le Monde* 1997: 43

Limits to the decline of conflict

The move towards the centre and the decline of radicalism in French politics is by no means uniform across the political spectrum. In particular, the rise of the National Front since the early 1980s and the more generalized rise in racism and anti-semitism over the same period represents a strong counter-tendency to the more general trend described above. Attracting considerable support, mainly around issues relating to immigrant workers and law and order, the FN expresses fairly popular political sentiments of an extreme variety. There seems little doubt that the relative success of the FN is precisely, in part, a result of the inability or unwillingness of successive governments since the early 1980s to offer any radical policies to remedy social crises of various kinds, including the lack of integration of immigrant workers and the question of unemployment; this is in part why the FN has been able to convince its followers of a causal link between the existence of immigrant workers in France and high unemployment. Another popular theme with Jean-Marie Le Pen and other FN leaders is the supposed corruption of virtually all mainstream politicians. In other words, it can be argued that the rise of the FN is in part a result of the lack of radicalism on the part of other, more established political parties, in particular the PS and PCF. For although transfer of allegiance between the PCF and the FN has probably been exaggerated, the decline of the PCF does seem to have encouraged the rise of the FN, in that the sum of the two electorates remained almost constant (Ysmal 1991). It would be wrong, however, to ascribe the success of the FN entirely to a reaction against the moderate nature of other political parties (see e.g. Mayer and Perrineau 1989). There has always been an extreme right in France, which took the form of Poujadism in the 1950s and the quasi-fascist *Leagues* in the 1930s, when intellectuals were also often on the extreme right, by stark contrast with the period after the Second World War.

Some other developments in the late 1980s and early 1990s serve to qualify further the view that the expression of strong political views is on the wane and these developments indeed highlight the partial nature of this consensual, more moderate situation during the 1980s. First, the PS was severely weakened by the early to mid-1990s and went into crisis, proving incapable, for the time being at least, of providing the moderate governmental stability it had offered earlier. Some of the main reasons for this were the PS's inability to solve the major economic problems of the 1980s and 1990s, the series of political scandals associated with the party after its presidential and legislative election victories in 1988, and the simple fact that the PS had dominated French politics since 1981, a question of supporter fatigue, in other words. Second, the centre-right's overwhelming parliamentary majority after the elections of 1993 disguised only thinly the fact that it attracted under 45 per cent of the vote, and increased its vote over 1988 by no more than 2 per cent. Indeed, in the elections in the early 1990s what might be described as marginal, anti-establishment parties and candidates attracted up to a third of the electorate, indicating a profound disillusionment with party politics and politicians of either the mainstream left or mainstream right. The ecology parties achieved reasonably high scores at some elections, with 10.6 per cent of the vote at European elections in 1989 and a record 14.4 per cent in regional elections in 1992, although the ecologists have fallen from favour since then. The National Front continued to receive at least 10 per cent of the vote and more, and there emerged rogue, protest candidates such as Bernard Tapie and Philippe de Villiers, often attracting disaffected right-wing voters and in some ways reminiscent of the maverick tycoons Silvio Berlusconi in Italy and Ross Perot in the US.

The 1995 presidential election campaign and results sum up neatly the limits to consensus politics in the mid-1990s. A substantial minority of the electorate was apparently disillusioned with the more dominant situation described above, where the mainstream parties increasingly vie with each other over the middle ground but where none are able to offer solutions to France's most pressing problems. In the 1995 elections the vote for the FN candidate, Jean-Marie Le Pen, reached a record 15.0 per cent and in fact the total vote for the extreme right was almost 20 per cent, as Philippe de Villier's 4.7 per cent must also be counted as extreme right. Second, although the PCF will never regain much of the ground it has lost since 1981, the fact that the PCF candidate Robert Hue received 8.6 per cent of the vote suggests that support for the PCF is not about to disappear altogether. To vote for the PCF is to vote for a party which has been highly critical not only of the right but also of Mitterrand's legacy – at least since the PCF left government in 1984 – although a clear majority of those who voted for Hue voted for Jospin in the second round, as directed by Hue himself. Next, another surprise came in the first round (along with Jospin's success) when it was announced that 5.3 per cent of voters had opted for the Lutte Ouvrière candidate Arlette Laguiller, a Trotskyist who has stood in three other presidential elections and has never before received as much as 2.5 per cent. Finally, political in-fighting between ecologist candidates over the past few years has substantially reduced the vote for the Greens, after their peak of 14.4 per cent in the 1992 regional elections, falling to 7.6 per cent in the 1993 legislative elections, and it is largely these divisions which explain the relatively low vote for Dominique Voynet. But her 3.3 per cent is still a factor that adds to the fragmentation of the party system. Put together, over 11 million people voted for the more marginal, anti-mainstream candidates in the first round (Le Pen, Hue, Laguiller, de Villiers, Voynet and the virtually unknown, extreme right-winger Cheminade), which amounted to 37.3 per cent of the total vote. Another phenomenon which must be counted as evidence of growing political dissent is the increasing number of spoiled ballot papers counted in the second round of the elections, a practice which in all elections has become more common since the mid-1980s. Spoilt papers amounted to 1.3 per cent of all second round votes at the presidential election of 1974, 2.9 per cent in 1981, 3.6 per cent in 1988 and 6.0 per cent in 1995. In other words there were signs that the new consensus of the 1980s was not as enduring as might have been predicted towards the beginning of that decade (*Le Monde* 1995).

The trends of the 1995 presidentials were largely confirmed by the results of the 1997 legislative elections. Although the left managed to achieve a majority, with its allies, the PS only received 25.5 per cent in the first round. The extreme right vote remained high, ecologists increased their share of the vote and the PCF also did slightly better than in 1995 (see Appendix B2).

It should also be pointed out that although traditional types of trade union struggle are now less common, the years since 1981 have seen unrest associated with social deprivation, industrial restructuring and international change, including rioting and looting mainly by youth in suburban areas with high levels of unemployment and poverty, and fishermen and farmers often reacting to new regulations from international organizations which, in the short term at least, affect them adversely. The demonstration by Breton fishermen on 4 February 1994, for example, ended with participants setting fire to the Breton parliament in Rennes.

French politics are thus very far from conforming to any sort of perfect liberal democratic model. However, the somewhat different types of protest seen in the 1980s and 1990s often do not take the same form or represent the same type of threat that for example the PCF (sometimes in alliance with the PS, the CFDT or the CGT) represented in the past. On the contrary, the new patterns of protest are more to do with a general disillusionment with the mainstream political parties and politicians, including those (in particular the PCF) which once were the very incarnation of protest. Protest movements are now often in defence of the status quo and against perceived threats to the status quo, rather than constituting positive action in favour of radical, often socialist-inspired change, as was often the case in the 1960s and 1970s. In general, there is much evidence that the rules of the game in French politics remain significantly different from the period before Mitterrand.

Explaining consensus: the 1980s as a moment of tripartite harmony

Despite the limits to the decline of political and social conflict in France discussed above, put together, we can call this series of inter-connected phenomena 'consensus' politics, imperfect though this term may be. For the first time in many years, and arguably ever, French politics could in the 1980s and 1990s be likened in a system-atic fashion to politics in other north-west European countries, and the PS governments of the 1980s oversaw the evolution of politics in a direction that had not occurred in France during the post-war period. These consensus politics have not remained wholly intact, as I explain above, but that they marked a critical turning point seems very likely; the decline of left radicalism and trade union militancy, in particular, would appear to be lasting developments. I have men-tioned some of the reasons for the developments as I detailed them, but I now wish to suggest that a more overarching explanation is pos-sible, without denying the validity of other, parallel explanations as well. In order to attempt to explain the rise of this new consensus I use the paradigm of the regulation school. We thus need to establish the extent to which this new consensus was achieved, as in other countries, usually many years earlier, via cooperation between the state, trade unions and employers; does a partial inclusion of the labour movement in mainstream decision making, and relative peace between employers and employees, so common in other countries in the post-war period, help explain the decline of radical politics in the early to mid-1980s and the lasting effects of this decline since then?

The labour movement

Turning first to labour movement–government relations, the labour movement was certainly not formally integrated into the governmen-tal process in the 1980s, as it had been in some other countries during the post-war period. There was no attempt by government to orga-nize widespread negotiations with trade unions in order to agree wage rises or limit industrial action, for example, partly because there was no one trade union body which could legitimately claim to represent the interests of the majority of workers. However, there were tremendous differences with the past with respect to government–trade union relations, particularly in the first few years of Socialist rule, which amounted to close cooperation. For the first time since the Popular Front – and arguably more so in 1981 than in 1936 – trade unions viewed the government as *their* government. As we have seen, before 1981 trade unions had negotiated very little with government and the governmental sphere had been largely distinct from the trade union sphere.

On the election of Mitterrand and the formation of a Socialist government with Communist participation after left victory in legislative elections, it was clear that, for the first time since 1947, the major union confederations wholly supported the political programme of the government. Indeed, the programme had been strongly influenced by key aspects of the two major left unions' political priorities. The Confédération Française Démocratique du Travail (CFDT) had a strong influence on the nature of the Auroux laws, which among other things increased trade union rights in the workplace and were inspired to an extent by notions of *autogestion*, so dear to the CFDT in the 1970s. Reduction in working time was another theme close to the hearts of CFDT activists. CFDT leader Edmond Maire went as far as to say in 1982 that 'there is no longer any pre-requisite to the construction of socialism' (quoted in Wilson 1985: 267). Nationalization of key industries was a policy closely identified with the PCF, and thus the CGT, and the usually highly militant CGT went out of its way not to encourage industrial action, in large part because there were four PCF government ministers between 1981 and 1984. One CGT leader had explained in 1982 that 'the government has options that are globally the same as ours. We are more listened to now than in the past. The laws we wanted are now being presented by the Government. Our ideas are often accepted in drafting the Government proposals' (Wilson 1985: 256). Another trade union leader commented: 'There is not a day when my union is not consulted by one ministry or another. The concertation is constant as decrees and directives are issued everywhere. And we are consulted on these matters *before* they are actually decided' (Wilson 1985: 275).

Although there was no structural link between any of the trade union confederations and the PS, the influence of trade union policy on ministerial advisory committees (*cabinets ministériels*) was considerable. The Socialist-leaning CFDT was particularly influential and during the period of the first Socialist government after victory in 1981 21 per cent of *cabinet ministériel* members were also members of the CFDT, which amounted to half of all unionized *cabinet* members. Moreover, 30 per cent of *directeurs de cabinet* were CFDT members (Dagnaud and Mehl 1990: 160). The *cabinet* of the Ministry of Labour was particularly closely associated with the CFDT in this respect and it was headed by Michel Praderie, who had long worked with the CFDT.

Trade unions went out of their way to limit industrial action and as we have seen the number of days lost in strike activity fell sharply during the 1980s. Union membership fell and, paradoxically, contributed towards creating a more consensual situation. This was a very different state of affairs indeed to that of 1936, when the trade union movement grew and rose up to push the Popular Front government further in its reforms, or even in 1947 when the PCF was obliged to leave government because of rank-and-file trade union activity.

The state of grace between government and trade unions lasted until 1984, when the PCF ministers left government and thus opened the door to more normal CGT militancy, and it is significant that the first national day of action organized by the PCF was in 1984. Crucially, however, by this time the government had already radically changed direction, particularly in the sphere of economic policy, with the governmental cooperation of the PCF. By this time government no longer relied on the support of the trade unions and trade unions were sufficiently weak not to pose a major threat. But the government had been able to implement reform in certain areas precisely because it had won the confidence of the labour movement. Had it not won this confidence the history of the 1980s might have been very different.

Government–capital relations

Turning now to government–capital relations, again there was no question, as I have said, of a formal arrangement. Mitterrand and the Socialists were elected on a radical – albeit far from revolutionary – platform which was widely interpreted as a substantial threat to the position of the capitalist class, which had been described by the PS as follows:

> We wish to establish as precise and concrete a method as possible to effect the transition from one economic, social, cultural – and therefore political – state in France to another, from the capitalist system to socialist society. (*Parti socialiste* 1980: 10)

This was a challenge which, the day after Mitterrand's election on 10 May 1981, sent the value of shares on the stock exchange into free fall, and the value of the franc to the lowest position which the European Monetary System would allow. The *patronat* was appalled by the victory of the left, with all it implied in terms of nationalization of key industries, wealth tax, higher wages, reduced working time, longer holidays and in particular the Auroux laws. This was a package which would, according to outgoing president of the CNPF François Ceyrac, create a 'pre-revolutionary situation' (quoted in Berger 1985: 227) and which incoming president Yvon Gattaz described as 'much more serious' than in 1936 (Gras and Gras 1991: 73). In short, the spectre which had long haunted the French *patronat* seemed to be striding boldly across France.

As time went by, however, and particularly after the U-turn in economic policy of 1982–3, the *patronat* acted in a far more benign way towards the Socialists. Indeed the PS achieved in some areas changes which the right had not been able to achieve when it was in government. Not only did the PS government generally create a more peaceful political and industrial relations climate in which French industry could do business and in particular help tame the PCF and its trade union adjunct, the CGT; it also managed to de-index salaries from inflation for the first time since the immediate aftermath of the Second World War, asserted the importance of private enterprise, and reinforced France's role in European business. *Dirigisme* in economic affairs, so well established in France, was finally challenged head-on not by the right but by a Socialist government which included four Communist ministers. In January 1984 Mitterrand said in an interview that the economic crisis had 'ennobled' the firm. He added:

> The French are beginning to understand that it is the firm which creates wealth, the firm that creates employment, the firm that determines our standard of living and our place in the world hierarchy of nations. (Quoted in Machin and Wright 1985: 3)

An illustration of the degree to which French employers came to feel they could work with Socialist rule was the relative ease with which they were able to implement flexible working practices, so dear to employers internationally in the 1980s. Chris Howell, explaining how the *patronat* used the new bargaining climate of the Auroux laws to introduce flexible working practices, has argued convincingly that:

in the space of a decade [1982–92], the degree of control exercised by firms over what they pay their workers, the kinds of employment contract they use, the ease with which workers can be fired, and the organization of working time has dramatically increased ... [T]he second striking thing about the introduction of flexibility in France is that it made its biggest advances under the aegis of a Socialist government, between 1981 and 1986, despite the fact that the Socialists were initially hostile to flexibility and that flexibility is usually considered *une revendication patronale*. (Howell 1992a: 72–3)

Howell defines flexibility as 'the attempt by employers to shift the locus of control over issues such as wages, the use of work time, hiring and firing, and, more generally, industrial relations from national or industry level regulation ... to the firm' (1992a: 71). As he points out, it is significant that the 1986–8 Chirac government did not alter the Auroux laws at all, despite the right having been up in arms about them in the early 1980s. Indeed a survey carried out in 1984 suggested that 66 per cent of employers believed that Socialist industrial relations laws had been beneficial (1992a: 91).

Finally, there was a certain amount of agreement, or at least less hostility, between capital and labour. First, the number of collective agreements at local level rose sharply, mainly as a result of the Auroux laws (*European Industrial Relations Review*, 1989). Also the fact that the trade unions – and the CGT in particular – went into decline reduced the overt antagonism between employers and trade unions. FO, always more willing to negotiate, maintained or even increased its strength. More specifically, however, the 1980s saw the rise of what has been described as 'enterprise-based trade unionism', where certain trade unions have sought to encourage new working practices such as Japanese-style quality circles. The CFDT has become particularly associated with this new sort of trade unionism, summed up by CFDT leader Jean Kaspar in November 1988 when he called for 'a more positive approach to the firm, which is also a place where interests converge' (in Noblecourt 1990: 182). In 1986 CFDT National Secretary Jean-Paul Jaquier had already written strongly in favour of 'trade union freedom' (*la liberté syndicale*) and the right to manage (*la liberté d'entreprendre*), saying that 'to recognize the existence of these two rights is the adult way of one side of industry accepting the other, without necessarily accepting what the other is demanding' (Jaquier 1986, quoted in Noblecourt 1990: 182). These sorts of new, conciliatory attitudes have been facilitated, as we have seen, by the Auroux laws.

It is most significant that it was during the Socialist 1980s that a far more peaceful industrial relations climate emerged, less eventful than at any time in the modern history of France, with the exception of the Second World War. A neat indication of this new-found peace was the slight rise in the value of shares on the Paris Bourse the day after Mitterrand's re-election as President in May 1988.

Consensus beyond tripartism

How, then, did these areas of informal agreement or cooperation contribute to creating the broader political consensus referred to above? First, the dissociation between the PCF and consistent extra-parliamentary radicalism and the association between it and 'management' government meant that the PCF became a far less credible radical left alternative. The fact that the PCF ministers stayed in office at the time of and beyond the economic U-turn of 1982–3 played an important part in the further decline of the PCF after the losses in 1981, when the party already dropped to 15.3 per cent of the vote in the legislative elections. This contributed further to the problems which socio-economic change had brought with the decline of the manufacturing sector. The break-up of Eastern Europe and thus the failure of the long Communist experiment in this region served to compound the PCF's problems, of course, as it did for all other communist parties in Western Europe. Next, the move to the right on the part of the PS and its espousal of market economics in particular was made possible by the indulgent attitude of the labour movement during the post-1981 honeymoon period. The decline of the trade unions was also in part a result of this, given that they no longer represented clear class-against-class positions. The main parties of the left, in the form of the PS and PCF, no longer represented the bastion of resistance to compromise with pragmatic government it had been during the period of the Union of the Left and which the PCF had been for far longer. On the contrary, both parties governed during a period where compromise with capital had become, according to the PS, not only necessary but desirable in order to escape the ravages of economic crisis. In other words, the mystique surrounding the left largely disappeared in the space of a few short years and many left supporters had apparently come to accept the need for greater moderation.

Finally, the problems of the right were in part caused by the centre-left pragmatism which was so prevalent during the 1980s, because the left seemed to have located itself on the centre ground which the right had long claimed to inhabit. The right could no longer credibly condemn the left as a whole as being intent on overthrowing Western liberal democracy and setting up a Communist regime, as being a Trojan Horse for Soviet Communism. It was clear that the PS, at least, was playing much the same political game as the centre-right. Instead of claiming to represent reason in the face of unreasonableness and extremism, the centre-right now found itself inhabiting much the same ideological space as the PS and competing for this centre ground.

The major aspects of these developments took place during a period of economic hardship, and moments of harmony between any of the three actors mentioned above were brief. But the effects were far-reaching. Thus, although France in the 1980s did not display exactly the same elements of the post-war settlement of either Britain, West Germany or Sweden, it shared enough characteristics for us to argue that similar processes were at work. The generalized move towards the politics of pragmatism can be understood partly in these terms. However, in subsequent chapters I examine other, broadly speaking 'modernizing' aspects of post-war political history which also contribute to an understanding of the less conflictual politics of the 1980s and 1990s.

5
Social Democracy and the Left

> I do not dream, my dear compatriots, of an ideal society. I wish to eliminate inequalities which are obvious and which can be dealt with immediately.
>
> *François Mitterrand (1988: 44)*

I argue in chapter 4 that the Socialist Party played a key role in contributing to the more consensual political situation which developed during the 1980s in France. The PS was able to come to power in 1981 because it had won the support of a large section of a formerly more radical left electorate which had believed in the necessity of a total break with the established order as a precondition for greater social, economic and political justice. Much of the organized working class had long been in favour of head-on confrontation with the ruling class and, by contrast with other countries of north-west Europe, France had not been able to construct a socio-economic Fordist compromise upon which it could build a more harmonious political arrangement. Politics and industrial relations had continued to be dominated by conflict or the threat of conflict. Although the situation had begun to change after the departure of de Gaulle in 1969, it was not until the 1980s that the really significant break with the past took place and the PS was the main party political vehicle which allowed for the emergence of more consensual politics along the lines of the compromise achieved earlier in other countries.

The Socialist Party defies easy categorization, precisely because the radicalism of the left and the intransigence of the ruling class in France meant that the social, economic and political environment was hostile to the fundamentally compromising nature of social democracy. As we have seen, by contrast with the relatively clear role of left reformist parties in other north-west European countries after 1945, the behaviour of the PS was replete with paradoxes. For much of the post-war period, the Socialist current was different from socialism in these other countries in that other parties had either never been greatly influenced by Marxism, as in the case of Britain or Sweden, or had abandoned Marxism, as in the case of Germany after the famous Bad Godesberg congress in 1959. Many socialist or social democratic parties participated either as the main party or as major coalition partners in governments of national reconstruction. In France, despite participation in some coalition governments, the Socialist current after the Second World War remained ideologically influenced by the politics of class struggle, largely because of the hegemonic position of the PCF in relation to the working class and a desire on the part of the French Socialists to win for themselves some of the PCF's working-class support. However, the actual practice of the French Socialists was often well to the right of other left reformist parties during the post-war era, notably over the question of the war with Algeria, during which the Section Française de l'Internationale Ouvrière (SFIO) participated in governments which pursued the increasingly discredited campaign against Algerian independence fighters. Another corollary of the more conflictual nature of French society was that the SFIO – and later the PS – was by no means a mass party of the working class, in terms of either the size and nature of its membership or the size and nature of its electorate. Again, this was a significant difference between socialism in France and the classic social democracy of northern Europe, particularly in Scandinavia, West Germany, Austria and Britain. Moreover, in France the Socialists had no institutionalized links with a large, unified trade union movement which were also so important elsewhere.

Despite these differences, I do not believe that the PS can simply be viewed as the odd party out in an otherwise conformist family of north European socialist parties and – by contrast with some writers – I do believe it is useful to describe the PS as social democratic. Given its deep-rooted commitment to compromise and reform, rather than to challenging the fundamental characteristics of capitalism, and given its dependence on the working class for electoral support, there is far more to unite the PS with other left reformist parties than to separate it from them. There is much to be gained from likening the behaviour of the PS to that of other such parties, and this helps explain its behaviour during the 1980s and early 1990s.

In this chapter I begin by looking at social democracy as a historical phenomenon and suggest that a broad definition of the term is helpful when attempting to explain the behaviour of parties which are broadly socialist. Next, I look more generally at the left panorama in France before examining the PS itself and commenting on how other writers have defined it. I also consider the idea that in order to understand the PS it is necessary to compare it with European socialist parties in Spain, Portugal, Greece and Italy. Finally, I suggest tentatively that after defeats in the early and mid-1990s, followed by victory in 1997, the PS is now more than ever like socialist parties in other countries and that we may be witnessing a Europe-wide crisis of traditional social democracy.

The history of social democracy

A brief look at the history of social democracy in Western Europe helps explain its place in modern politics. In the latter part of the nineteenth century and in the early twentieth century, political parties which described themselves as social democratic, in Germany and Austria in particular, already found themselves confronting a fundamental question: should they devote virtually all their attentions to the wider class struggle via mass action with a view to over-throwing the capitalist system in the long term, or should they concentrate on partial, more immediate reforms within the framework of capitalism? In practice, the social democrats during this period tended to take the latter course, but up to 1914 they still regarded themselves and were thought of by others as revolutionary parties. The first real watershed came with the First World War, when the social democrats supported their national governments and thus implicitly expressed the view that the working class of other countries was a greater enemy than the bourgeoisie of their own country; they put nation before class. The Russian Revolution of 1917 then drove the wedge deeper between left parties who had a firmly reformist orientation and the communist parties of the Third International which were created in order to spread the politics of Bolshevism to other countries. For the communists of the Third International, the term 'social democratic' was necessarily pejorative and when used to describe the socialist parties implied an accommodation with capitalism, a betrayal of the class struggle on the part of the leadership of those parties and therefore politics which were contrary to the interests of the working masses. In the 1930s communist parties blamed the social democratic parties for the rise of fascism and went as far as describing them as 'social fascist', or as Stalin put it 'the moderate wing of fascism'. Since 1917, then, the movement for socialism has essentially been split between supporters of communism in the Leninist tradition and social democracy, or reformist socialism (Bottomore 1983: 442). It should be said, however, that since the emergence of Eurocommunism in the 1970s and still more since the break-up of the Soviet Union in the late 1980s communist parties have been far more accepting of liberal democratic principles and more conciliatory towards other parties, although the PCF was for many years a partial exception to this rule. The PCF was slower than other European communist parties to accept what many other communist leaders came to regard as inevitable.

Social democratic parties thus lay in a moderate terrain between the extremes, compromising with capitalism but representing the working class. Throughout Europe, they concentrated on elections in order to gain influence, their strategic goal being to participate in government and transform capitalism through gradual reform, whereas, particularly in the early days (until the mid-1930s at least), the parties of the Third International believed that electoral influence and other short-term, partial measures were only a part of the broader struggle for the overthrow of capitalism. Ideologically, then, social democratic parties situated themselves between the radicalism of the communist parties and the elitist values of conservative or Christian democratic parties whose political orientation was explicitly and unashamedly meritocratic and whose economic policies were oriented in favour of the interests of business. As Padgett and Paterson (1991) point out, social democratic parties have tended to have a commitment to nationalization and redistribution of wealth, state intervention in the economy and social provision, and more generally greater material equality between individuals. The British Labour Party ideologue Anthony Crosland describes social democracy in his classic book *The Future of Socialism* (1956) as political liberalism, the mixed economy, the welfare state, Keynesian economic policy and a commitment to greater social equality. Social democratic parties often continued to have an anti-capitalist rhetoric, but were informed by the assumption that it was possible to abolish capitalism gradually, through reforms, and without an armed insurrection on the part of the organized working class. Little by little this became a belief in the possibility of reforming capitalism to such an extent that it could offer social, economic and moral justice for everyone.

The years of reconstruction after the Second World War constituted the most successful period for social democratic parties, both in terms of winning elections and in terms of the actual success of their policies. During the 30 years after the Second World War, they played a central role in governments in many countries in Western Europe; Anton Pelinka ranks the 'governmental power' of these parties between 1945 and 1973 as: (1) Sweden, (2) Norway, (3) Denmark, (4) Austria, and (5) Britain (Pelinka 1983: 80). The Benelux countries and West Germany should also be added to any list of countries where social democratic government was prevalent. In fact, it is no exaggeration to say that in northern Europe, especially in the period between 1960 and 1973, normal politics meant social democratic politics. This was an era of economic reconstruction and sustained growth, often enabled by Fordist compromise, and social democratic parties were often the major or the sole party of government. The inter-war Depression had discredited laissez-faire economic policy and the dominant role of the state during the war coupled with the enormity of the task of economic reconstruction also legitimized state intervention; Keynesian economic theory provided the rational argument to match the egalitarian spirit so prevalent after the Second World War. Moreover, the onset of the Cold War at the end of the 1940s meant that confrontational, overtly anti-capitalist political action and political parties became less acceptable for many left-leaning voters and activists, because of their association with the Soviet Union. Indeed during the 30 years after 1945 social democratic values (by now firmly distinct from communism) seemed to fit perfectly the mood of the time in north-west European countries and were virtually identical with the dominant values of Western society as a whole; political liberalism, Keynesian economic policy, the welfare state and full employment were not only generally viewed as desirable, but also enabled sufficiently high levels of profit to satisfy the bourgeoisie as well as the labour movement. The bi- and often tripartite compromises which were often struck did actually provide gains for both capital and labour (see chapter 2). Writing in the late 1950s, Crosland went as far as to argue that since the 1930s Britain had become so much more politically, socially and economically just that capitalism had been reformed out of existence:

> I personally think ... that the proper definition of the word capitalism is a society with the essential social, economic, and ideological characteristics of Great Britain from the 1830s to the 1930s; and

this, assuredly, the Britain of 1956 is not. And so, to the question 'Is
this still capitalism?', I would answer 'No'. (Crosland 1963: 42)

Although this approach to late twentieth-century capitalist society is
associated with the 1950s and 1960s in particular, reformist socialist
government in fact remained widespread in northern Europe well
into the 1970s. In the years 1974–5, there were social democratic
prime ministers in Britain, West Germany, Austria, Belgium, the
Netherlands, Norway, Denmark, Sweden and Finland (Anderson
1994: 2).

Since the mid- to late 1970s, however, the capitalist economies in
the West have become far less suited to supporting the politics of
social democratic compromise than they were previously and the
governmental influence of left reformism in the countries where
social democracy had been a major influence in the post-war era has
declined considerably. As Perry Anderson points out, the movement
of neo-liberal, right-wing government began with Thatcher coming
to power in 1979 and then spread to West Germany, the Low Countries and to parts of Scandinavia. Only Austria and Sweden did not
succumb during this period (Anderson 1994: 3). During this time, the
bi- and tripartite settlements characteristic of the heyday of social
democracy have become virtually impossible, with high unemployment, weaker trade unions and generally the balance of forces swinging in favour of the ruling class and away from organized labour.
There has been a widespread crisis of the welfarist, Fordist economic
paradigm and the right indeed often blames former social democratic
governments for today's economic problems, pointing to the supposedly over-nannying state and over-powerful trade unions of the post-
war years. This attack on traditional social democracy is indeed one
characteristic of rediscovered neo-liberal economic thought on the
right and among the ruling class more generally, which favours
deregulation, the free reign of market forces, an absence of negotiation between government and significant popular pressure groups
(notably trade unions) and generally the balance of forces between
capital and labour swinging considerably in favour of the former.

Since the late 1970s the social democratic parties in northern
Europe have suffered setback after setback. The British Labour
Party, for example, experienced four consecutive defeats by the Conservatives at general elections in 1979, 1983, 1987 and 1992. This
prompted a major split in 1981 when the Social Democratic Party
was formed, profound divisions within the Labour Party itself and a

rapid move to the right after 1994 when Tony Blair became leader. In Germany, the Social Democratic Party has been out of national government since 1982 and has likewise gone through much ideological and strategic soul-searching. In Sweden, although the 1980s and early to mid-1990s saw success at elections, periods out of government after 44 years of unbroken rule up to 1976 also indicated growing insecurity for the Socialdemokratiska Arbetarpartiet. In Norway the right came to power in 1981 for the first time since the Second World War and the same year Gro Harlem Brundtland became leader of the Norwegian Labour Party, marking a distinct move in the direction of pragmatism. Finally, in Denmark a government was formed in 1982 comprising Liberals and Conservatives and for over a decade Social Democrats were in opposition, by contrast with the ten years up to 1982 when the Social Democrats had led the majority of the coalition governments (Crewe 1991; Padgett and Paterson 1994; Pontusson 1994; Mjøset et al. 1994; Christiansen 1994). In southern Europe, however, the trend in the 1980s was on the contrary towards reformist socialism, a point to which I return below.

It remains to be seen whether the counter-trend towards highly moderate social democratic government in the 1990s is durable; analysts are also beginning to wonder whether among some centre-left parties of government there is not a real rupture with their socialist or social democratic roots.

The nature of the left in France

As the above discussion makes clear, when I use the term 'social democracy' I mean, very generally, a compromise between the interests of a party which emerged out of the labour movement on the one hand with the interests of the ruling class on the other hand. This has been described as 'the attempt to reconcile socialism with liberal politics and capitalist society' (Padgett and Paterson 1991: 1). Successful social democratic parties emerged in countries where economic development and class relations were such that the capitalist class was powerful enough to make economic, political and social concessions to the working class and to allow the autonomous organization of the working class without any danger of these parties attempting to overthrow the capitalist system (J. Ross 1982: 5–6). In these countries, which tended to be in northern Europe, the autonomous organization of the working class could be tolerated and accommodated without fear of substantial loss of economic and political control by the bourgeoisie and ultimately without substantial loss of profit. In some countries of southern Europe on the other hand, the fragile position of the bourgeoisie meant that working class organization was severely repressed and conflict between the two classes became acute.

France lay somewhere between these two extremes, although at some points during the nineteenth century it came close to the second tendency: the labour movement grew in nineteenth-century France, but was for many years repressed in various ways; the *patronat* (often with the support of the government of the day) was extremely hostile to workers organizing collectively and the nascent trade unions were soon much influenced by a tendency to direct action and a desire to overthrow rather than reform the capitalist system. This partly explains why for a large part of the twentieth century the social democratic current (in the form of the SFIO then the PS) was relatively small and the Communist Party was relatively large. In a comment which in a general way sums up the spirit of reformist socialism, the Swedish social democrat Ernst Wigforss once said that 'neither the working class movement nor private capitalists could hope to suppress the other altogether . . . they should recognize this fact, and should cooperate to achieve their common interest – increased efficiency in production' (in Padgett and Paterson 1991: 10). This, in essence, is what the social democratic parties of many advanced capitalist countries did after the Second World War, but the PS only managed to do this, to an extent, in the 1980s.

The anomaly of the French situation and in particular the tardy emergence of the PS as a real party of government, is explained precisely by the fact that in France neither the dominant working class movement – in the form of the PCF and the CGT – nor the capitalist class had given up hope of suppressing their class enemy, although the Socialists were prepared to compromise. In France the PCF was sufficiently powerful and the organized capitalist class sufficiently weak (and intransigent) to make systematic class compromise as practised elsewhere impossible. Relations between the classes remained antagonistic and the left was divided into a large Communist Party and a socialist current sitting uneasily between the PCF and centrist parties like the Radical Party. Far from emerging as a dominant, moderate force and encapsulating the liberal democratic, Fordist and Keynesian values so prevalent in other north-west European countries in the 30 years after the Second World War, the SFIO found itself playing a more subordinate and pragmatic role, firstly under the Fourth Republic as part of unhappy and increasingly discredited coalitions of parties who often had little in common with each other apart from a desire to govern, then as a fragmented rump under de Gaulle's Presidency, from 1958 to 1969.

In order to understand the historical trajectory of the Socialist current, further discussion of the role of the Communist Party is necessary. Adam Przeworski comments that European socialist movements which came about in the context of nascent industrial capitalism faced three choices. First, they had to decide 'whether to seek the advancement of socialism within the existing institutions of capitalist society or outside of them'; second, they had to choose 'whether to seek the agent of socialist transformation exclusively in the working class or to rely on multi- or even non-class support'; finally, they had to choose 'whether to seek reforms, partial improvements, or to dedicate all efforts and energies to the complete abolition of capitalism' (Przeworski 1985: 3).

If we consider the reaction of the left in France to these three choices from the 1920s onwards, it is clear that a large part of the left, in the form of the PCF, took the more radical, less compromising route, whereas the Socialist current was far more persuaded by compromise with capitalism, multi-class support and reformism. However, the PCF never completely ignored reforms under capitalism and has at times taken a far more frankly social democratic route. Most obviously, it did so when it supported the Popular Front in 1936, when it participated in government with the Socialists and MRP from 1944 to 1947, and when it took part in government again from 1981 to 1984, not to mention from 1997 onwards. It also manifested frankly acknowledged social democratic tendencies when it went through a brief Eurocommunist phase in the 1970s, although even in the mid-1970s the PCF displayed far less willingness to compromise or to distance itself from the Soviet Union than did its Italian or Spanish counterparts. Indeed, it might be argued that the PCF has long been half-hearted in its struggle for the abolition of capitalism and that now it is wholly social democratic. The Common Programme of Government, co-signed by the PCF and PS in 1972, was a clearly reformist programme which posed no threat to the existence of the capitalist system. But for most of its life the PCF has had a radical left membership, close relations with a pro-communist trade union confederation, the CGT, and a barely flinching loyalty to the

Soviet Union. As a result, it has had a relationship with liberal democracy which changed greatly according to both domestic circumstances and the demands made on European communist parties by the Soviet Union. It made only the briefest of attempts to establish governmental compromises with the centre or the right (the exceptions being in 1936 and 1944–7), and indeed would not have got anywhere had it attempted to do so in an ongoing way.

Certainly, this is not to say that the PCF has remained a truly revolutionary party, one that continued to take seriously the idea of an insurrectionary overthrow of capitalism modelled on the 1917 Russian Revolution, or even the ending of capitalism by some other means. But its relationship with social democratic socialism (first in the form of the SFIO and then the PS) has been to say the least very uneasy, partly because much of the rank-and-file membership of the PCF remained committed to a thoroughgoing ideological onslaught on the capitalist system and all those who they viewed as central to its maintenance, notably heads of industry but also government ministers, for example. In other words, a large part of the PCF's success with its own membership and the electorate more broadly rested with its image as an anti-system party, a party which fought for the oppressed and sought profound changes in the organization of the economy, society and the political system. The partial nature of its conversion to social democratic electoral, parliamentary and more generally reformist-capitalist compromise became clear during the period of PCF participation in a PS-dominated government in the period 1981–4, when the PCF, in a very junior position in government, found that its appeal in terms of an image of intransigent defence of working-class interests was severely compromised, with the government implementing an austerity programme and other measures which expected the traditional working class to carry much of the burden of the economic crisis. Indeed this compromise was a significant contributory factor to the PCF's decline. On the other hand, the PCF has long, ultimately, been committed to supporting a general coalition of the left, and since its departure from government in 1984 it has usually supported PS legislative proposals in the National Assembly and often arrived at some sort of mutually beneficial arrangement with the PS in elections, whether this be a joint PCF/PS candidate, or an agreement to withdraw in favour of the best-placed candidate in the second round. Robert Hue becoming leader in 1994 has certainly continued to propel the PCF in a more social democratic direction, in the world of post-Soviet communism.

Table 5.1 illustrates the extent to which the PCF dominated or deeply divided the parliamentary left in France for much of the twentieth century. From the end of the Second World War right up to and including 1973, the PCF received a higher proportion of votes than the Socialists. Even in the late 1980s and early 1990s, it received between a third and a half of the number of votes the PS received. Table 5.1 also illustrates how the PS successfully built itself in electoral terms at the expense of the PCF.

The uneven development and divided nature of the left in France is intimately connected with the weakness and fragmentation which has always characterized the trade union movement. The radicalism of the major trade union confederations, in particular the CGT, has meant that other confederations emerged which defined themselves largely in terms of difference between them and the larger organizations. This fissiparous history has meant that even today there are

Table 5.1 Communist and Socialist voting strengths, legislative elections 1924–97

	Communist vote (% of total)	Socialist vote (% of total)	Communist vote (% of Socialist vote)	Communist plus Socialist (% of total)
1924	9.5	20.2	47	29.7
1928	11.4	18.0	63	29.4
1932	8.4	20.5	40	28.9
1936	15.4	20.8	73	36.2
1945	26.1	23.4	112	49.5
1946 (June)	25.7	21.1	123	46.8
1946 (Nov.)	28.6	17.9	158	46.5
1951	26.9	14.6	184	41.5
1956	25.7	15.2	170	40.9
1958	19.2	15.7	122	34.9
1962	21.8	12.5	174	34.3
1967	22.5	18.9	119	41.4
1968	20.0	16.5	121	36.5
1973	21.4	20.8	103	42.2
1978	20.7	24.9	83	45.6
1981	16.1	37.8	42	53.9
1986	9.6	31.6	31	41.2
1988	11.4	37.6	30	49.0
1993	9.1	19.9	45	29.0
1997	9.9	25.6	39	35.5

Source: D. S. Bell and Criddle 1994: 167 (by permission of Oxford University Press) ; *Le Monde* 1997: 43

four major confederations – CGT, FO, CFDT and CFTC – which show no convincing signs of merging in the near future. These conditions are again far from ideal for the emergence of dominant (that is governmental) social democracy. In Sweden, Austria, West Germany and Britain in particular, the substantial size, the unity, the stability and the reformist nature of the trade union movement has meant that there has been a wider, moderate left social movement which included cooperative societies, social clubs and financial institutions, and which helped foster the conditions necessary for the ongoing success of a social democratic party. This does not mean that a party in a country such as France cannot be social democratic, but it does mean that its existence will be more precarious and that it will be more volatile and prone to changes of direction, instead of being organizationally and ideologically anchored by a stable and well organized working class. In order to govern, and carry on governing, a social democratic party is obliged to win and consolidate the confidence of a large proportion of the working class.

Characterizing the Socialist Party

After the creation of the Socialist Party in 1969 and its relaunch at the Congrès d'Epinay two years later, the party set great store by attracting both the working-class Communist vote and the support of well-educated middle class radicals who became converts to various forms of neo-Marxism in the wake of May 1968. In June 1972, Mitterrand commented famously that the PS's principal objective was to 'rebuild a large socialist party on the terrain occupied by the Communist Party itself, in order to show that out of five million communist electors, three million can vote Socialist' (quoted in Biffaud 1988: 71). However, the political orientation and strategy of the Socialist current has continued to be characterized by a willingness to compromise with forces to its right, in spite of a left gloss on much of its programme. This is also what unites the PS with other left reformist parties in Europe and what helps explain its role in achieving more consensual politics in the 1980s and early 1990s. Along with Jacques Kergoat, I believe that defining the nature of the PS primarily involves analysing the ideological orientation of the party and not first and foremost scrutinizing its structure or the composition of its membership (Kergoat 1983: 278). The PS, like social democratic parties elsewhere, has long had a political orientation which was typical of parties belonging to the Second International to the extent that it was keen to maintain its working-class electoral base but was at the same time prepared to make substantial concessions to the interests of capital, difficult though this juggling act was in a country like France where a culture of political compromise was so alien. The *Projet socialiste* manifesto of 1980, for example, certainly contained radical-sounding phrases about the PS planning to change people's lives, about breaking with capitalism, and so on. But in terms of actual proposals it was a typical left reformist programme, containing such measures as nationalization of certain key industries and financial institutions, stimulating demand, improving working conditions, a progressive social policy and on the whole moderate foreign policy (Parti socialiste 1980). The practice of the PS in government in the early 1980s was also typical of a party of centre-left class compromise, to the extent that it sought to satisfy some of the demands of the labour movement whilst at the same time taking into account the needs of capital. It began by implementing Keynesian-inspired economic and social policies reminiscent of the approach of social democratic parties elsewhere in Europe in the earlier post-war period. Once it became clear that these policies were unworkable, in particular because of the international economic situation and the influence of neo-liberal economic policy in the nations with which France traded, the PS changed tack and began to implement an economic programme which was influenced more by pragmatism than by left reformist ideology. It was in fact a social democratic party which had adopted a set of conservative policies through force of circumstance.

As I have said, an important characteristic of social democratic parties is their dependence upon the working class for electoral support. The PS certainly shares this characteristic, as long as the working class is defined as blue-collar *and* white-collar salaried workers, rather than restricting the definition to manual workers. (See Tables 5.2, 5.3 and 5.4.) This is not the place for a detailed analysis of the class structure of advanced capitalist societies, but I do believe that it is quite wrong to suggest that white-collar workers are not members of the 'real' working class. Certainly, they do not conform to the romanticized view of the blue-collar worker who toils alongside his (usually also male) fellow workers in keeping with the traditional image. White-collar workers in particular tend now to work in less homogeneous units and have less traditional patterns of work, especially working hours. But the structure of the relationship with the

Table 5.2 Correspondence between voters' sectors of work and voting intentions in the French legislative elections of 1988 (%)

	Self-employed	Salaried: public sector	Salaried: private sector
PC	7	40	53
PS	12	35	53
Ecologists	14	39	47
UDF	27	29	44
RPR	29	22	49
FN	17	27	56
All	18	30	52

Source: Bergounioux and Grunberg 1992: 395

Table 5.3 Correspondence between voters' occupations and voting in the French legislative elections of 1988 (%)

	Far left	PCF	PS and allies	Ecologists	UDF, RPR and allies	FN	Total
Farmers	0	3	13	0	81	3	100
Craftspeople, shop keepers	0	7	28	0	59	6	100
Managerial, liberal professions	0	5	39	0	46	10	100
Lower supervisory, nurses, primary teachers[a]	2	12	45	1	34	6	100
Clerical	1	16	40	0	35	8	100
Blue-collar	0	16	43	1	21	19	100
Not working (inc. retired)	1	10	37	0	43	9	100

[a] Professions intermédiaires.
Source: CEVIPOV 1995: 173

rest of society, and most notably with the ruling class, remains the same as that of blue-collar workers. Ralph Miliband argues in this spirit that the working class in advanced capitalist countries must be defined as a group which includes clerical workers, service and distributive workers, and public and state employees. These workers are often just as subordinate in their social and economic hierarchies as were traditional blue-collar workers and almost always as lacking in control. Thus although the manufacturing working class has been in decline for some years, the working class as a whole is in fact still

Table 5.4 Correspondence between voters' occupations and voting in the French legislative elections of 1993 (%)

	Far left	PCF	PS and allies	Other left	Ecologists	UDF	RPR	Other right	FN	Others	Total
Farmers	0	3	12	0	0	32	23	8	13	9	100
Craftspeople, shop keepers	0	4	9	5	4	20	32	5	15	6	100
Managerial, liberal professions	3	6	27	0	13	24	15	6	6	0	100
Lower supervisory, nurses, primary teachers[a]	3	11	27	1	15	15	16	2	8	2	100
Clerical	3	10	17	1	10	16	16	5	18	4	100
Blue-collar	2	14	18	1	7	17	16	3	18	4	100
Not working (inc. retired)	1	9	19	1	6	20	24	4	12	4	100

[a] *Professions intermédiaires.*
Source: CEVIPOV 1995: 215

growing, as the groups mentioned above increase in size (Miliband 1989: 41). André Gorz was quite wrong to argue, as he did in the late 1970s, that we must bid 'farewell to the working class' (Gorz 1980). Indeed it is striking how far white-collar workers are from enjoying the extensive technologically created leisure predicted by some writers two decades ago, and huge numbers of supposedly privileged white-collar workers in industrialized countries live with the very real threats of unemployment, deterioration in working conditions, and a decline in real income.

Throughout the 1980s the PS attracted a sizeable proportion of the working-class vote, although in the 1990s the working class began to vote in shockingly large numbers for the FN (in the 1995 presidential elections 27 per cent of manual workers voted for Le Pen and 21 per cent for Jospin; in 1997 the figures were 24 per cent for the FN and 49 per cent for the PS and ecologists).

Returning to the role of the PS in the 1980s and early 1990s, it is precisely the spirit of compromise (especially with the business elite), whilst drawing on working-class support, which allowed it to construct more consensus-oriented politics. This is what social democratic parties in other countries of northern Europe did in the post-war era, and in France it was the polarity of the dominant representatives of employers and the labour movement that had prevented the emergence of social democratic government at an earlier date. The major problem with France's social democratic experiment in the 1980s, however, was firstly that the world economy was weak and secondly that in many other countries around the world governments hostile to social democracy were implementing economic policies which, arguably, obliged the French Socialists to choose between a siege economy or adoption of neo-liberal economic policies. As we have seen, it did the latter.

Other authors draw quite different conclusions about the nature of the PS. Hugues Portelli (1988) argues that the PS is substantially different from other centre-left parties in Europe precisely because it has fewer, and weaker, links with the working class. Portelli's main thesis is that the PS – a 'party of the new middle classes' – is in fact very similar to the Radical Party, which was particularly influential in the Third Republic (Portelli 1988: 119). Lacking a trade union movement with which it could work closely, French socialism has not had a consistently working-class political orientation and the middle-class composition of the PS membership is both a result and a cause of this. He explains the tortuous history of the SFIO and the PS in a

highly illuminating way, particularly in relation to the Fourth Republic and the Algerian war, arguing that the absence of a structural link
with the working class permitted the SFIO to act in a way which was
characteristic of a more bourgeois party. But his final characterization of the PS is, I believe, flawed. Certainly, the absence of close
trade union links has meant that French socialism has had a less consistent political orientation than other European socialist parties,
because it has not been structurally and therefore ideologically
anchored by a large movement organically linked to the working
class. But in other countries Socialists were also often prepared to
make substantial compromises in order to come to power or remain
in government. The German SPD, for example, governed with the
centre and the right in the Grand Coalition from 1966 to 1969, and
the British Labour Party governed with the explicit support of the
Liberal Party in the 'Lib–Lab Pact' of 1977–8.

Portelli stresses the sociological composition of the party membership itself in an attempt to show that the reconstructed PS is far from
being a party of the working class, which social democratic parties
must be. He points out that the party was rebuilt not by the traditional working class but by intellectuals of various kinds: 'the party
has adopted the culture of the intellectuals, marginalizing all those
who are not university-educated and *professionnels de la parole*'
(1988: 126). The PS was indeed largely reconstructed by middle-class
intellectuals and para-intellectuals (such as schoolteachers, university
lecturers, researchers and journalists) and other members of the
'new middle classes'. But activist support for socialist parties is also
found among these groups in all other West European countries,
without exception. Perhaps it makes them more vulnerable to shifts
to the right, but these parties are nevertheless obliged to bear in
mind that to have any hope of participation in government they must
continue to appeal to a significant proportion of the working class.

Finally, the point about the Radical Party was that it occupied a
firmly centrist position between right and left, allying with one or the
other according to what was expedient at the time. As far as the PS is
concerned, it has certainly shifted towards the right since it has been
in government and indeed at one point (in the immediate aftermath
of the 1988 parliamentary elections) pursued a policy of *ouverture*
towards the centre-right and independents. As I have pointed out, in
its previous incarnation as the SFIO it compromised with the centre-
right in governments of the Fourth Republic. But the PS has by no
means departed from the left camp since 1981 and continued to look

for support from the PCF after the Communist ministers resigned from government in 1984, for example. After its defeat in the legislative elections of March 1993 and presidential elections of March–April 1995 the PS continued to look to the left for renewal; for example Lionel Jospin took an active part in the huge rally of the left as a whole (including Alain Krivine, leader of the Trotskyist Ligue Communiste Révolutionnaire) at Bercy in April 1996, an event organized by the PCF (*Le Monde* 4 April 1996). The left victory in 1997 seemed to confirm that this was a successful strategy, and the left–right split, although perhaps weaker than it was, is still intact.

One school of thought in political science defines social democracy by examining the *structure* of the large and highly successful left reformist parties in Europe in order to understand what unites them (e.g. Bergounioux and Manin 1979; Moschonas 1994). The centre-left parties in Sweden, West Germany, Austria and Britain are viewed as social democratic because they are in countries with large, moderate, unified trade union movements and are closely linked to them. Bergounioux and Manin go further and argue that in addition to this characteristic it must be understood that 'social democracy is not a political ideology but a form of *government*' [my emphasis], which is based on class compromise, redistribution of wealth and a well-developed state sector (Bergounioux and Manin 1979: 183). In terms of structure, and for a long time in terms of political orientation as well, this means that the French PS was far from being social democratic, whereas for instance the Swedish, Austrian or German Socialist parties were (1979: 187). I think Bergounioux and Manin are correct to the extent that there has not been a trade union confederation sufficiently large and also organizationally and ideologically close enough to the PS to prevent it from oscillating between periods of decidedly right-wing political practice and periods of left politics. As I have said, under the Fourth Republic the SFIO indulged in neo-colonialist practices in Algeria, broke up strikes violently, and generally shared policies with parties which were well to its right. But it is also true that the combination of a willingness to compromise with capital and a strong ideological orientation towards the working class means that there is far more to unite the PS with other organizations in the socialist Second International than to separate it from them. The Socialist current in France has also, in common with other social democratic parties, always had as its first priority success in elections. In short, the (subjective) will to compromise was there, to strive for left-leaning consensus, but (objective) circumstances prevented this from happening. The PS came to power in 1981 on a platform which contained most of the programmatic elements which Bergounioux and Manin identify as social democratic and, as I have argued elsewhere in this book, soon learned to compromise with capital again.

Over the past few years various writers have emphasized the differences between north European socialism and south European socialism in explaining the role and changing nature of centre-left parties. The French left is increasingly thought of as part of the southern European group of socialist parties. Perry Anderson has pointed out that in the nineteenth century and early twentieth century large social democratic parties emerged in Britain, Germany and Belgium based on the activities of major concentrations of heavy industry and therefore industrial workers, with strong trade unions. In Scandinavia similar parties were built on an alliance of small farmers with labour. Although the northern parties enjoyed early electoral successes, their major influence came in the post-war period and especially in the early 1970s, as we have seen. In France, Italy, Spain, Portugal and Greece, on the other hand, the development of industry was a far more uneven process, clerical and seigneurial influence remained strong in the still large agricultural sectors and the trade unions were far smaller. Anarcho-syndicalism was still a major influence in these southern European countries when the Second International was becoming established in the north and the communist parties on the whole became far stronger than in northern Europe.

In the final few decades of the twentieth century, however, the situation changed. By the early 1980s, whereas social democracy had lost much of its governmental power in northern Europe (the exceptions being Austria and Sweden), France, Spain and Greece had large Socialist majorities in parliament, and Italy and Portugal had socialist prime ministers which reflected an important – if not necessarily dominant – position of Socialists in government (Anderson 1994: 2–4). Paul Webb mentions that in addition to the common southern European socio-economic characteristics detailed above, 'the influence of the Roman Catholic or Orthodox church [was] strong and the rights of workers, women, the young ... minimal or non-existent.' More specifically, Webb argues that in the late 1970s or early 1980s, the southern European socialist parties became more internally cohesive, reorganizing around an impressive leader. They also became electorally ambitious, with centrist programmes (Webb 1994: 9–10). Whilst these parties rely on the working class for electoral support, they do not enjoy the militant, ongoing support of the working class in the form of party membership or institutionalized links with the labour movement. Ideologically, these parties have a Marxist, or at least anti-capitalist, rhetoric but little of real programmatic substance once the rhetoric is stripped away, a fact that allows for great flexibility when it comes to the tough job of actually governing. On the other hand, as Gerassimos Moschonas points out, in countries with large communist parties and weak and fragmented trade union movements (Spain and Greece in particular, but also France), centre-left parties tend to meet more obstacles when attempting to forge cross-class alliances than in countries where communism is weaker and trade union movements large and unified (Moschonas 1994: 58–60; also Przeworski and Sprague 1986: 70).

These are important points and ones which do shed light on the nature of the PS, particularly in terms of its position as a socialist party in a country where social, economic and political modernization came in an uneven fashion. To contrast north European and south European socialism is a way of highlighting the relationship between the development of political parties and socio-economic modernization. But, firstly, to suggest that either the PS or France as a whole belong to the southern European tradition is to underplay the more modern aspects of France's political system and political life more generally, not to mention the French economy, compared with the truly southern European countries. France is at least halfway between the south and the north in these respects, for although it did not industrialize as quickly as some of the north European countries, it has long been ranked among the leading industrialized nations in terms of GNP, trade and productivity of labour, for example, and has been a leading participant in industrialized countries' international economic organizations such as the European Union and the OECD. Certainly France in the Fourth Republic was very unstable politically and under de Gaulle governmental politics were in many ways authoritarian, reminiscent of a country whose pace of socio-economic development was slow and uneven. Care should therefore be taken not to exaggerate the extent to which the PS fits the modern model of socio-economic and political development. However, although the similarities between France and southern European countries are something which analysts have too often ignored in the past, similarities should not be exaggerated.

Anderson, for example, mentions Gaullism alongside the extraordinarily repressive regimes of Salazar in Portugal, Papadopoulos in Greece and Franco in Spain as evidence of an authoritarian political past. The comparison greatly overstates the repressive nature of Gaullism, for in Portugal, Greece and Spain opposition parties were in each case banned, whereas this was far from the case under de Gaulle, when even the PCF organized openly, despite being regarded by the Gaullists as enemy number one. Liberal democratic tendencies were far more in evidence under de Gaulle than during the southern European dictatorships. To suggest that socialism in France has some structural and sociological characteristics distinct from those of classic north European socialism does help explain the fluctuating nature of its programme and general ideological orientation. The development of the left in France was affected by relatively late and uneven industrialization, by the existence of small but radical trade unions and by the strength of the Communist Party. During the years of the first Cold War the SFIO could not contemplate an alliance with the PCF, so chose the centre parties and the centre-right as governmental allies; during reconstruction and its rise to power after 1969 an alliance with the PCF was more expedient; once in power, the PS moved rapidly to the right without pressure to do otherwise via formal links from the trade union movement. However, to suggest that this places France within a wholly distinct category of left reformist parties from those of northern Europe is analytically unhelpful. There is in fact much to unite the north European parties of the Second International with each other and with those of the south, and France to a certain degree bridges the gap between north and south.

The PS is a classic social democratic party in many ways. But the point about socialism in France is that by the time circumstances allowed it to govern, times had changed. As Jane Jenson puts it, 'the universe of political discourse within which the French left operated was still ordered by the major elements of the Fordist societal paradigm, although the economy was no longer operating according to Fordist principles' (Jenson 1991: 103). Alain Lipietz argues in similar vein that when the PS came to power in 1981 it was 'economically and ideologically too late. Fordism had entered crisis, both in France and internationally' (Lipietz 1991: 29). This line of approach thus helps explain the Socialist 1980s in France and helps us understand, in particular, why the PS's largely social democratic experiment came to grief. We are able to make some sense of the brief social democratic experiment in France and the PS's role in achieving a more consensual political situation in the context of broader West European political development.

The PS foundered on the rocks of a changed international economic and social climate and is at present suffering as well from not having a long track record of representing the key sections of the French working class in the post-war period. This makes the task of full recovery difficult. But there seems little doubt that the Socialist-dominated 1980s will continue to be identified as a turning point in the history of French politics, particularly because that decade sealed the fate of traditional left radicalism.

A crisis of social democracy?

From the mid-1970s onwards, changes in the economic conditions, social structure, and in particular the balance of forces between the classes in advanced capitalist countries have profoundly altered the environment in which political parties operate. These changes, which I have argued can in broad terms be associated with a change from a Fordist to a post-Fordist mode of production and social context are on the whole not conducive to the existence of social democratic government, at least in its traditional forms. As we have seen, traditional social democracy was most successful during the post-war period of bi- or tripartite compromise along Fordist lines, where favourable economic conditions could offer social democratic parties the opportunity to bring their working-class electoral base into a position of compromise with capital and, to an extent, achieve benefits for both of these essentially antagonistic forces. This, I have argued, contributed in an important way in France to the more consensual political situation in the 1980s.

However, social democracy in much of northern Europe has been in crisis since the end of the 1970s, whilst in southern Europe it came into its own as repressive regimes in Spain, Greece and Portugal gave way to more democratic political arrangements (see Grunberg 1996: 477). In both Spain and Greece PSOE and PASOK ruled almost without a break during the 1980s and 1990s. In Portugal the PSP was in government between 1976 and 1978, then from 1983 to 1985, and its leader Mario Soares was elected President in 1986. In Italy the PSI not only participated in government but its leader,

Bettino Craxi, was Prime Minister from 1983 to 1987. More recently, social democratic parties of southern Europe have also been in difficulty, most notably in Italy, where corruption scandals virtually destroyed the PSI. In Portugal and Greece electoral victories in the early and mid-1990s brought the social democratic parties out of periods of weakness, and in the case of PASOK the danger of disintegration as a result of financial scandal. Only in Spain did the social democratic party remain in power throughout the 1980s and beyond, and even here allegations of corruption and ineffectiveness of economic policy have greatly reduced its popularity at elections.

It would now be reasonable to suggest that there is a generalized crisis among social democratic parties, or at least a profound transformation taking place in social democracy across Europe, due largely to the highly unconducive socio-economic conditions of the present period. Moschonas identifies the following key developments when seeking to explain the inability on the part of the centre-left parties to achieve the bi- and tripartite pacts which were so crucial to the success of governmental social democracy in its heyday: (1) the crisis of the welfare state; (2) the fragmentation of the labour force and increased specialization; (3) growth in the number of workers with insecure or 'flexible' conditions of work (working in the informal economy, on flexible working time, on part-time or short-term contracts, workers alternating between periods in work and unemployment); (4) the growing prevalence of 'microcorporatism' (in the form of quality circles, for example); (5) widespread unemployment, which contributes to making the working class a less homogeneous entity and which weakens solidarity between workers (Moschonas 1994: 103–4). Each of these developments stems originally from the economic crisis which emerged in the early to mid-1970s and the now widespread acceptance that in order to achieve economic growth it is necessary to shift power and profits in favour of capital, rather than towards working people, which was of course one of the hallmarks of social democracy. Parties find it more and more difficult to mobilize people to join and work for them, as Table 5.5 shows for the PS.

It seems in fact that a new stage is emerging in the life of European social democracy. Social and economic conditions throughout Europe are becoming more homogeneous, with the south to an extent harmonizing with the north as the countries of northern Europe experience profound social and economic difficulties and the structures of their economies and societies become more fragmented and precarious. The Socialist parties of southern Europe, meanwhile,

Table 5.5 Membership of the Socialist Party, according to party sources, 1971–94

1971	80,300	1983	203,535
1972	92,230	1984	189,282
1973	107,757	1985	176,878
1974	137,000	1986	177,284
1975	149,623	1987	183,210
1976	159,548	1988	202,083
1977	160,000	1989	204,172
1978	180,000	1990	165,186
1979	159,000	1991	155,000
1980	189,580	1992	137,000
1981	196,501	1993	112,405
1982	213,584	1994	103,000

Source: Bergounioux 1996: 261

have experience of government and have as a result altered their programmatic orientation and strategy in a firmly pragmatic direction, a process which was particularly rapid owing to the difficult economic circumstances in which they have governed. (It is significant that a number of studies since the beginning of the 1990s seek to compare social democratic parties across Europe and often pay particular attention to comparisons between north European and south European social democracy (e.g. D. S. Bell and Shaw 1994; Grunberg 1996; Maravall 1992)). The Socialist Party, like its counterparts in southern Europe, has also become more similar than in the past to other social democratic parties in northern Europe, for its periods in power saw a rapid shift to the right and towards greater pragmatism. Unfavourable economic circumstances meant that traditional social democratic government based on compromise was impossible to achieve in France, although the PS's attempt to bring about compromise in part explains the more consensual nature of the period since 1981. As the PS attempts to recover from a large degree of discredit earned during the years in power, comparisons will inevitably be made with socialist parties in other countries. I have argued that the working class is certainly not dead, or even in decline, because the working class must be defined as including white-collar workers and not only manual workers in traditional industries. Throughout Europe, however, the labour movement is experiencing tremendous difficulties, due to the international economic crisis coupled with the prevalence of neo-liberal government economic policy. It is this factor which will continue to make the task of consolidation difficult for the PS, as a workable post-Fordist social democratic paradigm remains elusive.

The two related questions which must be posed about the French left and the left in other countries are: (1) can social democracy survive?; and (2), assuming it can gain a new lease of life, will it retain anything of the traditional socialism which sprang originally from the labour movements in different countries? In answer to the first question, although life is by no means easy for these parties, it seems that even in countries where there have been severe setbacks in recent years they are able to retain a certain credibility. This is now the case in Britain, of course, where more than a decade and a half of Conservative rule reshaped the country in many ways which are most unconducive to the aims of traditional social democracy. Conservative government both actively encouraged the economic restructuring of the country, including a severe and deliberate weakening of the trade union movement, and helped push the political and social ethos of Britain rapidly in the direction of free enterprise and individualism. However, Tony Blair and his colleagues managed to convince a large proportion of the electorate that New Labour has something attractive to offer, a development which could not have been predicted in the mid-1980s, when the Labour Party appeared to many to be in terminal decline.

In France, meanwhile, the PS suffered severe setbacks in the early 1990s, notably in 1993 when the PS obtained the lowest proportion of the total vote for 20 years (see table 5.1). Neither Michel Rocard nor Henri Emmanuelli, who became first secretary in 1993 and 1994 respectively, were able to inspire confidence as to the future success of the PS. But the PS has been able to maintain credibility as a party of government to the extent that its candidate in the 1995 presidential elections, Lionel Jospin, came first in the first round, with a respectable 23.3 per cent of the vote, and scored an equally respectable 47.4 per cent in the second round against Jacques Chirac. Jospin was made first secretary of the PS in October 1995 and socialists who were ambitious for governmental power began to recover from the blow which had come when Jacques Delors announced at the end of 1994 that he would not stand as PS presidential candidate. In the early 1990s one could have confidently predicted a very marginal role for the PS in French party politics up to the end of the century and beyond, as well as highly damaging fragmentation of the party, which is what happened to the Socialist current during de

Gaulle's Presidency. Instead of this, the PS remains in the late 1990s a credible alternative to the centre-right in many people's eyes, as victory at the 1997 legislative elections has shown.

As I point out above, times are nevertheless extremely hard for social democratic parties throughout Europe, largely because of their inability to marry traditional social democratic policies with the current economic climate, and, as I have also pointed out, there is now far more in common between the socialist parties in countries where social democracy took a classic, north-European form, and those of southern Europe. However, a new social democratic paradigm – either sociologically or politically – has not emerged (Moschonas 1994: 124). The reasons for this include: the decline of the blue-collar working class; the decline of the trade union movement; the inability of either centre-right or centre-left in government to solve any of the major economic problems of the late twentieth century; the rise of ecology groups and other new social movements; the break-up of Eastern Europe, which has undermined the credibility not only of communism but in many people's eyes any ideology which emphasizes the importance of social equality and defence of the disadvantaged; and finally the move to the centre by many social democratic parties which have experienced power and thus the proximity of centre-left and centre-right.

Marc Lazar suggests that these sorts of problems are not insurmountable and that social democracy is likely to continue to adapt and survive:

> Is the left not at present going through one of those periods of difficult adaptation to changes in European society and politics as a whole, that it has gone through in the past and resolved after a certain time? After having leaned to the left is it not in the process of 're-centring' itself in response to the external environment? Rather than experiencing an inability to adapt, the left, as we have seen, is suffering from the lack of a project, from a totally unprecedented breakdown in its system of relations with society, from a change in its sociological characteristics, from a complete change in its methods of organization and from an absence of strategy. (Lazar 1996: 50)

This may be a correct prognosis. Throughout Europe, whether or not it is in power, the left is either finding it difficult or no longer making a serious attempt to reconcile the traditional aims and values of the labour movement with the realities of government. This creates tensions both between party leadership and the rank-and-file membership, and between the party and the labour movement.

This brings us to the other question, of whether social democratic parties will retain enough of their original policy orientations for them still to be classed as social democratic, as parties which have close links with the labour movements of their country, at least ideologically if not structurally. If the crisis of direction for social democracy is as profound as Lazar suggests, will it not be reformed out of all recognition in an attempt to find a way out of the apparent impasse in which it finds itself? The answer to this question is more difficult to suggest. I point out at the beginning of this chapter that social democracy has a long history of compromise with the interests of capital, something which became one of its defining characteristics early in its development. But partly because of the weakness of the labour movement throughout Europe and beyond, the ideological distance travelled by social democracy since the mid-1970s has been great. In the case of the PS, we have seen that it was vigorous in its adoption of neo-liberal economics, promotion of the firm and its willingness to put the burden of the economic crisis onto working people. The British Labour Party, meanwhile, has bent over backwards under the leadership of Neil Kinnock, John Smith and in particular Tony Blair to distance itself from traditional socialist ideals, with much being made of the rewriting of Clause Four (which previously committed the party to common ownership of the means of production, distribution and exchange), the promotion of private enterprise and marginalization of the role of trade unions in Labour Party matters.

Perhaps, in the light of history, it is worth hazarding a guess that social democracy and also socialism will survive, but that they will do so not because of the actions of social democratic leaders. Rather, it will be social movements and struggles which, as in the past, ultimately determine both the survival and the nature of parties of the left. Among these parties of the left splits and fusions are likely to continue to take place and revolts and protest movements will continue to influence the PS and other social democratic parties. Whilst the structure and characteristics of the working class may have changed, many of the big questions which the left was created in order to tackle remain unresolved: the problems of social deprivation, inequality, and insufficient rights for minority groups remain as or more acute in advanced capitalist countries as they did during the post-war period.

6
The Paradoxes of
Gaullist Modernization

People are tired of this way of behaving. Always saying: 'If you don't vote YES then I'll leave.' Well let him leave.
Elderly Frenchwoman speaking in April 1969 (in von Braun 1990)

In the spring of 1958 it seemed as if the future of democracy in France was seriously in jeopardy, whether or not de Gaulle took control of things. The army was apparently on the verge of attempting a *coup d'état* in metropolitan France and General de Gaulle came to power with its open support. His exploitation of these extraordinary circumstances in order to obtain the type of political regime he had advocated for over a decade meant that while he was loved and revered by many ordinary French people and politicians alike, he was reviled and feared by many others, in particular large sections of those who identified with the left. But de Gaulle's Presidency must in any case be viewed as a significant turning point in the evolution of modern French politics. For despite the ominous circumstances in which it began and despite some democratically highly dubious moments and indeed ongoing practices, in the end it made a substantial contribution towards bringing about political stability. It is also necessary to explore the very real increased respect for the notion of formal democracy, often ignored by critics of Gaullism. Integral to the legacy are Gaullist foreign policy, particularly decolonization, and just as importantly modernization of the economy, an economy which came to resemble those of other advanced capitalist countries far more than it had done before. However, if de Gaulle and his policies were midwife to political and economic modernization and stability, this process was brought about in such a way as to deny certain key sections of the population material and political benefits which were available in other countries. Modernization was thus once again real but profoundly uneven, as it had been so often before in French history, and it was precisely these paradoxes which contributed towards making the internationally revolutionary year 1968 a moment of particularly intense revolt in France.

General de Gaulle was in many ways a deeply conservative man, steeped in the values of nineteenth-century France. In his memoirs he described rural France as the 'source of my life, the mother of our population, the basis for our institutions, the mainstay of our nation' (quoted in Gauron 1983: 68). Tremendously patriotic, he wrote in another famous passage how France was 'like the princess in fairy tales, the Madonna in frescos, destined for an eminent and exceptional place' (de Gaulle 1954: 1). The nation had to be steeped in glory if it was to be true to its worth and de Gaulle experienced the many humiliations of France's history almost as personal affronts, so the army, to which de Gaulle devoted much of his life, played a key role in defending this precious, Madonna-like nation. Sentiments such as these had been held by countless patriotic French people over the centuries, and de Gaulle might have seemed the last person on earth to bring about substantial political and economic modernization; political stability based on direct democracy, the consumer society and industry at the cutting edge of technological innovation appear far away from such a romantic, mystical vision of France, as does a substantial reorientation away from a national political ideology based on a simple pride in traditional French culture, the colonies and an inward-looking, traditionally structured economy, and towards monopoly capitalism and location of France firmly within the international economic and political community. Indeed as late as 1969 the Gaullist Party general secretary Robert Poujade described Gaullism as a 'mystical doctrine of national unity' (quoted in Charlot 1971: 67). But at the point when de Gaulle came to power, the French political elite had reached an impasse over the question of France's relations with Algeria and the most historically significant point about de Gaulle's rule was precisely the ability to appeal to some of the most traditional, often reactionary, values held by many of his most ardent supporters and at the same time achieve changes which previously had not been possible because of this very conservatism. However, in the absence of compromise between labour, capital and the state, modernization under de Gaulle took place via a quite different route from that in other countries, excluding many of the intermediary groups which were elsewhere important in the process of social and economic modernization. There was nothing inevitable about political or economic modernization, and just as likely an outcome of the turmoil of the end of the Fourth Republic was further, lasting conflict and instability, and increased isolation on the international stage. But history turned out quite differently. This conservative-minded general was to bring about Fordist modernization with the support of large numbers of French people who were in fact opposed to such a paradigm, and de Gaulle made these people – and ultimately himself – seem like an anachronism.

Authoritarian aspects of de Gaulle's rule

The circumstances of de Gaulle's coming to power in 1958 and many ways in which he went about conducting politics were at odds with how a political leader is expected to behave in an advanced capitalist country which claims to be liberal democratic. He came to power in the midst of a profound crisis over Algeria when there seemed a grave danger of civil war in France. The officer core of the army, far from being the unquestioning servant of strong government which it is expected to be in a liberal democracy, was, after defeat in France in 1940, further defeat in Indo-China in 1954 and fear of being abandoned in Algeria in the few years up to 1958, a highly politicized body beyond the control of the increasingly weak governments of the Fourth Republic. De Gaulle stepped in during a political power vacuum in May 1958 with the explicit support of the army, which was by now in open revolt against the government of the day. He became head of state on the express condition that the constitution would change along the lines he had discussed in the Bayeux speech of 1946, whose ideas were reinforced by the succession of short-lived and weak governments from 1946 to 1958. Many, particularly on the left, viewed de Gaulle's accession to power as a *coup d'état*, and these included François Mitterrand (Mitterrand 1964).

In some ways Gaullist politics were indeed a substantial step backwards compared with the political arrangements under the previous regime, and a step in the direction of bonapartism. The Fourth Republic had attempted, constitutionally at least, to correct the political and social injustices of Vichy France by making government directly accountable to parliament, giving substantial power to *députés* and electing them by proportional representation, thus stressing the importance of local interests in politics. But de Gaulle's rule was based on authoritarianism and populism, on a constitution which by the criteria of the Fourth Republic was democratically wanting, on threats of chaos and disaster if de Gaulle was not re-elected or if his proposals at referendum did not receive approval. The new constitution, designed largely by de Gaulle and for de Gaulle, was most importantly presidentialist, particularly after the introduction of the election of the President by universal suffrage in 1962. It reduced powers of parliament substantially and gave the President tremendous control over the composition of government and thus government policy, and direct control in the realm of foreign policy. Under the new regime the President was able to dissolve the National Assembly and call a referendum when he saw fit; article 16 was infamous for the 'exceptional powers' it gave the President in times of crisis, which de Gaulle used from 23 April to 29 September 1961, after a putsch by four generals in Algiers, when he made some reforms by decree. (In all de Gaulle took 18 decisions unilaterally during this period, including increasing the powers of the police and curtailing certain rights of military and civilian civil servants (Avril 1987: 54).) The President was only subject to re-election after seven years, compared with a maximum five-year term for *députés*, a difference which gave tremendous power to the President. The Fifth Republic and its presidentialism shifted the focus from the local, stressed under the Third and Fourth Republics, to the national. Under the Third and Fourth Republics it was the prefect, the *député*, the priest, the schoolteacher and the mayor who were the focus of political socialization, whereas under the Fifth Republic it was the President and national government which were the focus of attention, along with the top civil service, which was crucial in consolidating the new regime and in laying down plans for the future (Cerny 1988: 24–5).

It was as much de Gaulle's style of leadership as the details of the constitution which enabled the less democratic aspects of his rule to persist and which were accepted at first because of the exceptional circumstances of the Algerian war. For several years de Gaulle viewed himself and was viewed by many others as the only person who could effectively and safely lead France, a belief he expressed frequently in television appearances, the new medium which de Gaulle used to his great advantage. An example of the sort of threat that de Gaulle did not hesitate to use came when he announced on television on 4 November 1965 that he was standing for re-election as President in the elections on 5 and 19 December 1965:

If the huge majority of French citizens votes to keep me in office, the future of the new Republic will be assured. If not, there can be no doubt that the Republic will collapse immediately and that the French State will experience still greater confusion than in the past, this time without any possible salvation. (De Gaulle 1970b: 401)

This classic 'me or chaos' position was in stark contrast to the sorts of political arrangements which prevailed at the time in other European liberal democracies, where parties of government and opposition would put programmes forward and rarely imply that the alternative was at best utter confusion. It was in stark contrast to the peace, albeit sometimes superficial peace, which reigned in the other European countries as discussed in chapter 3. But this sort of speech on the part of de Gaulle, instead of discrediting him in his role as the political leader of an advanced democracy and putting people off voting for him, actually helped keep him in office, as the political situation was sufficiently volatile for these sorts of threats to be taken seriously. Many preferred a man who at times had a semi-democratic approach to running the country to the apparent risk of political turmoil again. However, by the time of the referendum of 1969 when de Gaulle warned once again that without him turmoil would ensue, the country was not only disillusioned with him but also stable enough not to believe the portents of calamity he once again uttered.

Under de Gaulle there was an attempt to depoliticize social and economic change, to achieve modernization through a combination of personalized, charismatic leadership and the use of a supposedly neutral instrument in the form of the state. De Gaulle's antipathy towards political parties and trade unions was part of this personalization of politics and of the ultimately self-destructive notion that France was not to be modernized according to a consensual paradigm of involvement of many different political and societal forces, including those radical pressure groups and parties which had made their mark so frequently in French history, but very much from above. The state was to play a crucial role in modernization, largely to the exclusion of these other actors; for de Gaulle, again by contrast with political elites in many other West European countries, political parties presented an obstacle to modernization because they represented sectarian interests, and, as he put it in 1946, were seen 'all too often overshadowing the higher interests of the country' (De Gaulle 1970a: 7). The state, on the other hand, more easily represented the interests of the nation as a whole. The problem of the exceptionally large Communist Party and the exceptional radicalism of the organized working class, not to mention the intransigence of the *patronat*, was thus for a time bypassed by means of a more centralized, more authoritarian, less participatory approach to politics than in other West European countries. In France the 1958 referendum campaign by the Gaullists over the new constitution and much that followed in the next few years warned electors against alternatives to de Gaulle, whether in the form of an army coup, communism, or simply the rule of parties, each pursuing their own interests, vying ineffectively and destructively against each other. In that referendum, on 28 September 1958, the 79 per cent of votes in favour of de Gaulle (for it was in fact a personal plebiscite as much as a referendum over a new constitution) was a historic confirmation of the success of fostering widespread support through personalization. Cross-class support and high popularity scores in opinion polls confirmed this (table 6.2). De Gaulle's attempt to depoliticize running the country was supported by the new Prime Minister Michel Debré when he said before the National Assembly on 15 January 1959:

> It is necessary, in the national interest, to remove our key problems from partisan discussions – to an extent to 'depoliticize' them ... To depoliticize the essential questions for our nation is a major imperative. (Quoted in Capdevielle and Mouriaux 1988: 57)

A situation where there was a relatively even match between government and opposition was not to be seen during this period. The severe weakening of the left in particular was a precondition for de Gaulle's initial success, as it represented a certain suspension of the party political arrangements associated with liberal democracy, a suspension of the arrangement which was encapsulated by government versus opposition, instead of which there was a personality cult which de Gaulle needed in order to maintain his rule. The left appeared to offer no credible alternative to Gaullist hegemony and the PCF was the antithesis of Gaullism, a party which was so obviously and tenaciously class-based and ideologically-specific. Table 6.1 and figure 6.1 show that between 1958 and 1962 the left suffered substantial losses in terms of votes, and even more so in terms of parliamentary seats, partly because the constitution of the Fifth Republic replaced the previous system of proportional representation with a majority voting system. Indeed the highest score in legislative elections for the entire period between 1958 and 1969 for either the PCF

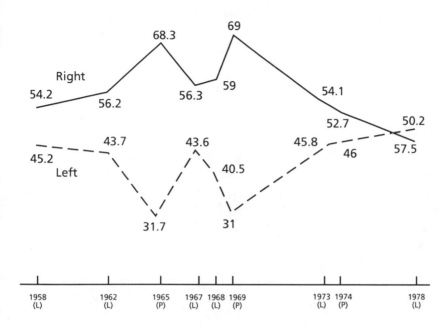

L = legislative elections
P = presidential elections

Figure 6.1 Balance between left and right in national
elections, 1958–78 (% of total vote).
Source: Portelli 1987: 328

or the non-communist left was lower than either of their lowest scores under the Fourth Republic. The PCF did particularly badly in the early years of Gaullist rule and for example it received 5.6 million votes in the legislative elections of 1956, but the total NO vote at the referendum on the new constitution amounted to only 4.6 million, with the PCF as the main campaigner against. But the centre-right also suffered as the years went by and arguably has never since been able to assert itself as a force wholly independent of Gaullism. Disunity was

Table 6.1 % of total votes and seats won by Communists and Socialists in legislative elections, 1956–68

	1956		1958		1962		1967		1968	
	Votes	Seats	Votes	Seats	Votes	Seats	Votes	Seats	Votes	Seats
PCF	25.9	26.7	18.9	2.2	21.8	8.8	22.5	15.3	20.0	7.0
SFIO/FGDS	15.0	16.2	15.4	8.6	12.5	14.0	18.8	24.9	16.5	12.1

Source: Cole and Campbell 1989: 86, 93, 96, 101, 103

prevalent among many parties at the time. As Jean Lacouture has pointed out, of all the political parties only the Gaullists, the Christian democratic MRP and the PCF were internally united in their approach to the referendum of 1958 over the new constitution; the Socialists in particular were divided between those in favour and those against (Lacouture 1986: 594; Duhamel 1989: 133). The SFIO, which had participated in many governments in the Fourth Republic, was profoundly split over whether to support de Gaulle or not and went into a prolonged crisis in the years after 1958. Parties which were the natural opponents of Gaullism were thus seen as divided and ineffectual, with the exception of the PCF, which was also weakened, as we have seen. A credible opposition did begin to emerge very slowly and in 1965 François Mitterrand received 45 per cent of the vote in the second round of the presidential elections as candidate for a united left. But it was not to be until after the departure of de Gaulle that the left began to be a properly viable political force again, partly because of the history of compromise with colonialism and divisions in relation to de Gaulle on the part of the Socialists. Even in the 1970s the road to power for the left was by no means clear of obstacles, and the 1970s was also a decade of exclusive rule by the right.

Developed liberal democracy is often associated with limited physical violence on the part of the state in order to maintain the status quo. Antonio Gramsci argues that, if the position of the ruling class is secure, it does not need to use a great deal of force in order to maintain its dominant position, because other classes and social groups accept its values and norms of behaviour. Bourgeois hegemony, he argues, 'presupposes that account is taken of the interests and tendencies of the groups over which hegemony is to be exercised, and that a certain balance of compromise should be formed – in other words that the leading group should make sacrifices of an economo-corporative kind' (quoted in Anderson 1976–7: 19). Gramsci stresses that if the ruling class is secure in its position it does not need to use coercion in the form of state violence in order to remain in power. But a particularly graphic manifestation of insecurity of the ruling class and the unevenness of political modernization in France during de Gaulle's rule was the persistent brutality of the police. Violence with obviously political ends, particularly on the part of state forces or on the part of the ruling political party, is indeed a reasonable indicator that liberal democracy has not become firmly established.

Writing from a different political perspective from Gramsci, Jean-Louis Loubet del Bayle suggests that the degree of legitimacy of a political system is in inverse proportion to the level of violence prac-tised by its police (Loubet del Bayle 1985: 552). Two incidents in par-ticular, both related to reactions in France to the Algerian war, illustrate the brutality of the police in a tragic fashion. First, during the night of 17–18 October 1961, after 20,000 Algerians had marched through Paris in protest against a curfew imposed on them, several hundred Algerians were killed by police in one of the most bloody nights of police repression France had seen for many years. The events of that terrible operation, ordered by Prefect of Police Mau-rice Papon, were for many years covered up and even now are little discussed. A few months later, on 8 February 1962, eight participants in a demonstration against the OAS were killed and over one hun-dred injured in charges by police at the Paris metro station Charonne. This is not to mention the police violence in May 1968, which played such a part in uniting students and workers in their revolt against aspects of Gaullism, or regular campaigns of violence against the nationalist population in Algeria. The activities of the shady and often thuggish Service d'Action Civique (SAC) attached to the Gaullist party reflected this sort of legitimized state violence.

It is helpful to locate de Gaulle within a bonapartist tradition, where an authoritarian but charismatic leader is able, for a relatively short period of time, to rule with an unusual degree of personal popularity within the framework of a strong state. Both Marxists (e.g. Brohm et al. 1974) and non-Marxists (e.g. Rémond 1982) have explained Gaullism in this way, and in a comparative historical study Choisel convincingly likens many details of the rule of Napoleon III to those of de Gaulle (Choisel 1987). Exceptional circumstances brought de Gaulle to power and exceptional circumstances helped keep him in power, namely the apparent danger of a return to political, social and economic instability. There was an attempt to ignore and deny class conflict and its institutional manifestations in order to unite the popu-lation around a set of modernizing, patriotic principles. However, de Gaulle's rule was far more akin to modern liberal democracy than the regimes of either of the real Bonapartes in French history.

The progress of political stability and democracy

Despite the very real authoritarian and anti-liberal democratic aspects of de Gaulle's rule discussed above, both the relative stability which de Gaulle's regime brought to French politics and the formalization of the notion of democracy, bonapartist though this was, must be viewed as being politically modernizing. The stability which the regime afforded meant that there was no longer the atmosphere of insecurity and at times crisis which had prevailed under the Fourth Republic. Governments lasted, policies were implemented and intentions were stated and on the whole adhered to. It was possible to declare an aim, plan for its implementation and put it into practice without too much risk of the government falling before there was time to see the measure through. This had not been the case under the Fourth Republic, particularly towards the end of the Republic's existence. Withdrawal from Algeria was an example of such a democratic process, in that government deliberated and proposals were put to the population via referendum and then acted upon. In spite of an attempted *coup d'état* by generals in Algiers in 1961 and bombings and attacks by the pro-French-Algerian Organisation de l'Armée Secrète (OAS) in France itself, including a very nearly successful attempt on de Gaulle's life at Petit-Clamart in August 1962, policy was implemented. Certainly, the electorate's hands were tied somewhat because of the fear of political and social instability if they rejected de Gaulle's proposals, but mass consultation was nevertheless championed by de Gaulle and his allies and was indeed used as a means to alter the political situation, frequently in the direction that was taken in other advanced capitalist countries.

Crucial to this process was the fact that de Gaulle himself stressed the need for democracy, for participation in voting for the people as a whole, though he did not advocate participation in other political processes such as joining parties and pressure groups. Formal democracy was thus emphasized as a way of achieving political progress and although deeply sceptical about the contribution which political parties and pressure groups could make to political life, de Gaulle was always at pains to stress the importance of the legitimation of politics by the electorate. In the 11 years of de Gaulle's presidency, there were ten national consultations (five referendums, four legislative elections and one presidential election), each one conducted with the certainty that the results would have direct and previously declared effects on the future of France. This was in contrast to the situation under the Fourth Republic where elections took place and *députés* were powerful but where governments implemented programmes based on compromise between parties which were able to put together some sort of alliance, but which represented poorly any of the various sections of the electorate and which changed so frequently as often to make consistency in policy impossible. In this respect de Gaulle was correct to criticize the Fourth Republic as being a 'régime des partis', as he did in May 1958. Direct democracy was an important element of Gaullism and a significant part of his legacy; this was a Rousseauist notion of democracy, a sort of direct expression of the General Will. To have such an independent relationship between himself and the people, independent of parliament and even government, was very important. Thus by the time he left office, although he was by no means respected by all French people, de Gaulle had shown that a political system could achieve stability, allowing modernization, *and* allow for the regular expression of the people as a whole. This combination of elements had been very rare in French politics since 1789. The election of the President by universal suffrage, for the first time since Louis-Napoleon Bonaparte came to power in 1848, was another prime example of this aspect of Gaullist politics; certainly the President was very powerful, and with a seven-year term he was in power unchallenged for longer than might be deemed democratic, but every adult French person had the opportunity to contribute directly to this choice in a way that was at the heart of liberal notions of democracy. These aspects of democratization, as opposed to simple stability, should not be overlooked.

It is probably true to say that without the democratic aspects of his political philosophy and practice de Gaulle would have been most unlikely to have stayed in power as long as he did, although, as I have said, his staying in power did partly depend on fear of political and social disorder if he departed. As it was, his populist approach was so successful as to earn him sustained popularity and electoral support from a remarkably broad section of society. This in part led Jean Charlot to describe the Gaullist Party as a 'voter party', with much in common with a (conservative) 'catch-all party', common in other Western industrial democracies, where 'a minimum of shared values is enough and this enables [the party] to appeal to a very wide clientele' (Charlot 1971: 64). Although this conclusion substantially underestimates the popular reaction induced by fear of the alternative – that is the exceptional nature of Gaullism – it does help explain the more liberal democratic aspects of Gaullism and how Gaullism successfully survived its founder, although weakened in the long term. Significantly, however, after de Gaulle's departure Gaullist Party support became far more traditionally that of parties of the

Table 6.2 Sociological composition of the Gaullist electorate, legislative elections, 1962, 1967, 1973 (% per category)

	1962	1967	1973
SEX			
Men	49	42	43
Women	51	58	57
Total	100	100	100
AGE			
21–34 yrs	28	29	24
35–49 yrs	24	26	29
50–64 yrs	28	26	23
64 yrs–	20	19	24
Total	100	100	100
OCCUPATION OF HEAD OF HOUSEHOLD			
Farmer	14	16	17
Industrialist, artisan, shopkeeper	10	11	9
Manager, liberal professions	5	5	7
Clerical worker, supervisor	19	16	19
Blue-collar worker	29	28	21
Inactive	23	24	27
Total	100	100	100

Source: Ysmal 1989: 287

right, as shown in table 6.2. The most striking change shown here is the decline in the blue-collar vote for Gaullism and the increased importance of support from supervisory and managerial workers (*cadres*).

Finally, the stabilizing legacy of the Gaullist period is particularly significant in that the constitution which de Gaulle introduced has not only lasted for nearly four decades, which was by far the longest, apart from the constitution of the Third Republic, since 1789, but has also seen the coming to power of a moderate left, well able to work within this constitutional arrangement and thus promoting the notion that the constitutional framework of the Fifth Republic is acceptable to left as well as right. *Alternance* is thus a possibility, which many on the left once ruled out, and a more institutionalized opposition has been established under this constitution, reminiscent of opposition in other countries. All major parties now accept the constitutional framework set up by de Gaulle and this will undoubtedly be, long-term, one of the most significant aspects of his legacy.

De Gaulle's foreign policy and the uses of *grandeur*

Typical of de Gaulle's peculiar mix of characteristics – conservative and modern, authoritarian and populist, autocratic and democratic – his approach to foreign policy is also unique and quite rightly a much-explored aspect of his rule (e.g. Barnavi and Friedländer 1985; Kolodziej 1974). One of the most obvious changes in foreign policy under de Gaulle was of course decolonization, mainly in the form of withdrawal from Algeria, which had been delayed in France partly as part of an attachment to the past in the absence of a clear view of the future. This was achieved despite the extreme hostility of certain sections of the population, including significant sections of the army. Solving the Algerian question constituted a huge step forward in terms of bringing France alongside other advanced capitalist countries not only as far as the reduction of overt political conflict was concerned, but also in terms of establishing France's place among countries whose economic orientation was towards other industrialized nations rather than towards its empire, not to mention removing a huge drain on the country's financial resources.

Moving beyond the Algerian imbroglio was also important in that France became once again an important and credible actor on the international diplomatic stage and generally a respected member of the West's international community. The construction and consolidation of Europe was another significant development, which was pursued despite de Gaulle's extreme wariness towards bodies which he perceived as a threat to France's sovereignty, including both the EEC and NATO. France also developed a defence policy which was much discussed both at home and abroad and which was underpinned by the new nuclear deterrent, the *Force de frappe*. The French deterrent in part conveyed the message to other countries that France was no longer weak and vulnerable to invasion as it had been for so many decades, but just as importantly boosted the confidence of the army and helped bring it back under full governmental control despite withdrawal from Algeria. In a not altogether convincing attempt to stress France's importance alongside the post-1945 superpowers, de Gaulle set out to establish France as a power which was allied neither to one nor the other.

Put together, these elements of foreign policy were to give France what de Gaulle described as a position of *grandeur* in relation to the rest of the world, but perhaps the most important point to make here with regard to Gaullist foreign policy is that, as Philip Cerny asserts most convincingly, the purpose of de Gaulle's foreign policy based on *grandeur* was for a large part ideological:

> [Its purpose] was not the attainment of glory and power for France for its own sake. Rather, *grandeur* refers primarily to the need to create a new and more profound sense of national consciousness, capable of transcending the traditional divisions which have characterised the French polity, thus allowing and reinforcing the development of a consensus supportive of a firmly established and active state pursuing the general interest, within a stable political system. (Cerny 1980: 4)

In other words, foreign policy served to bind the nation together and to distract attention from serious inequalities and conflicts of interest which could have, indeed in the end did, produce grave discontent and revolt on the part of some groups in French society. It helped achieve for a time what war can sometimes achieve in terms of 'linkage of foreign policy with a new structure of authority [that] can create a psychological association of national identity with authority, thus giving that authority a profound "legitimacy" ' (Cerny 1980: p. x).

Cerny does not refer to Gramsci in his book, but this interpretation of the situation is akin to Gramsci's notion of bourgeois hegemony, whereby the ruling class achieves cooperation on the part of the population at large because the ruling class creates an ideological system which also takes into account some of the interests of other groups and classes and not just the narrow, particularly economic, interests of the ruling class. The ruling class thus rules by consent, via some sort of compromise, as well as coercion, and the effectiveness of hegemony is often stronger at times of war between one nation and another. This sort of approach worked well in France, particularly at the beginning of de Gaulle's rule, when as we have seen a large proportion of the population supported him, and his role was most importantly one of achieving a solution to the Algerian question. But if traditional political and social divisions for a time played a less important part in political life, they had not gone away, as the events of May 1968 were to show so dramatically.

De Gaulle and the economy: modernization from above

The sharp contradictions between more democratic, modernizing aspects of de Gaulle's rule on the one hand and more archaic aspects on the other are particularly well illustrated by a look at governmental influence on the French economy during this period. Political stability under de Gaulle allowed his governments to encourage significant economic transformations, which went far towards bringing France more in line with other countries in this respect. (For a more systematic look at the economy under de Gaulle, see Braudel and Labrousse 1982; or Jeanneney 1992.) Certainly, since the Second World War the structure of the French economy had already changed greatly and some aspects of change under de Gaulle may be viewed as an extension of previous trends. There had under the Fourth Republic been substantial economic growth, increases in productivity, a huge rural exodus and thus urbanization, and substantial rises in the standard of living. Since the Liberation the state had played an important part in ensuring elements of this process, with widespread nationalizations, indicative state planning, and the immigration of foreign workers actively encouraged by the state, particularly from the Maghreb. The signature of the Treaty of Rome in 1957 signalled an intention to diversify trade away from French colonies and ex-colonies and towards the countries of Western Europe.

However, when de Gaulle came to power in 1958 France was still more marked by its past than other key industrialized countries. It remained more rural than its competitors, investment as a proportion of GDP was lower than in many other industrialized countries, firms were small and tended to be undercapitalized. Individually owned or family-owned firms dominated the economy and there was a business culture which meant that there was a widespread reluctance on the part of these businesses to move beyond this individual or family ownership and control. Trade was still predominantly oriented towards the colonies or ex-colonies, and exports compared with GDP put France at the bottom of that particular league table of north-west European countries (Eck 1990: 25; Jeanneney 1992: 25). In March 1957 the Minister of Finance Paul Ramadier commented:

> We are ... in the situation of a country which is perhaps not underdeveloped, but at least insufficiently developed, which has lost its position of advantage and is not managing to regain it in the same way in all sectors. (Quoted in Dreyfus 1982: 221)

Jean-Marcel Jeanneney, who was de Gaulle's Minister for Industry in 1959–60, argues that the weaknesses described above 'necessarily resulted' in the profound financial and monetary crisis of 1957–8 (Jeanneney 1992: 26). Thus when de Gaulle returned to power in 1958 this was one of the most pressing problems to be dealt with, with the help of Minister of Finance Antoine Pinay. Right from the start, the Pinay–Rueff Plan prioritized the fight against inflation, monetary stability and, perhaps most importantly, reducing barriers to foreign trade, thus subjecting French industry to the effects of direct competition with companies overseas.

De Gaulle's intention was to take the economy by the horns and transform it forcibly if necessary until it was more similar to economies of other advanced capitalist countries. State economic planning, with much input from large numbers of top civil servants, played an important part in de Gaulle's highly centralized, directive approach to the economy. Planning had been important under the Fourth Republic, but de Gaulle went further than the politicians of the immediate post-war period and promised that he would 'make sure that the preparation and the execution of the Plan assume an importance which they had not had before, by making it an "ardent obligation" and by declaring it my own particular interest' (De Gaulle 1970c: 171–2). In the same vein Prime Minister Michel Debré commented in 1961 that under the Plan 'the higher interests of the nation must take precedence over the particular interests of firms or groups of firms' (quoted in Birnbaum 1982: 88–9). The Fourth and Fifth Plans (covering the years 1962–5 and 1966–70 respectively) indeed reflected a significant shift in economic policy (P. Hall 1986: 149, 167; Howell 1992b: 62). Instead of targeting basic industrial economic sectors in their entirety, they set out to encourage state-of-the-art companies. The Fourth Plan targeted telecommunications, chemicals, construction and consumer electronics in particular, and the Fifth Plan large petro-chemical firms, electronics, aeronautics, pharmaceutical and data-processing firms. The declared aim of the Fifth Plan was:

> the establishment or reinforcement ... of a small number of firms or groups of international size ... in most industrial sectors (aluminium, steel, mechanical and electrical engineering, electronics, motor cars, aircraft, chemicals, pharmaceutical products, etc). The number of these groups should be very small, often even reduced to one or two. (Quoted in P. Hall 1986: 149)

These objectives, again in the words of the Plan itself, were pursued for instance via 'tax advantages, export assistance, price control exemptions, and investment funds' (quoted in P. Hall 1986: 167). The cult of the small firm was largely abandoned in France and large-scale firms were at last officially recognized as where the future lay. During this period many business people were converted to a new way of looking at the economy, which was less introverted and Malthusian than business attitudes prevailing under previous Republics.

Mergers played an important part in the modernization of the economy during this period, and often led to the significant productivity increases associated with economies of scale. The number of mergers per year in industry went from 32 in the period 1950–8 to 74 in the period 1959–65 and 136 in 1966–72, and between 1966 and 1969 the annual value of mergers was twice that of the total value of mergers between 1950 and 1960. The number of small firms thus diminished considerably during de Gaulle's Presidency, notably with a reduction in the number of firms with between 10 and 20 employees and a corresponding rise in the number of those with between 200 and 500 employees, although the number of firms with more than 1,000 employees did not grow as much (Berstein 1989: 156, 163; P. Hall 1986: 149).

Part of this process of concentration of capital was the promotion of leader projects, or 'national champions' as they were called, including such well-known firms as Péchiney-Ugine-Kuhlmann, Saint-Gobain-Pont à Mousson, Thomson CSF, Agache-Willot, Creusot-Loire and Dassault. The promotion of many obviously state-controlled projects served to show how the government set out both to intervene directly to change the structure of industry and to set an example to other firms and sectors, as well as demonstrating to other countries that France was one of the economic leaders of the world. Such *grands projets* included the building of Concorde with the British and the nuclear programme. Scientific and technological research was also reorganized and centralized under de Gaulle, a process which not only helped in a general way to foster industrial growth but also helped cross-fertilization between different sectors of the economy (Lelong: 1992). Economic modernization was thus a highly conscious process.

Such a *dirigiste* approach to rapid economic change was dependent upon a highly centralized state, which went hand in hand with the reinforcing of a meritocratic elite. The establishment of national state commissions such as the Delegation for Territorial Planning and Regional Action (DATAR) in order to control regional development meant that local interest groups and elites were largely bypassed and top civil servants were crucial to the formulation and implementation of local as well as national economic policy. Indeed the role of the civil service, in particular the Grands Corps, became generally far more important under the Fifth Republic, with some blurring of boundaries between government and civil service. All of de Gaulle's Prime Ministers were top civil servants (Michel Debré and Georges Pompidou were members of the Conseil d'Etat and Maurice Couve de Murville was an *Inspecteur des finances*) and many of de Gaulle's other ministers were former civil servants who often did not become *députés* either before or after becoming ministers. The importance of the connections among and job-hopping between political, civil service and business elites under the Fifth Republic has been well documented, in particular by Pierre Birnbaum, who emphasizes the importance of *pantouflage*, where former top civil servants take up leading positions in private industry, as well as public-sector firms (Birnbaum 1982: 103–9). Whereas the Fourth Republic was known as the 'République des députés', the Fifth Republic became known as the 'République des fonctionnaires', because of the close association between government and civil service. As Serge Berstein (1989: 205–6) has pointed out, this professionalization of business and political elites had the effect of undermining familial and hereditary aspects of political and corporate advancement, and reinforced the notion, at least, that a meritocracy was operating instead of the career advantages of inherited wealth and privilege. The *grandes écoles*, particularly the Ecole Nationale d'Administration (ENA), founded by de Gaulle's close associate Michel Debré in 1945, played an important part in training young people in this process, although in practice the *grandes écoles* were largely peopled by students from already highly privileged sectors of the population, often from Paris. Nevertheless, real competence as expressed in a prestigious educational qualification was now increasingly necessary in order to have an influence on the upper echelons of industry, politics or the civil service.

All this, helped by the favourable international economic climate, meant that the growth of the French economy in the 1960s was spectacular, ahead of all other leading industrialized nations apart from Japan in terms of growth of GDP, which had not been the case in the 1950s. The rate of investment was also impressive, already at 20 per

Table 6.3 Evolution of the geographical structure of French trade, 1949–73 (%)

	1949	1958	1969	1973
IMPORTS				
Developed countries	55.0	53.2	75.0	74.7
of which EEC	26.5	32.0	55.6	54.6
of which rest of OECD	18.7	21.2	19.4	20.1
Ex-French empire	24.7	25.4	9.6	6.1
Other countries	20.2	21.4	15.4	19.2
All countries	100	100	100	100
EXPORTS				
Developed countries	47.2	51.6	72.8	75.4
of which EEC	33.4	34.7	52.9	55.6
of which rest of OECD	13.8	16.9	19.9	19.8
Ex-French empire	38.2	24.0	12.1	9.1
Other countries	14.6	14.3	15.1	15.4
All countries	100	100	100	100

Source: Gauron 1983: 66

cent of GNP on average during the 1950s, a little behind other advanced capitalist countries, but reaching 25 per cent in 1969, locating France immediately behind Japan and West Germany. A more international orientation enabled also by decolonization and the establishment of the EEC played an important part in integrating France into the industrialized world economy: in 1958 exports only accounted for 10 per cent of GNP compared with 17 per cent in 1970, and EEC countries only received 10 per cent of French exports in 1960 with the franc zone countries receiving 30 per cent; in 1970 EEC countries received 50 per cent of French exports and the Franc zone only 10 per cent (see table 6.3). By 1965 France was the fourth most important exporter in the world, after the USA, West Germany and the United Kingdom. In terms of imports, the proportion accounted for by the franc zone fell from 23 to 9 per cent over the same period, whereas the proportion from the EEC rose from 30 to 49 per cent. Thus Europe replaced the colonies as France's major trade zone (Berstein 1989: 151–78).

It was during the period of de Gaulle's Presidency that the consumer society was consolidated in France. Indigenous population growth continued to be impressive and immigration added to this. The rural exodus progressed apace: 41 per cent of the population lived in rural areas in 1954, compared with 37 per cent in 1962 and 29 per cent in 1968 (*Quid* 1983: 1364). Higher real earnings and greater numbers of people living in towns meant that far more consumer durables were bought; not only did households increasingly have the basics of modern domestic plumbing such as hot and cold water, bathrooms and inside toilets, but ownership of motor cars, televisions, refrigerators and so on became widespread. As in other countries, a smaller proportion of consumer spending was oriented towards the bare essentials of life such as food and more was spent on clothing, housing, health, culture, leisure and above all transport.

The unevenness of socio-economic change

Under de Gaulle the economy thus became far more conventionally that of an advanced capitalist society and at last broke in many ways with the nineteenth century. But in order to understand the apparent paradoxes of this period it is necessary to point to some of its more archaic characteristics. Economic modernization was carried out, as we have seen, in an exclusive, rather than inclusive way without widespread cooperation with, or even consultation of, interest groups. In particular there was little cooperation between trade unions and employers. This was partly because of deep divisions among political and social forces, epitomized by the existence of a strong Communist Party and a dominant Communist-influenced section of the trade union movement, the CGT. French society and the French political arena still displayed more manifestations of dissensus than consensus, and economic modernization was carried out excluding precisely some of the organizations which represented (or should have represented) important sections of the new mass of consumers, mainly salaried workers. Some of the less modern aspects of the French economy and business culture were thus maintained. Indeed, de Gaulle's vision of political and economic modernization was only acceptable to key elements of the *patronat* precisely because it did not imply systematic compromise, or even negotiations with, organized labour. Employers were able to cling to archaic industrial relations attitudes based on patronage, and collective bargaining was at best patchy. In August 1967 Prime Minister Georges Pompidou actually wrote to national union and employers' organizations suggesting bilateral talks to resolve the problem of job losses and job reclassification as a result of industrial restructuring. But employers were extremely reluctant to agree to systematic negotiations and had only reached agreement with unions on the question of compensation for short-time working by the time events caught up with them in the form of May 1968 (Howell 1992b: 66).

With the Gaullist, top–down approach to economic modernization, the fruits of economic modernization were very unevenly distributed and certain sectors of the population remained greatly disadvantaged during these years of prosperity. Wages in some sectors remained low, and even discounting serious disparities between sectors, average hourly rates of pay rose less fast in France between 1958 and 1969 than in all other European countries except the UK and Switzerland (table 6.4). The disparity between pay in public sector and private sector was particularly pronounced and there was also substantial wage discrepancy between Paris and the provinces (Dreyfus 1982: 225, 230). Taxes were high and working hours were among the longest in the industrial world. This state of affairs led the economic historian Claude Fohlen to highlight the 'inequality of the share-out of the proceeds of growth' in the 1960s. He went on to say:

> While France has deliberately set out to create a consumer society, not all French consumers are getting fair shares of the benefits. Recent surveys based on comparisons with other countries have shown that the scale of wages and incomes in France is wider than elsewhere, with shocking discrepancies between the extreme social categories ... Whereas the condition of the skilled worker has improved continuously, that of the labourer has remained much the same, owing to the fact that the increases he gets through the raising of the minimum legal wage ... barely make up for the effects of inflation. (Fohlen 1976: 121)

Indeed the large number of workers on the minimum wage fared particularly badly, with the SMIC rising only 71 per cent between 1955 and 1967 compared with 156 per cent for blue-collar wages as a whole (Berstein 1989: 210).

There was relatively little overt industrial and political unrest in the years 1958–67, but it would be quite wrong to suggest that social, industrial and political conflict were absent. In the first few years of de Gaulle's rule there were violent clashes between small farmers and police in demonstrations over issues such as the abolition of indexation between agricultural and industrial prices. One person died in a demonstration in Amiens in February 1960. The miners' strike of 1963 was a moment of crisis, during which de Gaulle's popularity dropped significantly. After the generally calm industrial relations climate of 1964 and 1965, the following two years saw an upturn in strike activity, particularly in the provinces (Delale and Ragache 1978: 29; Capdevielle and Mouriaux 1988: 42–52). The enormous strikes and demonstrations of May 1968, then, did not come entirely out of a clear blue, strife-free sky.

Ironically, the close association between the state and private capital began to erode the mystique of the state and destroy the myth of it acting above sectional interests, an idea which had existed since the Revolution and before. The French state had been an apparently detached entity claiming to act for a set of interests superior to those of any one section of society, particularly in the realm of the economy. But in contradiction with de Gaulle's avowed philosophy, it was under de Gaulle that the state became a more obvious intervener in the wider mechanisms of society and more obviously not an expression of the General Will of the people. On the contrary, the state had become explicitly partial, a process which was taken further after the departure of de Gaulle (Birnbaum 1982: 92; P. Hall 1986: 180). Thus not only did significant sections of the working class feel excluded from the fruits of modernization both financially and politically, but the state was more explicitly acting on the side of capital, both private and public.

Several times during his Presidency, notably after the May 1968 crisis, de Gaulle attempted to implement an industrial relations strategy which allowed workers a share in profits, capital or management of the firm for which they worked, or all three. This policy, which he called *participation*, was a form of association of capital and labour which was based on patronage and which differed from cooperation between capital and labour in other countries. Elsewhere, the inclusion of the working class in the firm resulted from a recognition of the need to concede power because of trade union or political strength, or even because of the recognition that the working class was the central element of the new consumer society. But with de Gaulle's notion of *participation* the working class was to be included according to an old-fashioned, corporatist notion of class relations, which was a way of involving workers in the firm without a real compromise between the wider interests of the working class and employers. On 24 May 1968, in the midst of the student and workers' revolt, de Gaulle announced that there would be a referendum on

Table 6.4 Average annual rate of growth in various OECD countries, 1958–69 (%)

	France	Germany	UK	Italy	Netherlands	Belgium	Sweden	Switzerland	USA	Japan
Population	1.08	1.04	0.48	0.66	1.31	0.54	0.68	1.44	1.33	1.01
GDP	5.48	5.80	3.20	5.87	5.40	4.71	4.55	4.92	4.26	11.06
Added value per industry	5.74	6.40	3.36	8.10	7.52	5.31	6.11	5.30	6.06	14.86
Real salaries	3.62	5.28	2.98	4.32	4.76	4.21	4.24	1.89	1.57	6.26
Consumer prices	4.21	2.33	3.26	3.33	3.78	2.51	3.04	2.76	2.19	5.04
Exports (dollars)	10.25	11.46	5.81	14.96	10.83	11.44	9.54	10.55	7.21	16.95
Imports (dollars)	10.78	11.67	5.98	13.26	10.55	11.66	8.67	10.83	9.91	15.10

Source: Jeanneney 1992: 5

participation the following year. There was in the end no referendum specifically on this theme, but the government did attempt to implement *participation* to an extent anyway. One major problem with the scheme, as Chris Howell has put it, was that

> de Gaulle's plan was explicitly anti-union. Even after May 1968 and the creation of a legally secure position for union sections on the shop-floor, it was clear that de Gaulle did not acknowledge a role for labor unions in labor regulation. He regarded them as alien influences in the firm, detrimental to the notion of a classless capital–labor association. (Howell 1992b: 77)

It was indeed fitting that de Gaulle should spend the last year of his rule flogging a policy which suggested only a partial understanding of the modern epoch in which he lived and a policy which ultimately missed the point.

To conclude, it is worth quoting part of de Gaulle's last speech before the referendum of 1969, broadcast on television and radio, which turned out to be the last speech of his political career. It neatly illustrates the complex relationship between de Gaulle's political outlook on the one hand, and the nature of the society in which he lived, on the other:

> Your response will shape the destiny of France, because this reform is an integral part of the *participation* which is henceforth required in order to achieve stability for modern society. To refuse it is to oppose in a crucial sphere this social, moral and human transformation, without which we will suffer disastrous upheavals. To adopt it is to take a decisive step on the road which will lead us to progress in an orderly and harmonious way, profoundly changing relations between Frenchmen.
>
> Your response will shape the destiny of France, because if I am disavowed by a majority of you, solemnly, on this fundamental issue and no matter how great the number, the determination and the devotion of the army of those who support me and who, in any case, have the future of the country in their hands, my present duties as Head of State will obviously become impossible and I will immediately cease to carry out my functions. How, then, will the situation be brought under control – a state of affairs resulting from the negative victory of all those diverse, disparate, discordant and opposing forces, with the inevitable return to the rule of ambitions, illusions, alliances and betrayals – in the national disorder that such a breakdown will provoke?

If, on the other hand, I receive proof of your confidence, I will pursue my mandate, I will achieve, thanks to you ... the task I took on a decade ago to give our country democratic institutions which are suited to the type of people we are, in the society and times we live in, after the confusion, the troubles and the misfortunes which we have experienced for centuries ... Finally, once the end of the mandate has come, without crisis and without unpheaval, turning the last page of the chapter which I opened in our history some thirty years ago, I will transfer my official responsibility to the one you have elected to assume that duty after me.

People of France, in determining the future of our country, never has the decision of each and every one of you weighed so heavy! (De Gaulle, 1970c: 405–6)

De Gaulle once again attempts to persuade the French that without him as head of state the country will descend into chaos. However, if he stays, he promises not only stability and modernization but also emphasizes in particular *participation*, thus recognizing the absence of social reform during his Presidency, one of the causes of the uprising in May 1968. He also promises further democratic reform and assures his viewers and listeners that after a further three years (at the end of his presidential term) the country will be ready for a less exceptional head of state, for a politician with a less heroic past. He ends, however, by once again clearly threatening descent into turmoil if the French vote NO. That 53.1 per cent did vote against de Gaulle's proposals, provoking his instant resignation, is evidence that the threat was no longer taken seriously, a clear indication of how much the country had changed since 1958.

The Algerian question had been solved, the army had been brought to heel, the country had taken a significant step since 1958 towards becoming a liberal democracy where government depends directly on regular elections rather than on fear of further instability. Industrial restructuring and mass consumption had put France alongside other countries in terms of economic stability. In 1969 de Gaulle's prediction of violence after his departure is no longer taken seriously and on the contrary reminds electors of the very real anti-democratic and authoritarian aspects of his rule. The promise of *participation* is no substitute for genuine inclusion of labour and other interests in policy making, no solution to what Michel Crozier (1970) described as France's 'société bloquée'. As for de Gaulle's explicit reference to the modernization of France under his rule, a majority of the electorate no longer believed that this extraordinary man was the only person who could carry the process further.

France had changed but de Gaulle's ambivalent attitude towards modernity apparently had not. In May and June 1968 the people in the streets and the factories had sent the message to de Gaulle that his rule was anachronistic, but he had been saved by other demonstrators at the end of May, by a huge march on the Champs Elysées, led by André Malraux, Michel Debré and other ministers, who sang the Marseillaise and chanted, 'De Gaulle n'est pas seul.' This groundswell of support was confirmed by the 'rally of fear' elections at the end of June, when the Gaullists won a landslide victory. However, the result of the referendum of April 1969 informed de Gaulle formally that he was no longer wanted and no longer needed. In fact de Gaulle's project of political stabilization and economic modernization was so successful that he was rejected because of the more archaic aspects of his rule. France had changed and de Gaulle had served his historical purpose. He had become dispensable.

7
The Historical Significance of May 1968

From 20 May onwards, the roads from Paris to the Swiss border had never been so congested, even during winter sports at Christmas; and in the banks of Geneva, Lausanne and Berne French people queued up to rent safety deposit boxes and open accounts.

Pierre Vionsson-Ponté (1976: 250)

It has often been pointed out in recent years that the May 1968 student and workers' revolt is the last major political crisis France has known, the last in a long line of explosive historical moments which fall into the categories of revolt, revolution, counter-revolution, *coup d'état* or foreign incursion. This does not mean that deep conflict in French politics and society suddenly stopped in 1968, or indeed that there will be no more revolts of such intensity in years to come. However, the year 1968 was a watershed to the extent that since then French political life has come to resemble more than ever before the model of liberal democracy and political stability which many people the world over aspire to, although as I argue elsewhere in this book this process did not reach its apogee until the 1980s. May was clearly a historical moment at which the course of political and social history was changing in a concentrated, intense way, so it was a very conflictual but also a modernizing event. Just as importantly it is also a clear example of the openness, the lack of inevitability of political, social and economic history, despite a tendency for history to move in a particular direction. It is thus in keeping with the general aims of this book to attempt to establish if, paradoxically, May acted as a stabilizing influence on French political life and played a part in creating the more consensual conditions of the 1980s and 1990s.

It must be said at the outset that because May 1968, like previous revolts, provoked such powerful emotions – hope, sympathy and admiration on the one hand, outrage, fear and contempt on the other – analyses of the historical significance of what most writers agree was a moment of great importance in the post-war history of France tend to be superficial because they are often greatly influenced by a commitment to either the more revolutionary aspects of May or to the quelling of the uprising. As with so many conflictual moments in French history, it is rare to be indifferent in relation to May. It is therefore unlikely that an appropriately sober debate concerning the historical significance of May will become possible until more dispassionate historians of the events can emerge in generations to come, for it was the intellectuals who went on to write about May 1968 who had often been deeply implicated in it, be they students, academics, teachers or journalists, and many of them were in the streets before the traditional working class and trade unions became involved. It was they who bore the initial brunt of the state's heavy-handedness, in particular police brutality. By contrast with other subjects of modern historical study such as the Second World War, the Algerian war, Gaullism, the evolution of the French right, the PCF and so on, there are virtually no established academic authorities on May 1968, no interpretations which have gained widespread respect, and few doctoral theses. Evelyne Pisier has remarked that, 'absent from theses, dissertations and political science seminars, May 1968 has become a sort of scientific non-subject which a certain academic condescendence reserves for journalism which is necessarily superficial' (Pisier 1986: 15).

A wholly impartial view of history is never possible, but interpreting May has been particularly difficult to tackle with analytical rigour. Innumerable books and journal articles have been written on May 1968, but many seek to mark in a fairly superficial way an anniversary of 1968 rather than to contribute to a slowly growing corpus of knowledge about and interpretations of the events, as happens in relation to other historical phenomena. There were in particular clusters of publications around 1978 and 1988. Many of these books and articles are by former participants whose perspective is either very optimistic about the revolutionary significance of May (e.g. Bensaïd and Krivine 1988; Delale and Ragache 1978) or they are a friendly way of exorcizing a militant ghost from the past (e.g. H. Weber 1988; Hamon and Rotman 1987, 1988). Some are a largely anecdotal 'view from the other side' by policemen or civil servants (e.g. Grimaud 1977; Gaveau 1978). Extremely hostile views have also been published on anniversaries, including a book by Raymond Marcellin, whom de Gaulle made Minister of the Interior on 30 May 1968 with a brief to stamp out left-wing militancy (Marcellin 1978). Indeed strong partisanship of one form or another, whose death knell has been sounded so often in recent times, is still prevalent in relation to May. But even the terms of the debate are ill-defined, whether because of the levity, or the intense sympathy, or (more rarely) the hostility with which the subject is treated. This is partly of course because May 1968 is not yet far enough in the past to allow facts to be interpreted with the benefit of substantial hindsight, but also because of the very strength of feelings expressed in May itself. No one, not least myself, is immune from a feeling of *parti pris* in relation to May, but it is important to attempt to continue the debate about the significance of May in a serious fashion without being seduced either by nostalgic optimism or a temptation to simply catalogue facts.

In this chapter I critically examine two authors who place the events of May in the context of social, political and economic modernization, but whose approaches in relation to the place May occupies in this process of modernization differ somewhat. They are Régis Debray and Gilles Lipovetsky. Both their analyses, if read uncritically, neatly locate May in the evolution of French politics and society towards the consensual situation of the 1980s and early 1990s, so their ideas are of considerable importance for this book. I agree with some of the underlying assumptions in their analyses, in particular that May was in part a result of contradictory tendencies in the development of France after the Second World War and that it reflected a country in the process of profound and historic change. But their more general arguments, in both cases, are in my view flawed and need to be challenged in order for the debate to be carried forward.

Before embarking on such an exercise, it is worth briefly recalling some of the more important causes of the revolt and the nature of the events themselves (for a comprehensive account see Joffrin 1988). May 1968 needs to be understood in relation to the form which socio-economic modernization took in France in the post-war period. First, there was very rapid economic growth during the 1960s which gave rise to important social changes, such as rapid rural exodus and the consolidation of a consumer society. An important part of the modernization process was a huge increase in the number of students; between 1960 and 1968 the number of university students more than doubled from 215,000 to 508,000, although resources devoted to universities by no means kept pace with this expansion (Prost 1992: 123). Next, it is important to take into account the oppressive political and social climate of de Gaulle's rule, with often stifling bureaucracy, lack of dialogue between the state and interest groups (including trade unions), and a feeling among young people that government ministers and the President were as out of touch with the needs of French youth as de Gaulle himself, born in 1890, was remote in age. Finally, the 1960s were on an international scale a time of youth and in particular student rebellion, taking the form both of a revolt against the habits and views of the older, pre-1945 generation and on a more globally political plane against the behaviour of industrialized countries towards poorer countries, in particular the United States in relation to Vietnam.

In France the spring of 1968 and especially May saw widespread student strikes, occupations, mass meetings, and demonstrations in defence of various, often ill-defined, demands which reflected a generalized and profound malaise in French higher education. The government responded not with offers of negotiation but by closing universities, including the Sorbonne, and by sending in riot police whose brutality shocked even the most dispassionate of observers and often won their sympathy for the students. After days and nights of pitched battles with the police at the beginning of May, workers also began to take to the streets in mass demonstrations of solidarity with students against police repression. This was followed by a three-week general strike accompanied by widespread occupations, in support of many different demands and with little national coordination on the part of the leadership of the trade unions. It became the largest strike in the history of the French labour movement. The government became paralysed by the events and at a total loss as to how to control the insurgent workers and students. De Gaulle disappeared for several hours on 29 May without informing even Prime Minister Georges Pompidou of his whereabouts, in order to meet General Massu in Baden Baden, Germany. After his return de Gaulle at last managed to rally supporters to his defence, which took the form of a huge demonstration of support on the Champs-Elysées on 30 May. Negotiations between government, trade unions and employers at the end of May (the so-called Grenelle Agreements) resulted in significant financial benefits and increased trade union rights for workers across France, but the gains were in the end meagre compared with the scale of the protest in May. The strikes and occupations of universities, factories and other places of work slowly came to an end and the parliamentary elections called by de Gaulle for the end of June paradoxically resulted in a landslide victory for the Gaullists, a triumph explained largely by a backlash of fear against the May revolt. De Gaulle thus survived May 1968 and indeed increased his majority in parliament, but he resigned as President in 1969 after testing public opinion in a referendum and losing, a result usually attributed in large part to the May events.

Régis Debray and Gilles Lipovetsky: the ruse of reason

Both Régis Debray and Gilles Lipovetsky posit that there is a logical and clear connection between the events of May and the characteristics of the epoch of the late 1970s and the early 1980s in France, between the radicalism of May and the moderate nature of the later period (Debray 1978; Lipovetsky 1983; Lipovetsky 1986). Régis Debray identifies one of the main causes of the May revolt as being the contradictions inherent in what he calls a 'two-speed France' and he locates May as being the turning point between the traditional France associated with the nineteenth century and the modern France characteristic of the late twentieth century. He points out that economically France had undergone tremendous modernizing changes in the previous twenty years, including an impressive growth of GNP, the concentration of capital, the 'feminization' of the labour force and a vast increase in the number of graduates, whose historical task was precisely to manage the development of the economy. Socially, politically and ideologically, however, France was archaic and out of step with other advanced capitalist democracies; the authoritarian and nationalistic Gaullist regime was the party political counterpart of the anachronistic family where patriarchy reigned. In the typical French firm paternalism still flourished. Many other analysts would now agree that this contradiction was one of the sources of the revolt, but Debray contends that, far from May being a fundamental revolt against the society which carried this contradiction, it was ultimately a revolt on behalf of the modernizing bourgeoisie and was indeed the 'cradle of the new bourgeois society' (Debray 1978: 10). The ruling class needed May in order to bring France socially and politically in line with the needs of capital and 'if May had not taken place capitalism would have had to invent it' (1978: 17). Debray's style is characteristically tongue-in-cheek, but his thesis that May is a modernizing moment which inevitably benefited the capitalist system remains the serious core of his argument. This rather teleological interpretation leads Debray to suggest that 'the May revolutionaries were the entrepreneurs of the spirit needed by the bourgeoisie ... they accomplished the opposite of what they intended' (1978: 15), and the participants in the May revolt ushered in an era of truly modern capitalism in France and acted to 'correct a malfunctioning of the neo-capitalist machine' (1978: 23). This last quotation is particularly significant, for central to Debray's argument is a (largely unexpressed) belief that labour movement activism in the developed world is all but futile, for the Western working class can rarely effect change in a positive direction. At the very end of Debray's essay he comments that, while waiting for socialist change elsewhere, Europeans can only 'scrape their grain of sand from the ramparts of fortress West by lending a hand to the "barbarians" struggling outside the walls against our sophisticated barbarism' (1978: 89–90). Only at this point, then, does he state what has informed much of the analysis in his short book, namely a profound scepticism as to any transforming potential of labour movements in industrialized countries.

In similar, if less cynical, vein Gilles Lipovetsky argues that the May movement is best understood as part of a long-term drift towards individualism in advanced capitalist societies, involving the decline of the desire for collective action: 'just as the French Revolution carried on the centralising mission of the *ancien régime*, so the spirit of May 1968 encouraged under the banner of revolution the strong tendency towards the privatization of existences by stressing the subjective' (1986: 99). So despite the mass meetings which were such a feature of May, despite the enormous demonstrations, the three-week general strike and the widespread spirit of solidarity and enthusiasm for collective action, Lipovetsky believes the most historically significant aspect of May was the 'explosion of explicitly individualistic demands and aspirations' (1986: 93). Lipovetsky argues that the absence of common demands, the lack of a coherent idea of the type of society the revolutionaries were struggling for, the utopian ideas of many of the students and in general the lack of realism demonstrated by the activists, all pointed to a rise in the importance of the individual. The contempt for political parties, elections and trade unions displayed by many student activists was symptomatic of the same process and this crucial 'spirit' of May was expressed in much of May's famous graffiti: 'The economy is wounded. Let it die', 'Think of your desires as reality', 'Be realistic, demand the impossible', and so on (1986: 95). This 'first indifferent revolution' (1986: 95) was thus a catalyst to as well as an expression of a long process of individualization which subsequently became so manifest in the sphere of what we now call new social movements:

> How could one deny that the French May contributed at the beginning of the 1970s to the rise of various liberation movements, women and gays in particular? These movements, despite fighting collectively, stressed the desire for individual autonomy and concentrated on the need for immediate emancipation, on the validity of existential problems, on the exploration and conquest of subjective identity and the personality. (Lipovetsky 1986: 98)

May hastened the growth of apathy towards politics and, 'paradoxically, accelerated the decomposition of great collective movements for social change in favour of a hedonistic refuge in the Ego' (1986: 100). By contrast with what one might conclude, then, May is in part responsible for the preference in late twentieth-century France for jogging rather than taking part in street demonstrations, working out instead of trade union or political activism and DIY instead of discussing ways of changing the world.

Despite the very different theoretical influences on Debray and Lipovetsky (broadly Marxist and Tocquevillian respectively), their approaches are in some important ways similar. First, both authors argue that May hastened an evolutionary pattern that was already established, rather than representing a real break with what went before, still less any possibility of going beyond the established capitalist order. Second, the effects of May on French society were the diametric opposite of what most activists were seeking to achieve, or believed they were seeking to achieve; for Debray the capitalist system was consolidated and rendered more stable, and for Lipovetsky May helped reinforce the role of the individual in society and weaken the role of the traditional organized social groups. In both cases the hidden hand of history worked to mould the course of social and political developments in a way which no one was aware of at the time, an approach described by Ferry and Renaut as the 'ruse of reason' (Ferry and Renaut 1985: 80).

Both Debray and Lipovetsky present arguments which are attractive to the extent that they locate May in the context of modern

French history and the course which it has taken since the Second World War. May clearly needs to be viewed historically if it is to be understood in the context of post-war social, political and economic development, rather than either a historical aberration or a voluntaristic act of letting off steam on the part of students and workers, again somehow disconnected from the normal course of history. Both Debray and Lipovetsky relate the events to the period before May and to the period after May, and in the case of Lipovetsky to the fairly recent past as well. If valid, either of these accounts would help situate the revolt in relation to the more moderate course taken by French politics in the years since 1968, for both accounts seek to explain the contrast between the May revolt which shook France so deeply and the much calmer period which ensued. However, an overwhelming shortcoming on the part of both writers is to believe not only in the causal nature of the period before May, but also in the *inevitability* of the 'results' of May, rather than the openness of the possible outcomes. For them there is a logical progression from the nature of the events of May itself to the social and political situation of the following decades. Although I agree that May is in part a symptom of the uneven modernization of post-war France, I disagree with the chain of causality which both authors employ and below I examine the authors' arguments in relation to the social and political history of France since the Second World War.

Turning first to Debray's location of a major cause in the 'two-speed' France of the time, he is undoubtedly on firm ground. As I point out in earlier chapters, there was a sharp contradiction in post-war France between the fact that economically the country had joined the league of successful advanced capitalist countries, whereas politically and socially it still had some of the hallmarks of countries with less developed capitalist economies. Between 1945 and 1968 the proportion of agricultural workers in the working population fell a great deal, capital became far more concentrated, GDP and productivity increased at an unprecedented rate and foreign trade was less with colonies and ex-colonies and far more with other industrialized European countries. In the space of two decades France went from being a semi-rural nation of predominantly small-scale production units to being a fully-fledged industrialized society with an economy dominated by monopoly capital and a substantial urban proletariat. In other respects, however, France had hardly changed since the war. Relations between employers and trade unions, for instance, were very far from those in the more liberal capitalist democracies such as

Britain, West Germany and the Scandinavian countries. Employers often acted as if it was their absolute right to decide without consulting the workforce when and by how much to raise wages and when to introduce changes in working conditions, and company-level bargaining in particular was very weak. In case of industrial action of any intensity a vicious and well-armed riot police was available to physically beat protestors into submission rather than concede any real changes. Living standards among some sectors of the population remained low despite the economic boom, and welfare benefits remained meagre. Upward social mobility was less developed than in many other advanced capitalist societies and education was still in desperate need of modernization, despite expansion of higher education.

The Gaullist regime was in part responsible for maintaining this archaic system of social relations, although many aspects of it, including the extreme centralization of the political, administrative and legal system, had a longer history. As we have seen, because of de Gaulle's authoritarian approach towards ruling the country after his return to power in 1958, the continued modernization of post-war France did not take place along the lines of the liberal democratic model followed in other countries in many spheres, but according to the wishes of a backward capitalist class and a powerful bureaucratic elite. Indeed de Gaulle's approach was carved in the tablets of the constitution of the Fifth Republic, where the role of parliament and political parties is limited and the power of the President far-reaching. These factors were all aspects of what Debray describes as two-speed France. But in his analysis of Gaullist France Debray does not take account of the role of organized labour, or its relative weakness in France, which had been so central to the modernization process in other countries. It was in part the weakness of the organized working class at the end of the Fourth Republic that allowed de Gaulle to come to power in the first place and then allowed for the maintenance of an archaic system of social relations. In Debray's analysis of the background to May any real consideration of the role of the organized working class is absent, despite the central importance of the nine million-strong strike in May itself.

Between 1947 and 1968 the labour movement had very little direct influence on, let alone involvement in, the governing of the country. The SFIO participated in and even led a number of the short-lived governments of the Fourth Republic, but it was a party which had no direct links with the trade union movement. Once de Gaulle came to power, the Socialist current went into profound crisis and de Gaulle pursued a policy of modernization which excluded the trade union and labour movement instead of attempting to integrate it. To this extent, Debray's analysis is correct, for compared with other advanced capitalist countries there was indeed a 'malfunctioning of the capitalist machine', an exclusion of labour, which created profound tensions. However, in order to understand the significance of May it is also necessary to take account of the re-emergence of labour movement combativeness in the years before 1968. The first real sign of renewed militancy came with the miners' strike of 1963 and subsequently with strikes at many private and public sector firms: Rhodiaceta in Besançon, Berliet in Venisieux, Chantiers de l'Atlantique and Sud-Aviation in Saint Nazaire (Capdevielle and Mouriaux 1988: 239–40). It was this re-emergence of the working class as a force to be reckoned with and above all its frustration with suffering backward social conditions in a country where the economy was booming that made May in France so different from the revolts in other countries. It was only in France that the events of 1968 spilled over from the student movement into the labour movement to any significant degree, although as Colin Crouch, Alessandro Pizzorno and their co-authors have shown, the re-emergence of class conflict after 1968 was an international phenomenon (Crouch and Pizzorno 1978). In other words, it was not simply frustration at being denied certain gains which the working class had achieved in other countries which meant that May in France involved the labour movement to a huge degree, but also the fact that the labour movement had been becoming more militant, gathering confidence, during the 1960s.

Debray's analysis is useful to the extent that May did indeed reflect profound contradictions in the uneven social, political and economic development of France in the post-war period. It was in part a crisis of modernization, and in the decades since 1968 the various contradictions inherent in Gaullist society have gradually given way to a situation which is more akin to the more stable political and social conditions in other countries of Western Europe. The threat to the established order on the part of a Marxist-influenced socialist and trade union movement has declined, particularly in the period since the publication of Debray's piece (since when, incidentally, he has not, to my knowledge, published anything on the significance of May). However, Debray is wrong to argue that May was simply a manifestation of a self-correcting process somehow built into the capitalist system, and a moment when the protagonists were unconsciously but inevitably working towards the opposite of what they thought they were struggling for. This is crude economic determinism. Rather, the strikes in particular should be located as part of the re-emergence of the confidence of organized labour in the 1960s. May was certainly perceived by the government and by heads of industry as a tremendous threat to the established order and its energy carried on in various forms of protest in the early to mid-1970s, as I describe below. Successive (right-wing) governments introduced reforms, as new governments have often done in response to the revolts and revolutions in French history, which brought greater stability. But this by no means implies that the activists (students and workers) in May were somehow acting on behalf of capital, without realizing they were doing so. On the contrary, many were consciously anti-capitalist and acted accordingly.

The key to understanding May's place in the stabilization of the politics of post-war France is to interpret subsequent history in terms of a defeat, or at least only partial success, of May.

Turning now to Lipovetsky's argument, his approach is also superficially attractive in that it links what happened in May itself to major developments in the decade or so after May, most importantly the rise of new social movements and then the decline of collective action and more generally the decline of class conflict. As with Debray's historical situating of May, its attractiveness is in part its satisfying neatness, the feeling that his analysis is able to reconcile explosive May with the far more moderate nature of what has happened since. To argue, however, as does Lipovetsky, that the most historically important aspect of the events was an assertion of 'mass hedonism' (1986: 97), contributing to an acceleration of today's 'narcissistic individualism' which is largely indifferent to collective action (1986: 98) is quite wrong. He virtually ignores the longest general strike in French history, which was to change the nature of France's social relations more than any other event since the war and possibly since 1936. He ignores the fact that meetings and demonstrations were enormous and that France had rarely seen such widespread and wide-ranging discussions around questions of social change. The highly politicized nature of the student and workers' movement was displayed in a myriad of ways, not least by the often-chanted slogan 'Dix ans, ça suffit', 'Ten years [of de Gaulle] is enough'.

There are many examples from the general strike in May which bear witness to the tremendous collective spirit regarding not only

pay and conditions of work but also in relation to a more democratically organized society: in Nantes the strike committee controlled
traffic, distributed vehicle permits and blocked entrances to the
town; at the Rhône-Poulenc factories in Vitry strikers established a
system of direct exchange with farmers in the area; at several Paris
newspaper presses workers either insisted on changing headlines or
refused to print editions altogether where there were reports which
were hostile to the demonstrators and strikers. There are countless
other examples. The fact that the general public frequently displayed
solidarity with protesting students and workers also flies in the face
of Lipovetsky's interpretation of the events as an explosion of individualism. André Gaveau, a police superintendent in Paris at the
time, vividly describes how in the Latin Quarter at the beginning of
May local inhabitants brought food and water to battling students
and that 'despite widespread damage to people's cars and to the road
itself, a current of sympathy united students and "spectators"'
(Gaveau 1978: 70). As Cornelius Castoriadis comments in response
to Lipovetsky's interpretation, the dominant spirit of the May revolt
was in fact one of solidarity and of unity. Far from being itself an
expression of individualism, the movement was actually undermined
in the end by the reassertion of various forms of individualism:

> The weeks of fraternization and active solidarity, when you spoke
> to anybody in the street without fear of being taken as a madman,
> and when any car driver stopped to pick up a hitch hiker – is the sig-
> nificance of these weeks egoistic hedonism? Did the slogan 'Speak
> to your neighbours', written on the walls in May 1968, quietly pre-
> pare for today's isolation of individuals in their private spheres? . . .
> Order was finally restored when the ordinary Frenchman could
> travel in *his* car, with *his* family to *his* second home or *his* picnic
> spot. That is what allowed six out of ten ordinary Frenchmen to
> vote for the government a month later. (Castoriadis 1988: 186)

Of course there were innumerable examples of what might be
described as individualistic behaviour in May, ranging from the
invention of the often very imaginative and vivid graffiti which
became so well known to the celebration of freer expressions of sexuality than French society had previously been prepared to admit;
photographs of couples kissing on the barricades in the Latin Quarter summed up this new spirit of liberation (e.g. *Photo* 1978: 99). But
does not any revolt of any size bring with it a feeling of increased
personal and creative freedom where the individual feels able to

express himself or herself more fully than before, free from normal constraints? This was certainly the spirit which prevailed during the 1968 Spring Uprising in Czechoslovakia, for example, and more recently in the revolts against Communist regimes in Eastern Europe. Even fairly routine street demonstrations against public expenditure cuts or against nuclear arms often include participants who put on fancy dress, sing songs, carry home-made props or play musical instruments. Protests by ecology movements in the 1980s and 1990s have been particularly striking in the way participants express themselves individually in their dress, their music, their general lifestyles. This does not make the spirit of any of these demonstrations less collective, but illustrates the point that the aim of collective action is often, in part, personal freedom of some kind.

Perhaps the most eloquent testimony of this spirit in May was the slogan 'Tout est possible', which alluded both to the tremendously increased feeling of freedom in May itself and to the possibilities which May appeared to engender, in the realm of social and political organization in France, and the highly related realm of changes to individuals' lives. Many participants in the May movement felt they were playing an important part in shaping both politics and their own lives for the first time ever. The impressive posters of the Atelier populaire which appeared in such a short space of time are also a lasting reminder of the close relationship between political freedom and artistic expression (Atelier populaire 1969). There was certainly widespread expression of a desire to enjoy individual freedoms of various kinds in May, be they artistic, sexual or the desire to control one's own life in some other way (like the workers in Nantes in relation to the traffic they were surrounded by). But there was no indication that protesters believed they could bypass collective action as a means of achieving these ends, witness the huge demonstrations, the occupations and the mass meetings. In some cases groups expressed disillusionment with the often undemocratic, bureaucratic nature of trade unions and political parties, and libertarian influences were often in evidence, but this is something quite other than the events expressing a desire for selfish individualism.

In the final analysis, the aims of any social movement can be reduced to individual aspirations. A strike for higher wages will reflect a desire to overcome individual hardship caused by low pay, a demonstration against cuts in public expenditure will in part reflect participants' anticipation of lack of provision in the sphere of health-care or education for themselves, their families, their colleagues and their friends, and in May there was, ultimately, an expression of revulsion against the personal oppression, limited freedom of expression and in some cases real hardship which individuals suffered. But this did not imply that the events were somehow narcissistic, any more than the festive atmosphere which pervaded the departure of French workers and their families on their first paid holidays in 1936 meant that the movement which had won this right should be characterized as narcissistic. As the individual is both the main and the smallest sensuous unit, the level at which the basic physical and emotional experiences take place (pleasure, pain, hunger, thirst, distress, and so on), any collective revolt is bound to reflect experience at an individual level, any result will affect the experience of the individual.

Significantly, the two events which contributed above all others to bringing the May revolt to an end were firstly the huge right-wing demonstration on the Champs-Elysées on 30 May which re-established support for and thus the confidence of de Gaulle and his colleagues, and the national negotiations on pay, conditions at work and trade union rights, on 27 May (the Grenelle Agreements). Both phenomena, despite being very different in many ways, were an expression of collective wishes which in the case of the 30 May demonstration represented a collective expression of opposition to the May movement and in the case of Grenelle redirected energies in a more conventional, less threatening direction (for both the traditional labour movement and the Gaullist regime). It took these developments to inflict the first and most significant defeats on the movement.

The results of May

Passing now to the relationship between the events of May and subsequent social and political developments, the effect on what came afterwards was no more to consolidate capitalism or hasten the rise of narcissistic individualism than was the movement itself an expression of these tendencies. An examination of the post-May era shows how its impetus was also a collective and often anti-capitalist one and that it was in fact the substantial setbacks for the labour and other movements during the 1970s that meant that the radical impetus resulted in relatively minor reforms, rather than profound change. It should first be stressed that this impetus was weakened even before the end of the general strike, for two main reasons. First, as I have said, the wind was taken out of the sails of the strike movement when the leadership of the trade union confederations agreed to relatively meagre reforms and pay rises in exchange for a return to work, at the Grenelle negotiations. Crucially, the PCF leadership (with the support of much of its rank-and-file membership) had since the beginning of May decided to support striking workers only as long as they were demanding conventional reforms; none of the more far-reaching demands were regarded as legitimate. Second, there was a natural 'coming down' anyway when workers began to drift back to work and when life for workers and students was no longer structured around the next demonstration or meeting. In fact the PCF and the PCF-dominated CGT took much the same attitude in 1968 as they had in 1936 and immediately after the Second World War, when on both occasions the Communist Party decided to contain potentially lengthy strike movements for fear of losing control of them.

However, during the immediate post-May era there was indeed a surge of radical labour movement activism in many spheres, much of it outside the influence of the PCF and the CGT, the twin organizations which had dominated the organized working class for so long and the CFDT trade union in particular became far more radical after May, precisely because it was more receptive to change than the PCF-dominated CGT. CFDT General Secretary André Jeanson summed up the union's approach at this time when he declared at the congress of 1970:

> Let us say straight away that our strategy is one of class struggle. This expression is controversial and is for some out of fashion ... We will not enter into a debate on this, but can see easily enough that this is what we experience every day ... We live what is, I repeat, class struggle, we take on board the risks and limitations associated with it and it is via the conflicts it involves that we wish to transform capitalist society to its very roots. (Quoted in Capdevielle and Mouriaux 1988: 237)

Indeed in the five years following May the CFDT was in the forefront of many highly radical strikes which challenged traditional patterns of authority and went far beyond traditional demands about changes in pay and conditions. In response to intransigence from employers these movements often involved forms of direct action in addition to strikes, such as occupation of the workplace, sequestration of managing directors and occasionally industrial sabotage. *Autogestion*, a form of workers' control, became a widespread preoccupation, as did improvements in terms and conditions for women and immigrant workers, for example. The CFDT notably led strikes at Renault-Le Mans in 1971 and subsequently strikes at Pennaroya, Les Nouvelles Galeries de Thionville and Le Joint Français in St Brieuc. In 1973 the CFDT was still leading the most tenacious and imaginative struggles at Péchiney, Noguers, Salamander and Cousseau (Capdevielle and Mouriaux 1988: 239–40; G. Ross 1982: 230). The most celebrated struggle at this time took place at the Lip watch factory in Besançon, where workers occupied after notice to close the factory in June 1973. In a book about Lip co-signed by CFDT Secretary General Edmond Maire, he concludes that as a result of the struggle at Lip 'a majority of workers and the public in general has become more conscious of the need to overthrow capitalism' (Maire and Piaget 1973: 138). The CGT, meanwhile, was absent from many of these strikes and continued to argue for very traditional demands and traditional forms of action. It refused to support anything but peaceful, orderly work stoppages and picketing, objecting to illegal acts such as industrial sabotage. Often opposed to new types of demands, concerning notably the quality of work and *autogestion*, the CGT usually limited itself to conventional questions of pay, hours and working conditions. The radical strike movement which emerged in the years after 1968 was thus generally distinct from the traditional CGT-dominated part of the labour movement.

Far from helping to stabilize the capitalist system in the manner suggested by Debray, the post-1968 impetus disturbed the captains of industry considerably. The employers' leader François Ceyrac commented in 1973 that one was witnessing conflicts

> which have new and worrying characteristics . . . [with] a certain tendency towards radicalization; that is a refusal by workers' representatives to take account of the state of health of the company concerned and a wish to push for entrenched confrontation with no real desire to reach agreement

and he noted the 'weakening of the authority of trade unions before these new types of situation' (quoted in H. Weber 1978: 42).

The political parties of the left also entered a period of radicalization, largely as a result of May. The small Parti Socialiste Unifié

(PSU) became committed to a policy of *autogestion*, forged close links with the CFDT and in general became what was regarded as a 'laboratory of ideas', rather like the CFDT itself (e.g. Kesler 1990: 381–4). Meanwhile the neo-Marxist far left grew rapidly and the Trotskyist Ligue Communiste Révolutionnaire came to dominate this particular section of the left. Although tiny in terms of membership compared with many other political parties, during much of the 1970s the far left was able to mobilize tens of thousands of people in street demonstrations and in the 1973 legislative elections and the 1974 presidential elections in particular it did well in certain solidly working-class areas. In the 1974 presidential elections Lutte Ouvrière's candidate Arlette Laguiller received 10 per cent of the vote in the industrial sector of Orléans and 12 per cent in Charleville-Mezieres (H. Weber 1978: 42).

The most important development concerning political parties at this time, at least the one which had the most important long-term consequences, was the re-emergence, unification and radicalization of the Socialist Party. After years in the doldrums France's Socialist current regrouped at conferences in 1969 and 1971 as it became clear that a party of government of the left distinct from but in alliance with the PCF was once again a possibility. Certainly, in the long term the PS contributed greatly to the de-radicalization of the labour movement and of French politics more generally. But at the unifying conference in Epinay in 1971 François Mitterrand, who had just been elected leader, felt it appropriate to declare that 'violent or peaceful, revolution is first and foremost a radical break. Those who accept a radical break with the established order, with capitalism, can join the Socialist Party' (quoted in H. Weber 1988: 252). The new, more radical trajectory the PS was now on was confirmed by the fact that Jean-Pierre Chevènement, the leader of the CERES, Marxist-influenced wing of the party, was selected to draw up the PS programme and negotiate a common programme of government with the PCF. This programme was signed in 1972 and must be seen as, in part, a result of the radical impulse of May. However, the PS's uniting with the PCF was indeed double-edged, for although it was a result of a certain radicalization – particularly on the part of the rank and file – the PS strategy was to capture the moderate communist vote, a plan which in the long run has been successful beyond its wildest dreams.

Another important partial result of May was of course the re-emergence of the women's movement as well as other non class-specific groups such as the gay rights, ecology and anti-nuclear movements. For Lipovetsky this is further evidence to support his view that May was an expression of and acted as a catalyst to 'individualistic' revolt, as these groups were particularly concerned with 'personal' questions such as sexuality, contraception, abortion and domestic labour. It is of course true that the women's movement in France and elsewhere did much in the decade following 1968 to highlight the inextricable links between what was traditionally viewed as the realm of politics (government, elections, party activism, collective bargaining, strikes, demonstrations, and so on) and the traditional view of the (quite distinct) realm of the personal. But these new social movements were no less collective for emphasizing 'personal' issues, by contrast with what Lipovetsky argues. On the contrary, they stressed the common experience and solidarity of women with other women, gays with other gays, migrant workers with other migrant workers, where commonality of experience had previously been hidden or unacknowledged. Struggles around contraception, abortion and divorce which stressed the importance of changes in legislation for all women (but especially working-class women who could not afford to travel to another country to have an abortion, for example) led to changes in the law on each of these issues in the 1970s. Furthermore the forms of action which these movements adopted were unmistakably collective in nature, including street demonstrations, pickets, petitions and sit-ins. The famous *Manifeste des salopes* (literally 'Tarts' manifesto') where 343 well-known women signed a declaration in April 1971 claiming to have had illegal abortions, thus challenging the authorities to prosecute, is another example of a collective form of action in defence of a right which is generally perceived as being an individual one. Certainly, many issues in these protests were intensely personal in some respects and were often concerned with individual freedoms, but, as I have already argued in relation to Lipovetsky's analysis of May 1968 itself, all social movements relate to the individual's private sphere of existence at some level or another, without the implication that they are an expression of 'individualism'.

There is no doubt that in the decade following the events of May political and social changes took place which paved the way for a stabilization of relations between social classes, and it must also be said that political demoralization on the left and in the trade unions and the consolidation of consumer society did bring with them the rise of individualism. France was less and less socially and politically volatile as the 1970s wore on and still less so in the 1980s. Therein lies the rational core of truth in both Debray's and Lipovetsky's argument. However, the explanation for this lies in the failure of the spirit of May to continue to influence the shape of social and political change, rather than individualism being part of the spirit of May. By contrast with the logic of both Debray's and Lipovetsky's arguments, the 1980s and 1990s should not be seen as part of the heritage of May, but on the contrary should be seen as a result of many defeats for what the movement stood for.

The most obvious and indeed the most important formal political change brought about by May was the departure of de Gaulle in April 1969. After a landslide victory for the Gaullists in the June 1968 parliamentary elections de Gaulle attempted to further reassert his authority and reassert the appropriateness of traditional Gaullism by submitting two minor and mainly unconnected reforms for approval by referendum. He lost by a significant margin (52.4 per cent against) and was obliged to resign, which effectively sounded the death knell of traditional Gaullism.

The next President, Georges Pompidou, had been de Gaulle's Prime Minister for many years and had been groomed to succeed him. But under the circumstances Pompidou was obliged to innovate in significant areas. It was widely known that Pompidou differed from de Gaulle in his interpretation of the events of May. For de Gaulle the revolt was the result of a communist conspiracy and he was apparently incapable of locating and drawing any lessons regarding its social origins. Pompidou, on the other hand, acknowledged that significant sections of the French population had been deprived of a proper share in France's post-war wealth and that many were disadvantaged in the area of individual and social rights in comparison with other industrialized countries. With the appointment of Jacques Chaban-Delmas as Prime Minister there began a period of three years of liberal reforms and in a speech before parliament outlining his government's intentions in September 1969 Chaban-Delmas described his intentions for what he described as 'New Society' policies. The government would give priority to encouraging 'collective bargaining between the two sides of industry', he said, 'in order to go beyond the archaic and conservative nature of social structures' (quoted in Portelli 1987: 212). President Pompidou, going even further than his Prime Minister, claimed that:

My motivating idea is the transformation of social relations in France. It is unreasonable that in 1969 the relationships between management and wage earners should be those of endless conflict. We must establish new habits, built around the spirit of, and respect for, new contracts. (Quoted in G. Ross 1982: 217)

Inspired partly by the sociologist Michel Crozier's explanation of the causes of May as being the over-bureaucratized and generally ossified nature of French society, the Chaban-Delmas government effected reforms in industrial relations (Crozier 1970). In particular the government encouraged a sort of company-level social contract between nationalized firms and trade unions, which guaranteed improvements in workers' living standards in return for the maintenance of a certain level of productivity. Other changes included pressure on the employers' federation, CNPF, to negotiate systematically over differences with trade unions, a law allowing pay agreements at company level and a law which extended the right to training leave. This particular period of reform was brought to a close when elements of the parliamentary majority to the right of both Chaban-Delmas and Pompidou managed to have the Prime Minister replaced by Pierre Messmer.

That the era of Gaullism proper was certainly over was confirmed by the election of Valéry Giscard d'Estaing as President of the Republic in May 1974, after the death of Pompidou. Giscard had called for a NO vote in the referendum which sealed de Gaulle's fate in 1969 and epitomized liberal conservatism, professing faith in the rights of the individual, pluralism, free enterprise and social reform (Giscard d'Estaing 1976). Like Pompidou, Giscard began his period as President with a series of reforms which were implemented despite a Gaullist majority in the National Assembly and even a Gaullist Prime Minister in the form of Jacques Chirac. Giscard oversaw the reduction of the minimum age for voting from 21 to 18 years, the wider availability of contraception, the legalization of abortion, divorce by mutual consent, the reform of the social security system, a lowering of the age of retirement and the passage of laws on equal pay and employment opportunities for women and protection against redundancy. This reforming zeal only lasted about two years, partly because the economic crisis shifted the balance of forces between capital and labour and sent social reforms to the bottom of the agenda. But they were significant reforms and reflected an awareness that the old order had to be changed significantly or even destroyed completely if major conflict was to be avoided.

Successive governments, then, implemented reforms during the early and mid-1970s which meant that French society was less archaic than it had been under de Gaulle. These reforms did indeed help de-radicalize French politics and industrial relations and were partly a result of the May protests. However, the reforms implemented under Pompidou and Giscard d'Estaing were truly minor compared with the demands expressed in May, or, for that matter, during many of the disputes of the early 1970s. This is why I have argued that by contrast with what Debray and Lipovetsky maintain, the decline of militancy and the relatively moderate nature of politics since the mid-1970s is a result of the failure of the May movement, rather than part of its logic. A major setback for the post-May movement came in the early to mid-1970s with the onset of the economic crisis. It was in the mid-1970s that the wave of radical strikes came to an end and the strength of the far left declined in many areas. The change of climate in industrial relations was perhaps best illustrated by the trajectory taken by the CFDT in the late 1970s, when it began consciously to shed its radicalism and return to being a more moderate trade union confederation. In January 1978 the leader of the political section of the CFDT, Jacques Moreau, presented a historic report where he argued that 'in order to obtain concrete results, to give hope, we need to enter into necessary compromises with those who manage the economy and industrial relations' (quoted in Hamon and Rotman 1984: 300). The CFDT leader Edmond Maire also argued that the CFDT had moved too far in the direction of confrontationism and had been wrong to capitulate to the radicalism of the post-1968 era (Maire 1980). The women's movement began to go into a prolonged period of crisis at this time and there were in general fewer demonstrations and other sorts of protests.

The spirit of May and the Socialist years

Only in the most superficial way does the moderate nature of the period of Socialist presidency between 1981 and 1995 confirm the correctness of Debray's and Lipovetsky's analyses. Politics have moved towards the centre, union membership has fallen dramatically and many individuals have become overwhelmingly preoccupied with material consumption. Arguably, capitalism is more stable in

France than it has been for many years and socialist transformation more remote. In general the level of militancy of the working class has fallen and the individual French person has been more concerned with private life in an isolated way than ever before. All this has happened on an international scale, at least as far as Western Europe and the US is concerned, but how does this recent period in France relate to the May revolt? There is no doubt that the struggles in and after May 1968 helped reinforce the confidence of the left and thus ultimately helped secure the victory of the left in 1981. Indeed some aspects of the PS programme in 1981 were taken from the Common Programme of Government with the PCF signed in 1972: nationalization of major industrial groups and financial institutions, a wealth tax, a substantial rise in the minimum wage, the creation of jobs in the public sector, the raising of social benefits and increased negotiating rights for workers at company level (PCF and PS 1972). However, these already fairly moderate changes were complemented by inaction in other domains.

From the beginning it was clear that the Socialists did not intend to alter the constitution, despite a previous promise of reducing the presidential term from seven to five years, for example. Indeed little attempt was made to make the French political system more democratic, apart from laws on decentralization, which notably created a new, directly elected council at regional level; the relative weakness of parliament remained unchanged, as did the highly elitist and influential nature of the civil service. This situation was compounded by the fact that there was no popular mobilization after 1981 to push the government in a more progressive direction, as there had been in 1936 and after the Second World War. On the contrary, Socialist and Communist trade union confederations alike encouraged an already quiescent workforce to accept that overcoming deep-rooted inequalities would take time, and this resulted in the lowest level of trade union activism since the Second World War.

The first period of Socialist government was thus ambiguous in relation to May. There was an attempt to reduce some of the more glaring inequalities and deal with the more extreme injustices, but early indicators already hinted that traditional methods were eventually to prevail. That the spirit of May was largely already squashed was shown by the fact that the working class accepted in a fairly docile manner a series of austerity plans implemented by PS governments first led by Pierre Mauroy and then Laurent Fabius. Again, then, the 1980s and particularly the 1990s are far more a period which reflects a defeat of the spirit of May than a period which is in the logic of May. There have been noteworthy moments of popular and collective action since 1981, particularly in the public sector. In December 1986–January 1987 there were widespread strikes in the public sector. Then in December 1995 there was another wave of strikes, this time on a far greater scale, and Parisian public transport was at a standstill for several weeks, causing complete chaos in the capital. But on both occasions the movements were defensive in nature and contained little of the optimism of the struggles of May 1968 or the 1970s (see chapter 4).

Henri Weber suggests that some of the radical-left spirit of May was in fact translated into practice during the 1981–8 period of Socialist government. He contends, for example, that the 'democratic impulse of May resulted indirectly in the decentralization laws under Mitterrand and the liberalization of local radios' (H. Weber 1988: 208). But Weber is too keen to reconcile May and the period of Socialist rule, perhaps in part because he personally played an active part in both. The Socialist reforms were in fact far removed from the spirit of 1968 and related to May only in a way which was also informed by the significant setbacks discussed above. As many analysts have pointed out, the 1980s constituted a lowering of the sights for many former militants as far as a radicalizing socio-economic and political project was concerned, and as Weber himself points out, 'it was only in light of the experience of a united left government that there was a "decoupling" of democratization and principled anti-capitalism in left ideology' (1988: 157). May 1968 had by contrast strengthened, albeit temporarily, the 'coupling' of anti-capitalism and the struggle for democracy.

Locating May historically

How, then, should May 1968 be located in the history of post-war politics? Debray is certainly correct to identify May as being in part a result of tensions between different aspects of French social and political development in post-war French history. It is also useful to locate May 1968 in the socio-economic and political history of post-war France in relation to the greater degree of harmony and consensus in politics in the 1980s and 1990s, and a greater degree of individualism in society at large. This is in part what Lipovetsky sets out to do. However, the mistake that both Debray and Lipovetsky make is to assume that the events of May should be analysed as being part of the logic of consensus and individualism. In reality May came as a tremendous shock to the ruling class in France and elsewhere, and stringent attempts were made to ensure that damage was limited. In other words, it was understood that, in order to avoid further revolt, systematic appeasement had to take place in many realms, including education, industrial relations and the legal treatment of women. In general this proved a successful strategy; as had been the case in other countries in earlier times, the ruling class was able to limit the extent of revolutionary fervour, with substantial help in the 1970s from the economic crisis and rising unemployment. But it was precisely this reaction against the movement of May, this defeat for May, which meant that politics in France fell more into line with politics in other countries.

By contrast with the approaches of Debray and Lipovetsky, an attempt to define the historical significance of May 1968 in France must take into account the fact that social, political and economic change takes place as a result of tensions between different socioeconomic formations in society, most notably social classes. Debray's analysis is based first on a highly mechanistic, not to say teleological, view of history and a highly developed scepticism as to the ability of the Western working class to effect change in a progressive direction. For him the post-May era is a direct result of the 'hidden meaning' of May itself, rather than the compromise between opposing forces, which is often what history really creates, eventually, during a period of change. For Lipovetsky, one aspect of May 1968, namely the explosion of expressions of and demands for individual freedom, constitutes the essence of the revolt and the character of the two decades or so since 1968. In common with Debray, he mistakenly concludes that the main characteristics of the late 1970s, 1980s and now no doubt the 1990s are the logical result of May 1968. As I have attempted to show, Lipovetsky is more fundamentally wrong than Debray in his analysis of the nature of May itself, but their conclusions with regard to the post-May era are equally flawed.

8
The Waning of Intellectual Commitment

Ferry was pictured with his young daughter, his speed boat (*Le Ferry-Boat*) in St Tropez, his 'cello and the French Minister for Education, suggesting in order, family values, jet-set chic, profundity and political clout.

The Times *on philosopher Luc Ferry (8 June 1996)*

More than anywhere else in Western Europe, intellectual life in post-war France was associated with politics. To be an intellectual virtually obliged intellectual commitment, or *engagement*. One of the hallmarks of prominent intellectuals was that they took a stand on issues which did not necessarily fall within their immediate area of professional expertise and felt justified in giving views on political issues which were of general concern to ordinary people. We can be categorical in two other ways as well. First, prominent intellectuals were almost always located on the left of the political spectrum, often on the Marxist left, a position whose legitimacy was confirmed in part because of the existence of a large Communist Party. The second point is that intellectuals were very much in the public eye. They wrote in the leading newspapers, especially *Le Monde*, signed petitions which appeared in the mainstream press, spoke at political rallies, on the radio and on television, and went out of their way to associate themselves not only with particular political views but often with political parties as well. This meant that political life as a whole was imbued with a level of debate, including among rank-and-file activists, which was not found in countries where intellectuals played a less important role in politics and where there was a more established liberal democratic tradition.

Since the late 1970s and the beginning of the 1980s, the situation has changed dramatically. Two years after the victory of the left, in summer 1983, there was a lengthy debate in *Le Monde* on the 'silence of intellectuals' as far as politics were concerned. Many prominent writers condoned and indeed rejoiced in the general withdrawal of intellectuals from partisan politics, and one of the most lively journals of social and political debate of the 1980s and 1990s has been *Le Débat*, whose founders were explicit in their desire for intellectuals to be modest in their political interventions (Nora 1980). During the first period of *cohabitation* between Socialist President Mitterrand and a government of the right, the leading left sociologist Alain Touraine wrote in *Le Monde* that intellectuals should 'take advantage of this gentler form of politics, after being exhausted for so long by politics which were too harsh, too ideological, too Manichaeistic' (Touraine 1987). Perhaps most obvious of all, Marxism, which had already become less influential since the mid-1970s, went into what seemed like terminal decline. To be overtly Marxist became as discredited intellectually as being on the right had been in the decades after the Second World War, and many well-known former Marxists publicly recanted.

In this chapter I attempt to explain why intellectuals tended to be both politically committed and on the left in the post-war years and then why the relationship between intellectuals and politics in France has become more like that in countries known for more moderate, less ideologically explicit, liberal democratic politics. Intellectuals in France for many years publicly defended the battles that were being fought on the streets, in the workplace and, since the rise of the women's movement after 1968, in the home. But they also generated politics themselves, influencing and not only reinforcing the position of activists on the ground. Since the beginning of the 1980s intellectuals have assumed a role that is more marginal, more piecemeal, sometimes but not always more modest, and almost invariably with less of a 'world view'. The reasons for this changing role include socio-economic modernization, the changing nature of the French state, and a growing awareness of widespread human rights abuses in the Soviet Union. But the new relationship between intellectuals and politics came about in part precisely because party politics in the 1980s had become less ideological, less conflictual, less about challenging the social and political order as a whole and more about choices between options which were located firmly within the same, limited framework; the notion of a break with the past became far less popular. Since the early 1980s France has seen the emergence of a right-leaning liberalism among intellectuals, some of which is closer to the liberalism of Britain and America than to the traditional Republican liberalism of France. However, this phenomenon, despite the rediscovery of such writers as Raymond Aron, Julien Benda and Alexis de Tocqueville, often takes the form of reaction, sometimes revenge, against Marxism on the part of the liberal right rather than of a confident new political philosophy or political perspective.

The place of intellectuals in post-war political life

Some preliminary words are necessary regarding the nature and role of intellectuals, which will inform the discussion below. Defining the term 'intellectual' is notoriously difficult and writers diverge substantially on this (Saïd 1993: 3–17). My own view, in the tradition of the writings of Antonio Gramsci, is that ultimately, in order to speak meaningfully about the relationship between intellectual activity on the one hand and the nature of society and political life on the other, one has to take account of the fact that there is an intellectual contribution made by all those who help form the ideological orientation of a society or groups of people within it (Gramsci 1971: esp. 5–23). In a sense, then, virtually everyone is an intellectual, as almost everyone holds views and expresses them. But some people make a more obvious contribution to this process, including teachers, academics, journalists, priests, politicians and business consultants, whose 'social function', in the words of Gramsci, is being an intellectual (1971: 9). There are also those who are more conventionally regarded as intellectuals, who devote much of their time to writing and speaking about issues of public concern and exert a considerable influence upon many other people, who can be described as 'traditional intellectuals'. The importance of this approach is that while those who are generally taken to be intellectuals – the traditional intellectuals – have a special place in the production and diffusion of ideas, they by no means constitute the sum total of intellectual life. In practice, of course, whether one is dealing with the question of intellectuals from a historical, sociological or philosophical point of view, one is obliged to single out certain individuals who are deemed to be particularly influential, in order to make the task of analysing intellectual life more manageable. But it is important to stress that they are the highly visible (and certainly very important) tip of a far larger group of people whose social function is to be intellectuals. The more general intellectual climate of an epoch, its ideology, is created by an even broader group of people, many of whom may themselves not be aware of their contribution to this process. There is thus a symbiotic relationship between the various groups of intellectuals: the 'high' intellectuals produce the publicized ideas and the broader groups diffuse them more widely, critique them and alter them, which will in turn often cause the high intellectuals to refine their views. This approach differs from the classic view of Julien Benda, who in a famous book first published in 1927, *La Trahison des clercs*, treats intellectuals, *les clercs*, as an elite group of very gifted individuals, with whom he contrasts the mass of what he describes as 'lay' people, in other words everyone else. Indeed Gramsci's approach is very different from that of many intellectual historians, who are far more concerned with famous individuals treated in isolation than intellectual life in general.

As noted in chapter 2, part of the reason why intellectuals in France have, since the Revolution and before, often played an important role in politics is precisely because of the unstable nature of political life and the often contested position of political regimes and dominant political forces. The battles between church and state also contributed to strengthening the association between intellectual and political activity. But if the Dreyfus Affair at the turn of the century is often taken as the moment of birth of modern intellectual commitment, when Emile Zola and others lined up behind Captain Dreyfus to defend him against a clear case of injustice and inhumanity, intellectual *engagement* became far more taken for granted at the end of the Second World War. The credibility of any pretence of intellectual detachment had been scuppered by the inability of the Vichy compromise to stop the progress of fascism.

During the Occupation the choice of whether to resist or collaborate with the Nazis was in many cases a decision informed by reflection, and punishment meted out to suspected collaborators at the Liberation was certainly informed by reflection and discussion as to how to define collaboration and then how collaborators should be punished. (This is not to deny the role of emotions and often passion in this process, of course, particularly in the more extreme cases of summary punishment.) As James Wilkinson points out (1981: 25), the construction of the Resistance against Nazi occupation did not depend on a draft, but on the (illegal) choices made by individuals and groups. As France emerged from the period of Nazi Occupation between 1940 and 1944, politics had such a clear impact on everyday life that many writers regarded intellectual commitment not as a choice but as a precondition for intellectual work; well-known writers had in some cases substantial influence on other sections of the population and they often believed it was their duty to overtly defend the legacy of the Resistance, and in many cases to promote the cause of the left as well. There was a less stable social and political order than in many other West European countries, so social and political issues were not taken as given, were real issues for debate. Among the most famous intellectuals, Jean-Paul Sartre, Simone de Beauvoir and Louis Aragon, each in their own way, believed that to write necessarily implied commitment. Jean-Paul Sartre of course became the committed intellectual *par excellence*, arguing in the editorial *Présentation* of the first issue of *Les Temps modernes* in October 1945 that it was the intellectual's absolute duty to become involved in political debate, to take sides:

> We intend to work together in order to bring about certain changes in the society we live in ... We place ourselves on the side of those who wish to change both man's social circumstances and the conception he has of himself. Also, with regard to social and political events, our journal will take a stand in every case. (Quoted in d'Appollonia 1991: vol. 1, 67)

In *Qu'est-ce que la littérature?* Sartre develops this same theme in nearly 400 pages, arguing that the writer is not only committed but also necessarily on the left (Sartre 1948). This was entirely characteristic of the views of the time, and the already radical tradition among French intellectuals, although often on the right between the wars, was thus reinforced after the Second World War. In the cafés of St Germain in Paris discussions took for granted the importance of political commitment, whilst also embracing the necessity of theory. Several generations of university students, teachers, journalists, researchers in various different spheres, and many others as well, were deeply influenced by these thinkers. By contrast with other countries in Western Europe, where an intellectual consensus emerged after 1945 (except among the radical few, who were often influenced by French thought), in France both tradition and events decided otherwise. For example the exclusion of the PCF from government in May 1947, the onset of the Cold War, the size and influence of the PCF, the fact that intellectuals of the right had been thoroughly discredited during the war, and the already established tradition of profound involvement in politics on the part of intellectuals at all levels, including in the education system, meant that taking sides was almost inevitable.

Certainly, there were famous exceptions to the practice of left commitment, most notably Albert Camus and Raymond Aron, who both believed, in the tradition of Julien Benda, that intellectuals' first duty was to the defence of universal principles and not partisan politics. In 1955 Aron, who was a leading member of the Gaullist Rassemblement du Peuple Français (RPF), published *L'Opium des intellectuels*, which lambasted intellectuals who had embraced Marxism. However, writers who distanced themselves publicly not only from Marxism but from the left as well were in a small minority and their influence among other, lower-level intellectuals (and thus the trickle-down effect of their thought) was relatively restricted. Sartre, by supreme contrast, had an enormous influence and became little less than an intellectual hero for tens of thousands of students, teachers, journalists and many others. When he died in 1980 an estimated 50,000 people took to the streets of Paris to mourn his passing, a token of the respect many had not only for his ideas but also his political activities, which were in any case inseparable. As the crowd made its way to the Montparnasse cemetery in Paris, where Sartre joined other major intellectual names of the past, mourners were paying tribute to the man who signed more public petitions than any other post-war intellectual, wrote the Preface to Franz Fanon's powerful essay attacking imperialism, *Les Damnés de la terre*, spoke to the crowds in the occupied *grand amphithéâtre* of the Sorbonne in May 1968 and acted as editor of the banned Maoist newspaper, *La Cause du peuple*. It was this political commitment that the cortège remembered and which made Sartre such an emblem of his time, more than having written even such major works as *Critique de la raison dialectique* (1960) or *Qu'est-ce que la littérature?*

The relationship between intellectuals and the state is central to an understanding both of the characteristics of intellectuals in the post-war years and more recently the changing place of intellectuals in society. The history of a strong, highly centralized state since 1789 and before was one reason for their behaviour and orientation, and in particular their attitude towards politics. The state had for centuries been highly interventionist in many aspects of intellectual life, a fact which stemmed in part from an insecurity about governments' ability to defend the regime or the nation against domestic insurrection or attack by other countries, as well as by a desire to modernize. In the post-war period, the tradition of close state control and intervention in the realms of education, the arts, national and local administration, and the media continued and indeed was reinvigorated under de Gaulle. This close control by the state over many areas of intellectual activity had the effect of confirming the views of intellectuals working within the state in many different domains in their mistrust and sometimes hatred of the activities of the state. The state was their paymaster, but it also paid the soldiers who tortured in Algeria, the Generals who attempted to stage military coups in Algiers and Paris, and the riot police who beat protesters in the streets. As with other forms of political activity, because of the centralized nature of the state (and thus not only the 'great' intellectuals themselves, who were almost invariably situated in Paris, but also many others who were generally unknown), the effect of commitment was clear to see, and therefore intellectuals felt encouraged to do more.

The memory of the role the state had played during the Second World War also served to confirm the correctness of intellectuals' profound mistrust and particularly their view of it as partial, rather than unbiased, as is the claim of a liberal democratic or would-be liberal democratic state. After all, between 1940 and 1944, to break the law of the land became in retrospect the correct way to have behaved. By the same token, acting within the law and cooperating with the occupier became morally reprehensible. Unlike unoccupied countries during the Second World War, to be in the victorious camp at the end of the war as an intellectual was to be *against* the wartime state, to be committed not to a set of official institutions of authority but to a set of beliefs, an ideology, which was often associated with the left, but was in some cases a Gaullist set of beliefs or in others Christian democratic, for example. The fact that the Fourth Republic was incapable of providing a stable political framework and in particular incapable of offering governmental participation for two major ideologies – Communism and Gaullism – during much of the period between 1947 and 1958 continued to undermine any reputation the state might have had as an entity which catered for the needs of the vast majority of the French. De Gaulle's state after 1958 had the heritage not only of anti-Vichy activism and opposition to the constitution of the Fifth Republic but also, as time went by, opposition to the maintenance of French Algeria, which the Fourth

Republic had defended so vigorously. Likewise, the activities of the Gaullist state, so associated with the General's authoritarianism, anti-Communism, anti-Americanism and nationalism, were also so obviously partial.

In many other countries of Western Europe, intellectual activity was less radical and less challenging to the activities of the state. Certainly, in Germany and Italy in particular, and to a lesser extent in Britain, Marxist and other anti-establishment intellectuals existed, often university lecturers and the post-1968 generation of university students. But in these other countries, by contrast with France, intellectuals often contributed from 1945 onwards to reinforcing the Fordist socio-economic compromise, were often more accepting of the social democratic status quo which had contributed to the more consensual political and social situation. Intellectuals in other countries were certainly critical at times of the actions of governments, most prominently perhaps over government attitudes towards the United States' war in Vietnam, and in a less impact-making way in protests against domestic policy as the economic crisis of the 1970s began to bite, bringing rising unemployment and public expenditure cuts. But on the whole they condoned the moderate cooperation which often took place between the state, employers and representatives of the working class, for example. The predominant influence on intellectuals at all levels, including teachers, journalists and researchers, was left liberalism, an outlook which informed not only their thoughts but their actions as well.

From 1945 to the mid-1970s in France, by contrast, event after event seemed to confirm the correctness of French intellectuals who condemned the exploitation inherent in the capitalist mode of production, the brutality of the state and the injustices of Western imperialism. The French wars against the liberation struggle in Indo-China and Algeria drove the wedge deeper between the activities of the state and many intellectuals, whether they were the stars who were respected and read by so many, or the university lecturers, schoolteachers, students, trade union and scientific researchers, or journalists. As far as the Algerian war was concerned, for several years left and liberal intellectuals' voices were virtually the only ones heard speaking consistently in opposition to the torture meted out to Algerian rebels, and in September 1960 121 prominent intellectuals, including Simone de Beauvoir, André Breton, Marguerite Duras, Henri Lefebvre, Michel Leiris, Alain Resnais, Alain Robbe-Grillet and Pierre Vidal-Naquet signed a petition which concluded:

—We respect and consider justified the refusal to take up arms against the Algerian people.

—We respect and consider justified the behaviour of French people who believe it is their duty to give aid and protection to Algerians oppressed in the name of the French people.

—The cause of the Algerian people, which is contributing in a decisive way to bringing down the colonial system, is the cause of all free men. (Quoted in Eveno and Planchais 1989: 275–6)

The newspapers and news magazines *Le Monde* and *France Observateur* (which later became *Le Nouvel Observateur*), as well as *L'Express* and *Témoignage Chrétien* condemned the war, as did publishers Seuil, Minuit and Maspéro. Social and political dissensus more generally served as ground in which intellectual opposition flourished, the two phenomena reinforcing each other.

The phenomenon of Gaullism greatly occupied the minds of intellectuals, in part precisely because de Gaulle was an intellectual himself, with a 'total' (and in many ways radical) philosophy into which he had put much thought, which he had carefully put into words, and which had indeed attracted a certain number of professional intellectuals. The most famous of these pro-Gaullist intellectuals was André Malraux, who for ten years was de Gaulle's Minister for Cultural Affairs. But as Gaullism used the state as a vehicle for often controversial change, huge and rapidly increasing numbers of less prominent intellectuals who worked for the Office de la Radiodiffusion-Télévision Française (ORTF), in the civil service, local government, public sector firms, in universities and in schools felt negatively affected by Gaullism. Intellectuals featured large in the uprising of May 1968, of course, partly because they felt directly affected by the excesses of Gaullism, but also because they regarded themselves as acting as the conscience of the French working class and other oppressed groups. Throughout this period, protests against the United States' involvement in Vietnam reinforced many intellectuals' hatred of imperialism and US imperialism in particular. But beyond these more obvious examples of commitment, as Pierre Nora has pointed out, the popularity of the anthropologist Lévi-Strauss must be seen in the context of decolonization, that of Foucault in the context of counter-culture of the 1960s and 1970s and Lacan in the context of the personal exploration which sprang in part from the movement of May 1968 (Finkielkraut et al. 1987: 53). The success of feminist intellectuals in the 1970s, such as Kristéva, Cixious and Irigaray, and feminist literary criticism in particular, would of course have been unthinkable without the rise of the women's movement after the events of May 1968.

However, the other side of the relationship between intellectuals and the state during the period between the end of the Second World War and the mid-1970s is that changes often initiated by the state were taking place which were in time to contribute to reducing the radicalism of intellectuals and in particular the antagonism between intellectuals and the state. Francis Mulhern points out that the relatively late socio-economic modernization of France meant that intellectuals did not become part of the second industrial revolution until the 1960s, and remained far less a part of the new capitalist order, more of an outsider than the intellectual in Britain or America, in particular (Mulhern 1981: pp. xiii–xiv). But as socio-economic modernization closed the gap between France and other countries, the place of intellectuals in society changed. The opposite of many aspects of the French tradition of intellectual commitment is a more technical, specialized role for intellectuals, and this is a development which has become more obvious since the 1960s.

During the years of post-war reconstruction of the economy and the tremendous economic growth of what Fourastié (1979) described as the 'Thirty Glorious Years', the state put substantial resources into economic planning and the expansion of education in order to facilitate economic expansion. An important part of this investment was put into the post-school education of young people to consolidate the socio-economic structures necessary to achieve modernization. At the sociological tip of this process, many gifted individuals from the *Grandes écoles* joined state bodies which provided the information for the decision-makers in the realm of economic planning, transport, public works, trade, education, the arts, and so on. Many *Grandes écoles* graduates rose to the top of the civil service, universities, publicly owned firms and privately owned firms. A particularly large proportion of cabinet ministers under the Fifth Republic have been graduates of the *Grandes écoles*, often coming to government via the top civil service; this was a sort of technocratic political commitment as well as, or instead of, an ideological one, a far more pragmatic orientation. Intellectual energy was thus put into more mainstream activities which were more consensual and modernizing, including the elaboration and implementation of the economic plans, for example. Among the famous, the activities of Jean Monnet and Robert Schuman in relation to both planning and the construction of the European Union can be viewed in the same light, as can the political activities of Pierre Mendès France, for example, whose influence in terms of promoting the importance of modernizing measures far outstripped his formal political success. In the private sector as well, highly educated people were needed to conceive of, design and market goods and services for the burgeoning consumer society.

But the process was far more broad than this. Higher education produced intellectuals of many types who helped in the process of reconstruction and the consolidation of a modern economy. The post-war period was, after all, a time of greatly increasing importance for the social sciences. Generations of university students from the mid-1970s onwards became the lower-level intellectuals who were more moderate in their outlook. With the expansion of higher education came the transformation of universities into virtual student factories, and these institutions, which were the enablers of the semi-Fordist economic modernization of France, became almost Fordist in organization themselves. Intellectual activity in higher education was thus more practically oriented and those working in these institutions became less universalist in their outlook, less intellectually ambitious, less confident of their position as moulders of the country's political consciousness. In short, the predominantly left-wing university lecturers and researchers, whose position was also undermined by the various economic crises since the early 1970s, accepted a far more pragmatic position.

Certainly, some of the new intellectuals were radical, as discussed above, but in stark contrast to the more famous politically committed intellectuals and their followers, whose appeal was so much more obvious, the relationship between many of these less well-known, but no less important, modernizing intellectuals and the state was far less one of tension but of mutual dependence, and there was often integration and blending into what Althusser describes as 'ideological state apparatuses', particularly education, the civil service and the media (Althusser 1971). Once the obvious excesses of colonial war and Gaullism had also been overcome, these intellectuals were ripe in the party political realm for a more liberal democratic ideological orientation, offered in the 1970s and the 1980s by the Socialist Party in particular.

The decline of the left intellectual

Many of the most important figures of the French high intelligentsia after the war were either not members of the PCF, including Sartre, Beauvoir, Lacan, Lévi-Strauss and Foucault, or became dissidents within the PCF, such as Althusser, Ellenstein and Balibar. However, the importance of the PCF for offering the activist backdrop to left intellectual life in the 30 years after the Second World War can hardly be exaggerated. The Socialist current had not convincingly stood the test of Nazi occupation (many SFIO *députés* had voted in favour of Pétain becoming head of state) and was unable to emerge as a consensus-builder after the war. The SFIO's active involvement in the Algerian war compounded its intellectual isolation. A significant section of the right was of course profoundly discredited by its collaborationist activities between 1940 and 1944 and the Gaullist RPF was soon associated with the extreme right. The PCF, meanwhile, emerged in heroic mantle from the Occupation and indeed its intimate association with the Soviet Union served to consolidate this image rather than detract from it; an opinion poll conducted in September 1944 suggested that 61 per cent of Parisians believed that the Soviet Union was the country which had contributed the most to the defeat of Germany, compared with 29 per cent who mentioned the USA (d'Appollonia 1991: vol. 2, p. 12). Many intellectuals were drawn to the PCF, either through an affinity with the *Weltanschauung* it offered, or a belief in the Soviet Union, two approaches which were in any case closely connected. Certainly, visits to the USSR brought disillusionment for some intellectuals, and the Cold War separated others from the orbit of the PCF. But for many others Communism, or at least a view of the world strongly informed by Marxism, became the respectable alternative to the immoral and bullying behaviour of the West towards both the Eastern bloc and the Third World.

In the trade union movement, the largest confederation, the CGT, was an effective channel for the views of Communist militants or members who were fellow travellers. This is not the place for a systematic exploration of the gradual decline of the influence of the PCF in intellectual circles, which is carried out thoroughly elsewhere (esp. Hazareesingh 1991). But it is worth mentioning the Khrushchev report of 1956 which went some way to revealing the extent of Stalin's crimes; the invasion of Hungary, also in 1956, of Czechoslovakia in 1968 and of Afghanistan in 1978; mass killings in Cambodia by the Khmer Rouge; the flight of the boat people from Vietnam in the late 1970s; and the rise of Solidarność in Poland in the early 1980s. Closer to home, the PCF was extremely slow to oppose the French war against Algerian independence in the 1950s. Although the Union of the Left in the 1970s offered a substantial new lease of life to the PCF, a period during which membership rose greatly, with many new members coming from the new middle and intellectual classes, the PCF ignored the opportunity to adjust, despite a flirtation with Eurocommunism, from which it turned fiercely back to Stalinism in 1978–9.

All these developments, well before the break-up of the Eastern bloc in the late 1980s, contributed in the longer term to the weakening of the influence of the PCF and Marxism more generally. At the time of each of these developments, groups of intellectuals became disillusioned with the PCF and its often blind faith in the Soviet Union. But publication of the French translation of Alexander Solzhenitsyn's *The Gulag Archipelago* in 1974 can be singled out as a particularly significant blow to Marxist influence in France, finally dashing for many the hopes that the USSR still inspired, although it was no longer the beacon it had once been in any case. Intimately bound up with this was the lack of democracy which prevailed in the PCF, which brought public criticism from some of its own leading thinkers.

However, as we have seen, Marxism did not rely solely on the strength of the PCF for its continued popularity, and many non-PCF Marxist writers explicitly or implicitly defined themselves by contrasting their views with Soviet communism. Particularly after 1968 variants of Marxist theory which firmly distanced themselves from PCF orthodoxy flourished within the universities and left publishing houses. The publishers Maspéro, La Brèche and Syros did well, bringing out new editions of the works of Gramsci, Mao, Trotsky and others, and publishing contemporary theory which was within a new left framework. Nevertheless, much of the underlying confidence for these ventures still stemmed from the fact that the Marxist project had mainly gained strength since the war owing to the PCF. Certainly, the PCF was often viewed by new left writers as undemocratic and no longer able to lead a transition to socialism. But firstly it provided them with a source of hope in the French (and therefore more generally Western) working class, which continued to join and vote in large numbers for the PCF, and secondly it provided a constant

point about which they could debate. The PCF might be an organization which had degenerated, but it was still a large and influential
party of the working class which was very much in the Communist
tradition.

Two other strands of the pre-1980s left need mention in order to
understand the subsequent decline of the influence of the left intellectual. First, the period after 1968 saw the growth of the far left in
France, by which I mean groups which were revolutionary Marxist in
orientation, to the left of the PCF. They drew theoretical legitimacy
from the writings of Marx, Engels and Lenin, but also Trotsky, Mao
and Rosa Luxemburg, among others, and contemporary analysts
such as the Belgian economist Ernest Mandel, the French Trotskysts
Henri Weber and Daniel Bensaïd, and the Third Worldist Marxist
Régis Debray. Far left groups, such as Jeunesse Communiste Révolutionnaire (later called Ligue Communiste Révolutionnaire), Lutte
Ouvrière and Gauche Prolétarienne were popular mainly among
university students, but had a greater influence beyond this milieu
than their counterparts in many other countries. These groups were
particularly theoretical in orientation, devoting much time to study-
ing the Marxist classics, the nature of the Soviet Union, the role of
the Western working class, the character of the capitalist state, and
so on. This orientation is explained in part by an eagerness to explain
the difference between themselves and the PCF, given that they
also often claimed to be the true inheritors of traditional Marxist-
Leninism. They were also highly theoretical because they needed to
demonstrate what distinguished them from each other, in a culture of
stunning sectarianism. Although they had memberships of only a few
thousand at the most, they contributed towards consolidating the
Marxist tradition, particularly among students and teachers. Indeed
for many university students Marxism was redeemed by the interpretations of these groups and non-PCF intellectuals (Hauss 1978).

The second, and in the longer term more important left current of
the 1960s and 1970s is what has been described as the *deuxième
gauche*, meaning the section of the left around the trade union CFDT
and the Parti Socialiste Unifié (PSU) (e.g. Hamon and Rotman
1984). In the years after May 1968, the CFDT attracted many people
who were influenced by Marxism, but who were also influenced by
and involved in the modernization of France, in a sense combining
the characteristics of those who worked within the state to modernize France and those who were vehemently opposed to some of the
activities of the state. This *deuxième gauche*, sometimes described as

a 'laboratory of ideas' was particularly associated with the notion of *autogestion*, or workers' control over production. Crucially, it also took into account the interests of the huge numbers of new white-collar workers, far more than did either the PCF or the CGT. Some leading members of the PSU joined the PS in the early 1970s, including Michel Rocard and Lionel Jospin, and had a strong influence on the Socialist Party as it was emerging from the doldrums in the early and mid-1970s (Kesler 1990).

In relation to the decline in importance of the intellectual within all these various strands of the left, the victory of the PS in 1981, its subsequent failure to produce the socialist goods, its electoral defeat in 1986 and finally its problems after further defeat in 1993 are all significant. Certainly, much of the left high intelligentsia was working at a level of abstraction which may have seemed well removed from the down-to-earth and sometimes mundane preoccupations of political parties, particularly the preoccupations of the social democratic PS. Even the CFDT's struggles around *autogestion* did not assume that it was immediately possible to embark on a transition to socialism, and therefore it too took the long and thus fairly theorized view. Also, there was already a degree of disillusionment among left intellectuals and a certain amount of recanting, in particular on the part of the generation whose intellectual development was influenced by the events of May 1968. (This is described in a lengthy account by Hamon and Rotman entitled *Génération*, where the authors trace the path of the 1968 generation during *Les Années de rêve* (volume 1) from 1960 to 1968 and then *Les Années de poudre* (volume 2) from 1968 to 1975 (Hamon and Rotman 1987 and 1988).) But 1981 nevertheless represented a moment of great hope for left intellectuals, many of whom had by 1981 become supporters of the PS, or at least believers in the idea that a left government would create conditions for a more radical change. For some, who had lost faith (or never believed) in the idea of a sudden, revolutionary break with capitalism, the PS was the best hope for the defence of progressive interests in France.

Previously prominent members of far left groupings had in some cases become integrated into the apparatus of the PS, such as Henri Weber, who went from the leadership of the Ligue Communiste Révolutionnaire in the early 1970s to being an adviser to the leadership of the PS in the 1980s. Serge July, formerly a leading member of Gauche Prolétarienne, was editor of the centre-left newspaper *Libération*. Régis Debray, a former comrade of Che Guevara, became a close adviser of President Mitterrand and published works which made peace with the political establishment (e.g. Debray 1990). For others, notably those still in groups to the left of the PCF, 1981 brought the hope of a wave of strikes that would push the left government in the direction of more radical reforms, which is what had happened in 1936. This, they thought, could be built upon to construct a left alternative again. For the PCF, it was an opportunity to participate in government for the first time since 1947. The consensual situation which emerged after 1981 was, as we saw in chapter 3, dependent on a lowering of the sights of virtually all sections of the left, including the sights of intellectuals who helped formulate policy in the parties and trade unions. However, the great moment of hope turned out to be a defeat for much of what the left had stood for. As we have seen, it was the Socialists, with the governmental participation of the PCF and the acquiescence of the trade unions, who introduced firmly neo-liberal economic policy, de-indexed pay from inflation, elevated the status of private enterprise and generally reformed in favour of capitalism. These were developments which would have come as little surprise from a government of the right, but were hard to accept from a government of the left.

In the 1980s, then, many of the remaining left intellectuals were either voluntarily silent as far as politics were concerned or became part of the moderate establishment. So much intellectual energy had been pinned on the victory of the left in 1981 and so much rigour sacrificed in its wake, in intellectuals' eagerness to support the new, governmental left initiatives, that once the economic crisis and policy U-turn had effectively consigned any governmental radicalism to the past, many left intellectuals had burned their extra-governmental bridges and thrown their lot in with the ailing Socialist Party.

In stark contrast to the situation in the three decades following the Second World War, and more in keeping with the orientation of intellectuals in other countries of Western Europe, many intellectuals thus became more conformist, and they became in Gramscian language the organic intellectuals of the socio-economic and political status quo, rather than thinkers who systematically challenged the ruling class, as had previously been the case. This did not mean that they shunned political pronouncement altogether, or even some protest. But political intervention tended to be general in nature, or on safe ground, or both. In particular, well-known intellectuals intervened around issues concerning human rights, both in France and elsewhere. One example of intellectual intervention in the political arena came with the drawing up of a list of candidates in the 1994 European election campaign in defence of Bosnia, a list headed among others by the self-styled centre-right intellectual and ex-pupil of Althusser, Bernard Henri-Lévy. (The list dissolved itself before the elections took place.)

The relationship between the high intellectual and society at large, which is dependent on a whole layer of less prominent but extremely receptive intellectuals, has also changed. The intellectual in the public eye has become less of a guru, less of a mandarin. Indeed old age and ill health took their toll on many of the old-style leading intellectual lights in the early 1980s, leaving gaping holes in the Parisian high intelligentsia: Sartre and Barthes died in 1980, Lacan in 1981, Foucault in 1984, and Beauvoir in 1986. Poulantzas had committed suicide in 1979, Louis Althusser was confined to a mental institution after killing his wife and he died in 1990. No one of similar stature has as yet replaced these figures. There is, however, a new generation of intellectuals-cum-media stars epitomized by Bernard-Henri Lévy, who is in the tradition of some of the post-war big names only to the extent that he receives (and certainly craves) much public attention. The striking difference between Lévy and the previous generation is that he is virulently anti-communist, indeed as confident in his anti-communism as he and his 'new philosopher' colleagues had been in their Marxism before recanting; in this respect the often painfully moderate, qualified liberalism of many intellectuals of Britain or the USA has still only a partial hold on the French intelligentsia.

Some writers have pointed to the influence of the mass media in the decline of the intellectual tradition in France. Régis Debray convincingly argues that the 'Media Cycle' is the most recent of three great ages of intellectual development in France (Debray 1979 [1981]). First there was the University Cycle, from 1880 to 1930, when the universities replaced the church as centres of intellectual authority and debate. Next came the Publishing Cycle, from 1920 to 1960, when publishers largely determined which authors and which ideas became well known. Since 1968, Debray argues, the media rules in a more absolute way than either academe or the publishing houses before it, giving most space to ideas which are usually superficial but attract the all-important large audience: 'the information apparatus has outclassed and therefore subordinated and restructured the pedagogic, religious, trade union and political apparatuses – and a fortiori, the cultural apparatuses' (1979 [1981]: 79). Alain

Finkielkraut also points to mass communications when explaining the general decline of knowledge and culture:

> At the very moment when technology, in the form of interactive computers and televisions, seems to be able to bring all knowledge into all homes, the logic of consumption is destroying culture. Words remain but they have been emptied of any educative value, of worldliness, of soul. The pleasure principle – the postmodern form of individual interest – reigns over spiritual life ... A jumble of fleeting and random needs, the postmodern individual has forgotten that freedom is anything except the power to change television channel, and culture more than a satisfied impulse. (Finkielkraut 1987: 150–1)

To an extent popular culture has indeed replaced 'high' culture, the visual and pictorial has replaced the written word, and with this development has come the tendency to simplify for easy consumption in an age where the consumer reigns. This certainly has played a role in the decline of the quality of intellectual life; the rise of the mass media, television in particular, is indeed part of the process of socio-economic modernization which has changed the political and cultural landscape of France so profoundly.

The re-emergence of liberal political thought

An important development of the 1980s and 1990s is the re-emergence of centre-right liberalism, in particular as applied to the analysis of politics and history (Lilla 1994). The liberal tradition in France is weak and since 1789 both political practice and political thought have tended to be organized around and concentrate on ideologies, on socio-political solutions to problems intimately connected with the human condition as a whole, which tend to be more ambitious, more all-embracing than liberalism elsewhere. In other words, there has been little agreement that the current way of organizing or thinking about politics is on the whole satisfactory and that the most important thing is to guarantee certain minimum rights. By contrast with Britain or the USA, but also other countries of Western Europe since the Second World War, such as West Germany, Sweden, Austria, Denmark, Norway and the Netherlands, there has been little room for political ideas which have as their organizing principles

such notions as the defence of the rights of the individual, free association and worship, private property, limited government, the rule
of law and equality before the law. Certainly, the Third and Fourth
Republics were designed in order to defend certain liberal notions,
as was, to a lesser degree, the Fifth Republic. Republicanism as both
regime and ideology is itself in some respects liberal, although to
what extent is a matter of debate. Likewise, some political parties
have come close to representing liberal beliefs, in particular the Radical Party in the late nineteenth century and early twentieth century.
Giscard d'Estaing can also be located within this tradition to an
extent, with his defence of individual rights and, broadly speaking,
social progress (Giscard d'Estaing: 1976). As far as philosophy is
concerned, in the nineteenth century such thinkers as Benjamin Constant, Germaine de Staël, Alexis de Tocqueville and François Guizot
were all situated within the liberal tradition. The Radical philosopher Alain is certainly part of the tradition as well, with his strong
belief in limited government, individual rights and private property.
More recently, the writings of Raymond Aron were also firmly in the
liberal mould, although he like other liberals had marginal influence
until the 1980s (Lilla 1994: 8–12). Very often in modern French political history, either the formal political arrangements have been obviously anti-liberal, during periods when there were authoritarian or
dictatorial regimes, or there has been substantial opposition to more
liberal political arrangements, often from both the left and the right.
In other words, political instability has been the norm, which itself is
not conducive to the milder-mannered characteristics of liberalism.
As I say at the beginning of this chapter, the Second World War was
effective in putting a stop to some vestiges of liberal thought, a
process already begun by the First World War and the 1917 Russian
Revolution.

In the 1980s, this situation began to change rapidly. Into the void
which was created by the sharp decline in the influence of Marxism,
Hegelianism and structuralism, and with rise of the more moderate,
consensual politics of the 1980s, stepped a series of influential writers
who are firmly located within the liberal-right tradition. Writers such
as Luc Ferry, Alain Renaut, Marcel Gauchet, Pierre Manent and
Gilles Lipovetsky became influential through writings which ten or
fifteen years earlier would probably not have been published and if
they had, would certainly hardly have been read (e.g. Ferry and
Renaut 1985; Gauchet 1985; Manent 1986; Lipovetsky 1983). Associated with anti-communism and more generally 'anti-totalitarianism',

the way had been prepared in the 1970s for these intellectuals by the so-called new philosophers, a loose grouping which attained its peak at the end of the 1970s and which included such people as André Glucksmann, Bernard Henri-Lévy, Christian Jambet and Guy Lardreau. Many of these young writers were former activists on the far left in the immediate post-1968 period, and their main claim to a rather brief fame was anti-communism and their condemnation of totalitarianism of either right or left, and their influence reached its highest point in the run-up to the legislative elections of 1978, when the Communist and Socialist Union of the Left for a time seemed likely to win. In the 1980s, in addition to the emergence of new writers mentioned above, who were explicit in the renouncing of the intellectual trends of the 30 years after the war, there was also a certain rediscovery of earlier French liberal writers, including most notably Alexis de Tocqueville and Raymond Aron, both of whom rapidly attained renewed respect. Reviews and journals sprang up and blossomed which had the declared aim of providing a forum for liberal ideas and as a conscious arena for non-Marxist and non-structuralist views. These included *Le Débat*, founded by Pierre Nora and Marcel Gauchet in 1980, and *Commentaire*, founded by Raymond Aron the same year, a journal now edited by Jean-Claude Casanova (Aron died in 1983). Also notable are the numerous American and British writers whose views became popular after being virtually unknown in France. These included Karl Popper, Friedrich von Hayek, John Rawls and the German-American Hannah Arendt.

One of the important new directions among the new liberal intelligentsia was revisionism in the study of the history of the French Revolution, led by François Furet. For many years, the historiography of the French Revolution had been dominated by Marxist or quasi-Marxist interpretations, which stressed the importance of socio-economic conflict, and in particular class struggle. Just as importantly, 1789 had come to be seen as a sort of ideal type of Revolution which had since been played out again and again in various guises and in various countries, most notably in 1917 in Russia. This dominant view among historians had helped to reinforce the legitimacy of the legacy of 1917 and Bolshevism, which was according to this interpretation in the same historical line of descent as 1789, and Jacobinism in particular. A former Communist himself, Furet and his team began to make a serious impression on French historiography at the end of the 1970s with a book entitled *Penser la*

Révolution française which included an introduction by Furet entitled 'The Revolution is Over' (Furet 1978). The meaning of this controversial and provocative statement was twofold. First, in late
twentieth-century France, where modernization and liberal democracy had according to Furet succeeded in eliminating ideological conflicts, the notions of revolution and counter-revolution were no
longer relevant, or at least far less so. Second, historians had always
accorded too much importance to 1789, in the mistaken assumption
that social and political history was more about sudden, revolutionary breaks with the past than about a slower and less dramatic evolution. Over the next ten years, Furet came to dominate both academic
and more popular debates about the Revolution, which were increasingly influenced by Tocqueville. Drawing benefit from the anti-communism of the time, he argued that the Terror of 1793–4, far from
being an unfortunate result of an event in a revolutionary period
generally to be applauded, was an integral and indeed inevitable part
of any revolution, as had been shown so tragically in the Soviet
Union and elsewhere.

In 1988, the year Mitterrand was re-elected President of the
Republic after two years of *cohabitation* with the right, François
Furet contributed a chapter entitled 'La France unie' to a book
about the more liberal democratic, consensual politics of the 1980s,
La République du centre. In this he asserts:

> For a long time the idea the French had of the Revolution allowed
> them to cement their political unity around their conflicts. It was the
> basis of their political perceptions, the issue over which they argued,
> separated into different camps and in the end attempted compro-
> mise … But in the space of 20 years two crucial phenomena have
> disappeared, namely the idea of the Jacobin state which under-
> pinned that of the Revolution, and the conflict between Catholics
> and non-Catholics which focused on the question of schooling.
> (Furet 1988: 53)

Furet's contribution to French historiography in some ways sums up
intellectual change in France. First, 1789 was no longer to be seen as
a revolution to be glorified and if possible re-enacted. Revolution
was no longer seen as the motor of history or necessarily progressive.
Second, the past was most usefully interpreted by historians of liberal persuasion who were less obviously politically committed; a
more detached approach was the way to achieve greater insight.
Finally, the French as a whole had, at least implicitly, come to these

conclusions as well, as demonstrated by the more consensual political and social climate of the 1980s. It should also be pointed out, however, as Robert Gildea has done, that the bi-centennial celebrations of 1789 were by no means a picture of harmony: 8 July 1989 saw a left-wing demonstration which marched to the Place de la Bastille, led by the PCF, the Trotskyist Ligue Communiste Révolutionnaire, the CGT, anarchists, Kanak autonomists from New Caledonia, Palestinians, Basques and Kurds. They marched separately from the official celebrations in order to make the point that the bourgeois governments of the West should in no way be allowed to claim as their own the slogan Liberty, Equality and Fraternity. The anti-revolutionary right also demonstrated, although in smaller numbers (Gildea 1994: 14). These public displays of dissent from the official celebrations, although they represented minority views and emotions, were a reminder that even in the apparently consensual 1980s conflict and divisions symbolized by the Revolution were not over, that peace had not entirely broken out.

A sea change has taken place in the orientation of French intellectuals to politics. Many intellectuals have become profoundly disenchanted with Marxism and the various parties and other organizations influenced by it. Instead of a belief in a better world for which there was not yet a model, but which would be some variant of socialism or communism, intellectuals have become interested in less contentious issues and ones which arouse fewer objections. Liberal critiques of society abound, which include defence of human rights and discussions about the reduction of poverty and injustice, but rarely belief in the possibility of their elimination. But intellectuals have not, on the whole, reverted to the extreme right ideologies of the 1930s, although of course the politics of fascism are present in the form of the National Front.

The modernization of France from a socio-economic and political point of view means that the tensions which had created and sustained a radical intelligentsia are less pronounced. But it is important not to take the new role of the intellectuals, as defined by themselves, entirely at face value. With the establishment of a left government and its subsequent move to the right, the decline of the Marxist left and the rise of political liberalism and economic neo-liberalism was so striking that it became taken for granted that the change was permanent. It was no accident that intellectual life reflected, albeit in an imperfect way, the politics of governmental and extra-governmental power, which had become the politics of superficial consensus, politics where there was an absence of hope for profound change. Certainly, intellectual commitment in modern France has many significant landmarks, including the Dreyfus Affair, the battle between left and right in the 1930s, Nazi Occupation, colonial wars and May 1968. None of these moments have been of immediate importance during the 1980s and 1990s and there has been no major revolt since 1968. On an international scale, the major ideological divisions which have dominated the twentieth century have declined.

However, intellectuals have not even begun to come to grips with the real nature of the emerging and massive questions which are likely to dominate the next century, although these will no doubt still be concerned with exploitation of humans by other humans, particularly North versus South, and also the exploitation by human beings of nature. These questions may well in time create the sorts of tensions which gave rise to belief systems and forms of commitment which are on the same scale as those which sprang from the 1917 Russian Revolution.

But even now French intellectuals fool themselves if they believe they have become independent of politics. Instead, they have achieved, perhaps temporarily, the somewhat uninspiring place which many intellectuals in other countries achieved earlier: they have learned to conform, to blend in with their ideological surroundings, to accept all but the most glaring forms of exploitation and deprivation, against which it is safe to protest without compromising one's liberal credentials. Suggestions about how to tinker with the present social and political arrangements are seen as legitimate, but bolder visions of a more just future for the mass of humanity are not. If France is experiencing the decline of the intellectual, it is in part because they no longer strike notes of discord, no longer offer hope for widespread emancipation, but confirm and conform to the moderate and safe politics of liberal democracy. They have, for the moment at least, fallen into line.

9
Conclusions

Democracy does not exist simply because the law declares individuals
equal and the collectivity master of itself. It still requires the force of the
demos which is neither a sum of social partners nor a gathering together
of differences, but quite the opposite – the power to undo all partner-
ships, gatherings and ordinations.

Jacques Rancière (1995: 32)

I have argued throughout this book that it is not sufficient simply to
record political developments, or even to order political phenomena
according to whether they are indicators of conflict or consensus,
stability or instability, progress or reaction. To do so is interesting
and necessary, but not enough. We also need to attempt to explain
the underlying reasons for general patterns of development in politics and related areas in order to achieve a greater understanding of
them. If the PCF becomes less popular, the PS moves to the right,
the Gaullists shed their traditional orientations and trade unions
become weaker, we need to take a historical and general view of
what is happening to politics in France, as well as look at the details.

I have argued, by contrast with what postmodernists might claim,
that there is indeed an overall logic to the way in which capitalist
societies evolve, and therefore to the way in which politics in capitalist societies change. It is correct to argue that there has been a series
of distinct but overlapping stages in the evolution of capitalism,
although this does not mean that every country inevitably goes
through the same stages, which is what the modernization theorists
of the 1950s and 1960s argued, for example (Lerner 1958, 1968; Coleman 1968). For one thing, the international social, economic, diplomatic and cultural influences of one country on another must be
taken into account when assessing individual countries' evolution.
Neither should we fall into the trap of crude economic determinism;

the development of the capitalist economy certainly plays an important part in shaping social and political developments, but actions of
individuals and groups also play a significant and sometimes determining role in countries' evolution. In chapter 3 and below, in this
chapter, I suggest that the framework of the regulation school is useful in attempting to explain some of the changes in capitalist societies
since the 1970s, although the regulationists probably exaggerate the
degree of change.

Certainly, one can only be struck when looking at economic, social
and political developments in the various leading industrialized
nations over the past quarter-century by the degree of similarity
between them. To mention just some of the most obvious examples,
they were all severely affected by the international economic crisis at
the beginning of the 1970s. After a period of crisis management during the remainder of the 1970s (and for some countries the early
1980s as well), almost all of these countries adopted similar economic
policies, influenced by neo-liberalism. Virtually all now have deep-
rooted social problems such as high levels of unemployment and
homelessness, which have often been compounded by these market-
led approaches. A significant minority of the population is forced
onto the very margins of society, a phenomenon which the French
aptly call *exclusion*. In the political sphere, the left has either been
marginalized or has transformed itself almost out of all recognition in
an attempt to lure back voters who came to believe that only the
neo-liberal right could defend their country against the buffeting of
international economic storms. Trade unions are weaker than in the
past. Finally, the extreme right has benefited from these developments and in several European countries it has grown significantly
since the early 1980s.

On a supranational level, organizations like the European Union
are constantly pushing member states in a similar direction. At the
time of writing all member states of the EU are trying hard to reduce
their public deficit in order to qualify for membership of a unified
monetary system, which itself will bring further convergence, if successful. One effect of this is to erode further some of the social welfare services which were provided by the state for the first time in the
post-war period.

In France, I have argued, there have certainly been some sea
changes in the political sphere since the early 1980s, which I have followed others in calling, broadly speaking, consensus politics, or the
'end of French exceptionalism'. There is little doubt that the country

Seymour Martin Lipset believed in 1959 belonged in his (certainly over-schematic) list of 'unstable democracies and dictatorships' of Europe and Latin America rather than among the 'stable democracies' of those same parts of the globe, or which Jean Blondel 15 years later suggested still had elements of a 'developing country' as well as a 'modernizing state', has become more similar both to its West European neighbours and to the United States (Lipset 1959[1960]: 49; Blondel 1974: 33–44). But once this change has been established, it is necessary to go further and attempt to understand the historical motor forces which underlie these changes. The overall concept I have adopted for exploring these changes is that of socio-economic and political modernization. But it should be stressed that modernization is not always beneficial to an overwhelming majority of the population, although it can bring real advantages to many people at certain times. Modernization has often been and continues to be a double-edged sword, as the increasing injustices and material inequalities of the 1990s illustrate, an age which is technologically speaking so modern. In the middle of the nineteenth century Marx, demonstrating characteristic skill in standing back from the immediate and the particular and highlighting broader trends, pointed out the profound contradictions of the modern era. In a speech made in 1856 which seems almost as apposite today, he said:

> On the one hand there have started into life industrial and scientific forces which no epoch of human history had ever suspected. On the other hand, there exist symptoms of decay, far surpassing the horrors of the latter times of the Roman Empire. In our days everything seems pregnant with its contrary. Machinery, gifted with the wonderful power of shortening and fructifying human labour, we behold starving and overworking it. The new-fangled sources of wealth, by some strange weird [sic] spell, are turned into sources of want ... At the same pace that mankind masters nature, man seems to become enslaved to other men or to his own infamy. Even the pure light of science seems unable to shine but on the dark background of ignorance. (In McLellan 1977: 338)

These are contradictions which may seem obvious and highly apparent, but which are on the other hand often overlooked in the complexity of daily events, in the constant attempts to explain more particular and less overarching developments. This is relevant to the more consensual politics of France since the early 1980s because the French have at least superficially become more accepting than they used to be of the unjust aspects of modern society as well as of the more equal, more just results of social, economic and political modernization. The benefits of socio-economic modernization are there, but so are the severe drawbacks.

Let us look briefly at two attempts to theorize the profound changes which are taking place in advanced capitalist societies the world over. Both are close to the concerns of this book in attempting to understand an apparent decline in political and social conflict.

The end of history

A famous attempt to understand the current social, economic and political period in a holistic fashion came in 1989 from Francis Fukuyama, who claimed that we were witnessing what he described as the 'end of history'. Perhaps one of the most significant points about Fukuyama's original article, entitled simply 'The End of History', was precisely that it aroused interest not only in academic and intellectual circles, but also in newspapers and news magazines throughout the world; there appeared to be widespread thirst for and receptiveness to ideas which sought to explain social and political developments of the late twentieth century in a global way, although much of the response to the article when it appeared was critical. This widespread interest continued after the publication in 1992 of Fukuyama's 400-page book *The End of History and the Last Man*, which was a further elaboration of his theory.

In a nutshell, Fukuyama's approach as expressed in the original article is that liberal democracy world-wide has triumphed over other ideologies, in particular hereditary monarchy, fascism and most recently communism (Fukuyama 1989: 8–12). Fascism had been conquered during the Second World War and communism was in terminal decline in Eastern Europe and elsewhere. Liberal democracy and capitalism were replacing these other ideologies and socio-economic systems and there was widespread consensus concerning the legitimacy of this form of government. Moreover, Fukuyama argued that liberal democracy represented the 'end point of mankind's ideological evolution' and the 'final form of human government', and therefore constituted the 'end of history' (1989: 4). Conflict might continue, he argued, and some states might remain with or fall back into some form of non-democratic government shaped by nationalism or religious fundamentalism in backward parts of the Third World. But there was no longer a viable, long-term alternative to Western democracy: 'the basic principles of the liberal democratic state could not be improved upon' (1989: 5).

When the article first appeared, critics argued that Fukuyama's central thesis was quite wrong because political conflict and strong ideologies were prevalent in many parts of the world and there was no reason to doubt that they would continue to be so in the foreseeable future. But as Perry Anderson points out, this sort of criticism in fact missed the point of the end of history thesis (Anderson 1992: 333). Fukuyama did not argue that conflict had ceased, but that no other ideology or form of government could compete effectively with liberal democracy and capitalism as practised in OECD countries. Fukuyama had thus covered this type of criticism in advance. More convincing critiques were elaborated in response to his view that liberal democratic states, and the US in particular, were basically just societies, where 'the root causes of inequality do not have to do with the underlying legal and social structure of our society, which remains fundamentally egalitarian' (Fukuyama 1989: 9). This is a point to which I return below.

When Fukuyama expanded his argument in book form and took into account the views of his critics, he once again sought to answer the question as to 'whether, at the end of the twentieth century, it makes sense for us once again to speak of a coherent and directional History of mankind that will eventually lead the greater part of humanity to liberal democracy. The answer I arrive at', he continued, 'is yes, for two separate reasons. One has to do with economics, and the other has to do with what is termed the "struggle for recognition"' (Fukuyama 1992: pp. xii–xiii). He goes on, in an account which he describes as a new Universal History, to explain that he takes a dual approach in relation to the 'end of history' argument. First, because of the impact of natural science, there is a strong tendency in the logic of economic development on a world scale for economies to develop in the direction of an advanced form of liberal capitalism, a 'final result' which is a process which 'guarantees an increasing homogenization of all human societies, regardless of their historical origins or cultural inheritances'. However, Fukuyama argues that this does not explain the evolution of government in the direction of liberal democracy. In order to explain this phenomenon, we must turn, second, to Hegel's non-materialist account of history, based on the 'struggle for recognition'. The distinction between animals and human beings, he says, is the existence among humans of non-material needs, in particular the need to be recognized as a human being. This, according to Hegel, is what drives history forward (1992: pp. xiv–xvi). For Hegel, history ended with the 1789 French Revolution; for Fukuyama, history ends with the advent of widespread liberal democracy:

> The desire for recognition, then, can provide the missing link between liberal economics and liberal politics that was missing from the economic account of history in Part II [of Fukuyama's book]. Desire and reason are together sufficient to explain the process of industrialization, and a large part of economic life more generally. But they cannot explain the striving for liberal democracy, which ultimately arises out of *thymos*, the part of the soul that demands recognition. (Fukuyama 1992: p. xviii)

I believe that Fukuyama's general instinct is correct, to the extent that he believes that important aspects of the post-war paradigm are coming or have already come to an end. Fukuyama's arguments are important, partly because they come the nearest yet to laying down a philosophy of history which seeks to explain in universal terms the apparent triumph on a global scale of capitalism and liberal democracy in the late twentieth century, particularly over communist systems in Eastern Europe. His arguments also have merit in that they attempt to reassert the validity of an overall logic to the course of history, which is at present a fairly unfashionable position to take up; analytical trends in the social sciences, arts and humanities are on the whole divided between those who argue from a more or less postmodern position that it is not possible to analyse in general terms, only in piecemeal fashion, and on the other hand those who work within an almost entirely empirical framework. Fukuyama also argues that there is a tendency for liberal democracy to emerge at a certain point in the history of capitalism, which I also agree with, although this is by no means always the case and, as Fukuyama points out, regimes which practise liberal democracy can sometimes slip back into more authoritarian forms of governance.

Fukuyama's argument is, however, seriously flawed in a number of ways. First, he makes sweeping statements about the extent to which liberal democracy has triumphed over other forms of governmental arrangements in recent history; as Anderson points out, it is highly questionable whether, for example, the thriving capitalist economies of the Republic of Korea, Taiwan or even Japan are accompanied by true liberal democratic systems. Certainly, liberal capitalism has firmly taken root in these countries, but Fukuyama himself notes that 'Japanese democracy looks somewhat authoritarian by American or European standards' and 'one could say Japan is governed by a benevolent one-party dictatorship' (1992: 240–1). Second, he is relatively uncritical of the tremendous harm which capitalism has done in advanced capitalist societies, especially since the beginning of the economic crisis in the early 1970s. In the 1980s and 1990s in particular, many advanced capitalist countries have seen the decline of traditional forms of left–right or industrial conflict, but with this have come growing disparities between rich and poor, high levels of unemployment, rising levels of urban decay and urban crime, poverty in old age, endemic discrimination against women, racism, and increasing ecological threats. These are no mean problems. How can late twentieth-century capitalism be presented as a benign form of social and economic organization which is able to offer the preconditions for the consensual and fair 'end of history' when it is so rife with inequality and so prone to structural crisis, with unpredicted – and apparently unpredictable – crash and recession becoming a way of life?

In a general way, Fukuyama has far too much faith in the ability of liberal democracy and capitalism to deliver a just form of socio-political arrangement. Liberal democracy is in fact a minimalist form of democracy, which purports to guarantee equality before the law but which does nothing to guarantee the right to more equal material treatment in terms of such fundamental considerations as health, education, nourishment, warmth and shelter. Thus the advanced capitalist societies, which have seen increasing disparities between rich and poor, high levels of unemployment, extreme poverty and rising levels of homelessness, are not deemed by enthusiasts for liberal democracy to be any the less democratic, simply because people still are viewed as equal before the law and are all eligible to vote in elections. In fact, one of the motive forces of individuals within contemporary capitalism, particularly the more neo-liberal variants, is this very inequality and the struggle for a better way of life than one's neighbour's. Inequality is an important part of the fabric of capitalism.

Interestingly, Fukuyama makes many of the same mistakes as the modernization theorists of the 1950s and 1960s in that he is over-optimistic, believes in the ability of liberal democracy to provide a 'final' and fair governmental arrangement, and believes the Third World is following in the footsteps of the advanced capitalist societies, largely ignoring the impact of advanced capitalist countries on the Third World. The modernization theorists appeared also to be claiming the ultimate triumph of liberal democracy as capitalism developed. There are other elements of Fukuyama's approach in what other analysts who arguably fit into a general modernization approach have said. Daniel Bell claimed that conflict over material considerations was less acute the more the 'knowledge society' became the norm (Bell 1973). In postmodernists' writings there is a distinct feeling that history proper has finished and that there is no longer any real logic to history, as there had been during the more truly modern period.

It is also worth mentioning similarities with the historiography of the ex-Communist French historian François Furet (see chapter 8). Furet too argues that one particular form of conflict – class conflict – which had largely determined France's history since the 1789 Revolution has both ceased to determine the course of history and ceased to capture the imagination of the French people, in particular since the beginning of the Mitterrand era. Put another way, for Furet history as it had been experienced and interpreted for centuries had ended (Furet 1978).

Coming as it did when the Eastern bloc was disintegrating and when it seemed that the West had finally won the ideological battle between East and West, Fukuyama's thesis appeared to explain observable facts within a sound theoretical framework. But on closer inspection it becomes clear that it is a superficially attractive paradigm which falls down largely because of excess faith in the ability of liberal democracy and liberal capitalism to bring about just, therefore stable, societies.

Fordism and post-Fordism: the regulation school

Parts of the argument expressed in this book are strongly influenced by the notion that it is helpful to view recent socio-economic and political developments in advanced capitalist societies as part of the process of transition from Fordism to post-Fordism. According to these theories, the economies of advanced capitalist countries are moving out of one phase, which is described as Fordist, into another, as-yet ill-defined phase, which is described as post-Fordist. There are, in fact, three major perspectives within the general post-Fordist literature, which can be described broadly as the *neo-Schumpeterian*, the *flexible specialization* and the *regulation* perspectives. In the discussion here I look only at the regulationists, who place more emphasis than the other two approaches on industrial relations and, to an extent, on politics and government; the other schools are more exclusively concerned with economic development. As I point out below, however, the more strictly political implications of even the regulation approach remain, as yet, relatively undeveloped. (For a discussion of Fordist and post-Fordist theory more generally, see A. Amin 1994: 7–16; and Elam 1994.)

Based notably on the pioneering work of French political economists in the 1970s and 1980s (Aglietta 1976; Coriat 1979; Boyer 1986; Lipietz 1985, 1987), the regulation project is an attempt to explain in particular the crisis of the world economy since the mid-1970s and more generally the dual tendencies of the world economy to go through periods of instability and crisis on the one hand and periods of success and stability on the other, including, notably, the post-war boom. Like Fukuyama's interpretive schema discussed above, the regulation school separates capitalist development into stages and seeks to understand the different economic and social parameters which determine the nature of the current epoch compared with the features of the classically Fordist post-war period characterized by economic growth, rapidly rising living standards, increased leisure time, cooperation between capital and labour, and consolidation of the welfare state.

Fordism as a dominant form of socio-economic organization, in the framework of these analysts, had its heyday during the welfare capitalist years of the 1950s and 1960s, when both the production and management practices which were characteristic of the American motor car manufacturer Henry Ford (in the 1920s and 1930s) were widespread. Lipietz describes the essential elements of the Fordist paradigm thus:

[1] The organization of production is best restricted to dominant groups (employers, technocrats), by extension of the Taylorist industrial model, which denies mere 'operatives' any intellectual involvement in the labour process. [2] Wage-earners and indeed the whole population will, in the normal course of things, recoup some of the productivity gains through a set of legislative or contractual

forms of regulation, in such a way that, as purchasing power
increases with productivity, full employment is virtually ensured. [3]
People should receive this directly through wages or through the
welfare state; but in any case in the form of money giving access to
traded goods and services. [4] Full employment and the advance of
mass consumption are the goals of technical progress and economic
growth, and the state's role is to make sure these are achieved.
(Lipietz 1989 [1992]: 11)

Meanwhile, the broader socio-political context of the post-war heyday of Fordism is described by De Vroey as follows:

> In most countries, the golden age was a period of social consensus,
> interrupted only by short phases of social upheaval. Capitalist soci-
> eties had not of course forgone their invariable features: exploita-
> tion and domination were still present. However, the two main
> classes, employers and wage earners, had come to a mutually advan-
> tageous compromise. Workers benefited from a stronger institu-
> tional and political collective position. Regular increases in wages
> gave them access to a consumption pattern undreamt of by their
> parents. Unemployment was low, while workers were provided with
> insurance systems and a network of collective goods and services.
> Despite revolutionary rhetoric, in practice this was seen as sufficient
> compensation for darker aspects of the wage status: submission in
> the workplace, increases in labour-intensity, exploitation. For the
> capitalist class, the advantages were obvious: the attainment of
> social peace and class collaboration, minimizing halts in production
> and gaining outlets for the increased production. The cornerstone of
> the consensus was the linking of real wages to improvements in pro-
> ductivity. (De Vroey 1984: 56)

These are, of course, descriptions of Fordism which are abstracted
from actual examples of national economies, but key elements of
them can be identified in the economies of many advanced capitalist
countries in the post-war era. In chapter 3 I discuss some examples of
the often consensual governmental and industrial relations arrangements of this era in Britain, Germany and Sweden and argue that
Fordism was far weaker in France.

Passing on to the aspects of the regulation argument which deal
with post-Fordism, the crisis of Fordism since the mid-1970s has
resulted in the slowdown of growth and in the recessions which have
become characteristic of capitalism in the late twentieth century. But
what has caused these profound crises? According to Nielson there

are four factors which have contributed to the crisis of Fordism. First, productivity gains decreased because of such factors as technical limits to efficient mass production, and resistance on the part of the organized working class to modern production methods. The resulting slowing down of investment compounded the decrease in productivity gains. Second, mass production spread to more and more countries and domestic markets were no longer large enough to absorb the ever-growing quantity of consumer products. The resulting internationalization of trade and increasingly global competition meant that national economic management was less effective, in part because foreign products were more prevalent in domestic markets. Third, as Fordist mass-production techniques cannot be applied to many parts of the service sector, in particular education, health and housing, this has led to social expenditure being increasingly costly relative to the cost of mass-produced consumer goods. This in turn has resulted in structural imbalance and inflation. Fourth, consumers gradually became less content with standardized products, which had lent themselves more readily to mass production. Instead, the post-Fordist consumer has become far more desirous of individualized items, traditionally associated with luxury goods. This leads to a segmented consumer market (Nielson 1991: 24).

Fordism has not, according to the regulationists, been replaced by a fully formed new socio-economic system. Indeed most analysts working within this conceptual framework are at pains to point out that to talk of 'post-Fordism' is not to describe a fully-fledged new era, but is a way of suggesting that the defining characteristics of the old era (Fordism) are now far less prevalent than before. However, certain characteristics of the emerging era can be distinguished. For example, the information technology revolution has enabled firms to introduce production techniques which rely on 'flexible specialization' in certain types of goods, allowing these firms to cater for the new patterns of consumer demand; this is described as producing for 'niche' markets. On a wider, political and institutional level, the passage from Fordism to post-Fordism involves: less regular, systematic collective bargaining, thus helping shift the balance of forces away from labour and in favour of capital; various forms of labour 'flexibility'; a move away from universal welfarism towards more piecemeal social safety-netting; a more modest role for the state in the management of the national economy and industrial relations practices, implying a greater emphasis on the market; greater social polarization along the lines of ethnic origin, gender and region. These measures are of course associated with the rise of neo-liberal policies since the end of the 1970s and generally with what is now described in a nutshell as the ideology and policies of Thatcherism (e.g. Jessop et al. 1988: 129).

Criticisms of various kinds have been levelled at the arguments of the regulation school and the most systematic have come from members of the British Conference for Socialist Economists (e.g. Clarke 1988; Bonefield 1993; Psychopedis 1991). For example, some analysts are dubious as to how widespread the characteristics of Fordism actually were in the labour process during the post-war period. Does calling the period Fordist not ignore the fact that the labour process at this time took a variety of different forms, not only one approximating to the ideal-type Fordist model? Also, according to its critics, Fordist literature under-emphasizes the increasing dominance of multinationals in the post-war industrialized world, and also pays too little attention to the commercial and financial sectors which have become so important during the period since the mid-1970s. Regulation theory has also been criticized for over-stating the degree to which there is a break between one stage of capitalist development and another; should the period since the early 1970s not be characterized as being one of adjustments within the same general (Fordist) framework, rather than a real break with what went before? Finally, does this conceptual framework allow enough room for the effects of social action, conflict, and in particular class conflict? Does it not dwell too much on system at the expense of examining agency? (A. Amin 1994b: 10–11; Clarke 1988; Bonefield 1993.)

It is indeed clearly necessary to avoid an economically or technologically determinist interpretation of the current stage in the evolution of capitalism, and it is important to stress that the basic mechanisms of capitalism are still very much intact. Indeed in some respects these mechanisms are strengthened by the current crisis, especially in terms of the fundamental ability of capital to exploit employees in order to extract profit. This is at the heart of the neo-liberal agenda, and many characteristics of post-Fordist methods of work organization serve to increase the power of capital over labour. I agree to an extent with critics who suggest that this approach does not give enough emphasis to the role of the action of individuals and social groups on the course of history and in particular class struggle. However, regulation theory does have considerable merits as a paradigm for attempting to account for the profound changes which are taking place in the structure of the economies and polities of advanced capitalist countries and relating them to the more successful period of capitalism in the quarter-century or so after the Second World War. In particular, it is useful in that it attempts to account for changes in the present scheme of things without resorting to explanations which paint an over-optimistic picture of the future, or make confident assertions about models of future development when it is clear that such models are only one possible vision of the future; as Jessop puts it, 'a well-developed and relatively stable post-Fordist social formation remains an as-yet unrealized possibility' (Jessop 1994: 260). Far more than other theories of socio-economic and political change such as Daniel Bell's 'post-industrial society' thesis, or Fukuyama's 'end of history', the regulation school, whilst working within a broadly neo-Marxist framework where changes in the economy and production process are ultimately attributed a determining role, protagonists do in fact stress the *openness* of the historical process. The societal paradigm in regulationist literature is, after all, bound up with institutional and, ultimately, political structures which provide a framework for economic development and which are themselves by no means determined solely by economic structures.

However, although the potential is there for more in-depth treatment of political characteristics, regulation theory, despite its ambition to sum up the socio-economic and political totality of the period it is dealing with, has so far dealt very little with the political structures of the current epoch. By contrast with Fukuyama, who argues that liberal democracy is a key characteristic of the era he claims represents the 'end of history', regulation theory is first and foremost an economic theory which deals in particular with changes in the labour process.

Some analysts working within a regulation approach have dwelled somewhat on other developments. For example, Stuart Hall has argued that social, political and cultural aspects of Thatcherism can be explained in part by reference to post-Fordism (S. Hall 1988). More specifically on post-Fordism and the nature of the state, Jessop argues that there is a 'hollowing out' of the capitalist state; the state becomes on the one hand more international and also more local (Jessop 1994). It becomes more international because with greatly increased economic competition on an international level the state is obliged to turn its attention to the question of the country's international competitiveness. If the state does not do this, it risks seeing its own country's economic performance suffer greatly, particularly with growing competition from newly industrialized countries.

The role of the state on a national level therefore changes, as its former, welfarist and Keynesian priorities become subordinated to those of international competitiveness, flexible production and generally to responding to the demands of the market, instead of constructing and maintaining the conditions of a demand-oriented economy, as the Fordist state had done. Other internationalizing pressures include global environmental risk, which requires international action and therefore also weakens the power of the state on a national level. It becomes more local, in part because, as some of the national state's attention is turned towards the international economy and its transnational institutions, the local and regional level becomes more important as far as economic regeneration is concerned, with all the implications of this in such areas as education, training, investment and research. Sabel argues that the state also becomes more local because the passage from long-run, mass production to flexible production lends itself to reorientation towards the local, a smaller and more manageable market (Sabel 1994). A result of this is that there are now more contacts and cooperation between local and regional states, again, in part, because of the diminished role of the national state. Jessop depicts what he calls the new, 'Schumpeterian workfare state' thus:

> In abstract terms, its distinctive objectives in economic and social reproduction are: to promote product, process, organizational and market innovation in open economies in order to strengthen as far as possible the structural competitiveness of the national economy by intervening on the supply side; and to subordinate social policy to the needs of labour market flexibility and/or the constraints of international competition. In this sense it marks a clear break with the Keynesian welfare state as domestic full employment is downplayed in favour of international competitiveness and redistributive welfare rights take second place to a productivist reordering of social policy. In this sense its new functions would also seem to correspond to the emerging dynamic of global capitalism. (Jessop 1994: 263)

Alain Lipietz, one of the pioneers of the regulation approach and primarily an economist, has also turned his hand to the political aspects of the contemporary period. However, rather than presenting an analysis of what the weakening of Fordism has generated in terms of political structures, he presents a political programme which he believes is appropriate to the post-Fordist era. In *Towards a New Economic Order*, in particular, he argues that given the changes to basic socio-economic premises, 'we must agree on new promises and projects; we must invent a new "grand compromise" which is appropriate to the new conditions' (Lipietz 1989 [1992]: 24). This programme is couched in fairly general terms, but includes ways of involving workers in their work via such innovations as: stressing the importance of workers' skills; giving them more control over their work; far shorter working time; increased leisure time; and emphasis on ecological concerns. On an international level, Lipietz argues, there must be a new, non-aggressive international economic order where debt becomes a thing of the past (1989 [1992]: esp. 144–5; 1994). In short, Lipietz's writing about politics is normative rather than analytical and perhaps pre-figurative – even utopian – rather than realistic. In stark contrast to his economic analysis, his approach to politics lacks rigour.

Despite the fact that relatively little has been written from within a regulation framework on post-Fordist political developments (with the important exception of the evolution of the state), and despite the other misgivings I express above, regulation analysis does provide a convincing general framework for interpreting the contemporary era. It is able to explain the transition from one phase in post-war socio-economic development to another without claiming that we are on the threshold of, or already in, a phase of societal development whose economic, social and political characteristics are entirely new. The degree of change and the extent to which regulation analysts feel able to predict change both remain modest and relatively open.

Theorizing change

The two conceptual frameworks discussed above take for granted the notion that it is possible to interpret social, economic and political developments in industrialized countries since 1945 in a global way and that there is a logic to the development of capitalism. Theories of postmodernism, whilst claiming that grand theories, or 'meta-narratives' are not capable of explaining the contemporary world and are therefore not conceptually sound, themselves also largely fit into the category of totalizing theories, or metanarratives. In addition, the conceptual frameworks discussed above are attempting to come to terms, in one way or another, with the fact that the period of relative social, economic and political stability in the post-war period has come to an end. This, in essence, is what I have been attempting to do in a more applied way in relation to France in other chapters in this book.

With hindsight, it is clear that most periodizing socio-economic theory about the present or the recent past overstates the case for newness of the stage under examination and exaggerates the speed at which changes are taking place. It is perhaps inevitable that proponents of new theories should overstate their case and also that some critics should be unhelpfully dismissive in the polemic which ensues. The point is to try and tease out what is valid in these theories and to treat with greater caution what is obviously a reaction to newness and perhaps extrapolation, that is, discard what is clearly excessive enthusiasm, without throwing the baby out with the bath water. There are elements of both of the theories discussed above which are useful in determining the nature of the current epoch. Both approaches are, to an extent, types of modernization theory, though not as crude as the theories named as such put forward in the 1950s and 1960s. Each emphasizes the importance of socio-economic changes on other historical developments. I agree that we have entered a qualitatively different phase from the post-war period, or are at least at a transitional stage between two phases of development. However it is wrong to interpret developments as they appear at present as generally positive, as does Fukuyama, among others. In France and in other countries of the industrialized world, including newly industrialized countries, many characteristics of the current epoch are most undesirable compared with the characteristics of the post-war period in the West. Whether there is superficial consensus or not, a key part of the developments over the past two decades has been increased social deprivation and disillusionment with mainstream politics, without there being obvious, progressive alternatives.

Returning now to the case of France, instead of suggesting implicitly, as some writers have done, that more consensual, more liberal democratic politics are necessarily more just, we need to take account of the fact that less polarization in politics, less participation in conflictual activities does not necessarily reflect more satisfaction with the way things are. It may mean defeat (perhaps only partial and temporary) of

forces which informed more conflictual politics in times past, such as
trade unions and left-wing parties, but not acceptance of the aspects
of politics and society people were struggling against. Indeed we
know that the French in particular, in what is again a more general,
international trend, are profoundly disillusioned with the centre-left
and centre-right politicians who are the main public representatives
of liberal democracy. According to opinion polls the French believe
that a majority of politicians are profoundly untrustworthy and that
they are less and less concerned with what ordinary people want; to
the question 'Are politicians interested in the concerns of the
French?', 48 per cent replied 'Very little or hardly at all' in 1979 and
the proportion rose steadily to 63 per cent in 1994. This left 47 per
cent who replied 'A lot or a little' in 1979, compared with only 36 per
cent in 1994 (Colombani and Portelli 1995: 57). This in part explains
why the French are once again voting in increasing numbers for parties of protest, especially the National Front. The period since 1981
may have been one in which some important conflictual forces have
been weakened, but it has also been one in which disillusionment
with mainstream politics has increased, which among other things is
a reaction against the widespread pragmatism of politicians of both
centre-left and centre-right. Indeed there is a new political vocabu-
lary to sum up the gloomy facts and the despondent spirit of the
time, including *affaires d'Etat* to describe numerous cases of political
corruption since the early 1980s and *morosité* to describe a general
spirit of disillusionment and a dearth of positive political ideas. Certainly, there is widespread belief in the importance of building a
stronger Europe, for example, but the plight of the unemployed, the
very poor and the homeless is never far from people's minds. To date
there has been limited public disorder relating to *exclusion*, mainly in
the socially deprived suburbs of large cities. But as the mainstream
current affairs magazine *L'Express* warned, the level of social and
political discontent below the surface in France indicates that French
society is 'like a well stopped bottle, but one which is full of a volatile
and inflammable liquid, a Molotov cocktail liable to explode at any
moment, as our past bears witness' (*L'Express*, 5–11 Sept. 1996).
Any conclusions regarding the decline of conflict in France must be
carefully qualified.

The debate around the nature of consensual politics also touches
in an immediate way on one of the most important notions in politics, that of democracy. This is not the place for a thorough exploration of its meanings and implications, of course, but democracy is

too relevant a concept to ignore completely. As Rancière suggests in the epigraph at the head of this chapter, democracy is far more than the formalities of participation in voting, open government, ruling according to the country's constitution, equality before the law, and so on. These are among the commonly accepted characteristics of liberal democracy. But for democracy to be realized more fully than in these very important but nevertheless limited ways, huge numbers of citizens would have to participate directly in making decisions and would need to become far more involved than the simple act of casting a vote every few years in favour of often remote politicians who go on to construct an even more remote national or local government. So instead of welcoming what in some respects is the depoliticization of the population in the form of consensus politics, instead of striving to achieve supposedly as neutral as possible management of society, which is what praise of consensus politics often implies, on the contrary analysts should recognize that profounder democracy involves participation by the people at every possible stage. It involves decisions which are arrived at after regular discussion by large numbers of people, it involves debate and disagreement, the right to recall elected officials if they become unpopular as a result of their actions. It gives rise to alliances and oppositions which evolve and dissolve frequently. As Rancière also comments:

> The folly of the times is the wish to use consensus to cure the diseases of consensus. What we must do instead is repoliticize conflicts so that they can be addressed, restore names to the people and give politics back its former visibility in the handling of problems and resources. (Rancière 1995: 106)

Such changes are certainly difficult to achieve, but because they are so difficult does not mean we should be content with far weaker forms of democracy. Nor is this to deny the advantages of liberal democracy over certain other forms of political arrangements. There is no doubt that to have the limited, formal mechanisms of political systems which have become characteristic of the West in the twentieth century are a real improvement compared, for example, with authoritarian systems where opposition parties are banned or restricted, where civil rights are minimal and intimidation a constant feature of political and civil life. With regard to France, the political situation since the early 1980s is preferable on the whole to the situation under de Gaulle, for example, when threats of mayhem, strong-arm tactics and close state control of the media undermined liberal democracy. But de Gaulle's rule itself certainly allowed for more democracy than the army would have brought in 1958 if it had succeeded in effecting a *coup d'état*.

The advantages of liberal democracy over other forms of political arrangements notwithstanding, another precondition for greater democracy is more equal distribution of wealth. Liberal democratic regimes often do virtually nothing to tackle the problem that greater power is intimately related to greater wealth in capitalist societies. The profoundly uneven distribution of wealth in advanced capitalist societies means that power is also extremely unevenly distributed. So until there is a more equal distribution of wealth, including of course ownership of the means of production and of property more generally, a profounder democracy will remain elusive. Indeed with growing material inequalities in many industrialized countries over the past 15 years, conditions for a profounder democracy have in this respect been undermined. But there are other, sometimes related inequalities which severely undermine the democratic credibility of liberal democracy, including inequality between the sexes, inequality according to ethnic origin, age and physical ability.

But is pointing out the shortcomings of more consensual politics and the passing of profound political conflict in France simply a form of nostalgia? Is it a way of glamorizing the times when it seemed that radical and democratizing change was both easily attainable and imminent? Does less conflict not in fact partially reflect the fact that for a majority of the population living standards are now higher, many people have more leisure time and formal politics are more stable? To an extent, yes. The modernization of French politics and society has resulted in fewer sources of discontent in some traditional areas of discontent. But the dwindling of conflict has not on the whole been accompanied by positive feelings about the status quo or even about constructing alternatives. Instead, there is widespread apathy. Fukuyama is partially correct to suggest that there now appears to be no alternative to liberal democracy, for the time being at least. But he is wrong to be complacent about it. The consolidation of liberal democracy has happened in part because the most radical progressive experiment in social, political and economic change in the twentieth century, in the Soviet Union after 1917, turned to dictatorship and tragedy, and grew to fit the picture of horror which the ruling classes in the West immediately tarred it with. The degeneration of the Soviet Union and the rest of the Eastern bloc into profoundly undemocratic, bureaucratized states, then the disintegration of the Eastern bloc from the late 1980s onwards confirmed the West in its feeling of superiority, of correctness, even though what is growing up in parts of the former eastern bloc illustrates the worst aspects of the ruthlessness of capitalism. The Soviet Union, greeted with such enthusiasm at its inception by the labour movement of many countries, has therefore also been among the greatest obstacles to the creation of progressive alternatives in the twentieth century. But because capitalism has won the battle against communism, this does not imply that liberal democracy is the highest possible form of democratic politics.

Without wishing to be falsely optimistic, it does seem as if the next twenty years might see quite different forms of politics emerging, which analysts will regard as constituting part of a new political era. The Fordist socio-economic and political paradigm appears to be exhausted without there being as yet anything constructive to put in its place. The anarchy of the market is the only alternative systematically posed so far by governments and political parties. In the advanced capitalist countries, neo-liberal economic policy has failed to deliver what Keynsianism had brought in the post-war era, that is, greater material wealth for large numbers of people and greater equality. Instead, the decline of traditional industries and traditional labour movement-based politics and industrial relations has brought impoverishment and despair for a significant section of many industrialized nations. In the Third World, wars, famine and huge movements of populations displaced by war are still common. There is also the re-emergence of religious fundamentalism, which has encouraged politicians in the West to begin to demonize parts of the Third World as it once did communism in the Soviet Union. However, the current state of affairs in the industrialized countries, at least, might not last. Neither the labour movement nor left politics are in terminal decline, despite the severe setbacks of the last quarter-century. New forms of politics are emerging in various countries based on alliances of Green activists, labour movement activists, feminists and the left. There is in particular growing awareness that the present socio-economic arrangements in the West are a serious threat to the ecological balance of the globe and therefore, ultimately, to the very existence of human life on earth. This may well be one of the routes which will be taken back into more creative, more humane forms of politics.

But the study of politics itself should change in some respects, or should at least be augmented in order to explore politics in a different way. At present there is a tendency for political theorists to remain firmly in the realm of theory and for analysts of political developments on the ground virtually to ignore theory in their examination of government, elections, political parties, pressure groups, and so on. The academic study of politics since the Second World War in particular has often concentrated on describing institutions and mechanisms of government, political parties and pressure groups. In France much political science either examines constitutional law, or is almost exclusively concerned with analysing election results and opinion polls. But the study of politics should be much more besides. Rather than attempting to separate it from other branches of the social sciences, analysts should recognize that politics stretch into many other parts of society. Societies should in fact be studied as totalities and can be understood only to a limited extent if broken down into (often falsely) separate component parts, labelled 'political', 'social' or 'economic'. Also, none of the social sciences can be value free, and to acknowledge this is in fact a more honest approach than that of the self-proclaimed, or at least implied, objectivity of some writers. To bridge the gap in a thorough and scholarly way between the more theoretical branch of politics on the one hand and the more empirical on the other is a challenge which should be addressed.

This also touches, finally, on the theme of responsibility of writers and teachers, of intellectuals, dealt with to an extent in chapter 8 of this book. The temptation is particularly intense at present to conform, both in one's actions and in one's writings, for much the same reason that other workers in other parts of society hesitate more than they used to before rocking the boat. But as people who are able to stand back a little and pose sometimes awkward questions about the contemporary world, intellectuals are able to speculate about and suggest change in a way which is more awkward for people who have less potential for intellectual distance from their immediate circumstances. As others have pointed out, this position and responsibility may not always be an easy one; it may at times be isolating and views expressed may be unpopular. But to write and speak without excessive regard for hostile responses has always been at one and the same time a privilege and a most uncomfortable experience.

In this conclusion I have touched on some vast and in any immediate sense unanswerable questions, which could only be adequately addressed in a separate work, or works. But in a book on something as apparently uncontroversial as increased consensus in the politics of France today, it is necessary also to pose some more overarching questions, to pose questions to which there are no immediate answers. When analysing any country, we need to point out the more obvious but also the profoundly and irresolvably puzzling nature of some aspects of politics.

Appendices

Appendix A Regimes in France since 1789

	Regime	Ended by
Up to 1789	Bourbon Monarchy	Revolution
1789–92	Constitutional Monarchy	Fall of Monarchy
1792–9	First Republic	*Coup d'état* (18th Brumaire)
1799–1814	Consulate of Napoleon and First Empire	War (Napoleonic Wars, abdication of Napoleon)
1814–30	Bourbon Monarchy	Revolution
1830–48	July Monarchy (Louis Philippe)	Revolution
1848–52	Second Republic	*Coup d'état*
1852–70	Second Empire (Napoleon III)	War (Franco–Prussian War)
1870–1940	Third Republic	Invasion (by Germany)
1940–4	French State (Vichy)	Invasion (by Western Allies)
1944–6	Provisional Government (de Gaulle)	Transition to Fourth Republic
1946–58	Fourth Republic	Quasi-*coup d'état* (de Gaulle)
1958–	Fifth Republic	

Appendix B Results of national elections in the Fourth and Fifth Republics

Table App.B1 Legislative elections in the Fourth Republic (% of total vote and seats)

	1945 %	Seats	June 1946 %	Seats	Oct. 1946 %	Seats	1951 %	Seats	1956 %	Seats
Turnout (% of electorate)	(79.9)		(81.9)		(78.1)		(80.2)		(82.8)	
PCF	26.2	161	25.9	153	28.2	183	26.9	101	25.9	150
SFIO	23.4	150	21.1	129	17.8	105	14.6	107	15.2	99
Rad., UDSR, RGR	10.5	57	11.6	53	11.1	70	10.0	95	15.2[a]	94
MRP	23.9	150	28.2	169	25.9	167	12.6	96	11.1	84
Ind./Con.	15.6	64	12.8	67	12.9	71	14.1	108	15.3	97
Gaullists					3.0		21.6[b]	120	3.9	22
Others	0.1	4	0.1	15	0.8	22			13.2[c]	50

[a] Radicals split into two factions.
[b] RPF.
[c] Mainly Poujadists.

Table App.B2 Legislative elections in the Fifth Republic (% of total vote, first round)

	1958	1962	1967	1968	1973	1978	1981	1986	1988	1993	1997
Turnout (% of electorate)	77.1	68.7	81.1	80.0	81.3	83.4	70.9	78.5	65.8	78.9	68.0
Communists	19.2	21.7	22.5	20.0	21.4	20.7	16.1	9.7	11.3	9.2	9.9
Socialists and allies	15.7	12.6	19.0	16.5	20.8	25.0	37.8	32.1	37.5	20.3	25.6
Radicals	8.3	7.8	—[a]	—[a]	—[b]					0.9	
Other left	—	2.4	2.1	4.7	3.6	3.6	1.9	2.2	0.4	1.8	3.1
Total left	*43.2*	*44.5*	*43.6*	*41.2*	*45.8*	*49.3*	*55.7*	*44.0*	*49.2*	*32.2*	*38.6*
Greens	—	—	—	—	—	2.1	1.1	1.2	—	7.6	3.6
Opposition centre	11.1	9.1	13.4	10.3	13.1						
Gaullists and allies	19.5	37.8	37.7	44.7	36.0	43.9	40.1	43.1	40.5	39.5	36.2
Other right	22.9	8.6	4.9	3.5	5.1	4.7	3.0	1.9		4.7	
National Front	—	—	—	—	—	—	—	9.8	9.9	12.4	14.9
Other	—	—	—	—	—	—	—	—	—	3.7	1.9

[a] Radicals allied with Socialists.
[b] Radicals split.

Table App.B3 Presidential elections in the Fifth Republic (% of total vote)

	Gaullist/Centre	1	2	Left	1	2	Green	Ext. right
1965	*de Gaulle* Lecanuet	43.7 15.8	54.5	Mitterrand	32.2	45.5		5.3 (Tixier)
1969	*Pompidou* Poher	44.0 23.4	57.6 43.4	Duclos (PC) Defferre (PS) Rocard (PSU) Ext. left	21.5 5.1 3.7 1.1			
1974	*Giscard d'Estaing* Chaban-Delmas (UDR)	32.5 14.6	50.7	Mitterrand Ext. left	43.4 2.8	49.3	1.3	0.8 (Le Pen)
1981	Giscard d'Estaing (RPR) Chirac (RPR) Debré (Gaullist) Garaud (Gaullist)	28.2 18.0 1.7 1.3	48.2	*Mitterrand* Marchais (PC) MRG PSU Ext. left	25.9 15.4 2.2 1.1 2.3	51.8	3.9	
1988	Chirac (RPR) Barre (UDF)	19.9 16.5	46.0	*Mitterrand* Lajoinie (PC) Juquin (PC – diss.) Ext. left	34.1 6.8 2.1 2.4	54.0	3.8	14.4 (Le Pen)
1995	*Chirac* (RPR) Balladur (RPR)	20.8 18.6	52.6	Jospin (PS) Hue (PC) Ext. left	23.3 8.6 5.6	47.4	3.3	15.0 (Le Pen) 4.7 (de Villiers)

Turnout (% of electorate)	1965	1969	1974	1981	1988	1995
1st round	85.0	78.8	84.9	81.1	81.4	78.4
2nd round	84.5	69.1	87.4	85.9	84.1	79.7

1 = 1st round; 2 = 2nd round.
Sources: Frears 1991: 225–7; *Année politique, économique et sociale*, 1993: 138; 1995: 179; *Le Monde* 1997: 43.

Appendix C Presidents of the Republic and Prime Ministers, 1959–97

Presidents of the Republic

1959–1969	Charles de Gaulle
1969–1974	Georges Pompidou
1974–1981	Valéry Giscard d'Estaing
1981–1995	François Mitterrand
1995–	Jacques Chirac

Prime Ministers

1959–1962	Michel Debré
1962–1968	Georges Pompidou
1968–1969	Maurice Couve de Murville
1969–1972	Jacques Chaban-Delmas
1972–1974	Pierre Messmer
1974–1976	Jacques Chirac
1976–1981	Raymond Barre
1981–1984	Pierre Mauroy
1984–1986	Laurent Fabius
1986–1988	Jacques Chirac
1988–1991	Michel Rocard
1991–1992	Edith Cresson
1992–1993	Pierre Bérégovoy
1993–1995	Edouard Balladur
1995–1997	Alain Juppé
1997–	Lionel Jospin

Bibliography

Abélès, Marc (ed.) 1991: *Faire la politique. Le Chantier français*. Paris: Autrement.

Aglietta, Michel 1976: *Régulation des crises du capitalisme*. Paris: Calman-Lévy. (Translated by D. Fernbach as *A Theory of Capitalist Regulation: The US Experience*. London: New Left Books, 1979.)

Alexander, Jeffrey C. 1995: 'Modern, Anti, Post and Neo'. *New Left Review*, 210 (Mar./Apr.).

Almond, Gabriel and Verba, Sidney 1963: *The Civic Culture*. Princeton: Princeton University Press.

Althusser, Louis 1971: 'Ideology and Ideological State Apparatuses (Notes towards an Investigation.)' In *Lenin and Philosophy and Other Essays*, London: New Left Books, 121–76.

Amin, Ash (ed.) 1994a: *Post-Fordism*. Oxford: Blackwell Publishers.

Amin, Ash 1994b 'Post-Fordism: Models, Fantasies and Phantoms of Transition', in Amin 1994a.

Amin, Samir 1976: *Unequal Development: An Essay on the Social Formation of Peripheral Capitalism*. Brighton: Harvester.

Anderson, Perry 1976: *Considerations on Western Marxism*. London: New Left Books.

Anderson, Perry 1976–7: 'The Antimonies of Antonio Gramsci'. *New Left Review*, 100 (Nov.–Jan.), 5–80.

Anderson, Perry 1992: *A Zone of Engagement*. London: Verso.

Anderson, Perry 1994: Introduction to Anderson and Camiller 1994: 1–22.

Anderson, Perry and Camiller, Patrick (eds) 1994: *Mapping the West European Left*. London: Verso.

Année politique, économique et sociale 1989, 1993, 1994, 1995: Paris: Evénements et Tendances.

d'Appollonia, Ariane Chebel 1991: *Histoire politique des intellectuels en France 1944–1954,* 2 vols. Brussels: Editions Complexe.

Apter, David E. 1965: *The Politics of Modernization*. Chicago: University of Chicago Press.

Apter, David E. 1987: *Rethinking Development: Modernization, Dependency and Postmodern Politics*. London: Sage.

Aradeth, Maxwell 1984: *The French Communist Party: A Critical History (1920–84)*. Manchester: Manchester University Press.

Armstrong, Philip, Glyn, Andrew and Harrison, John 1991: *Capitalism since*

1945. Oxford: Basil Blackwell (2nd edn).

Atelier populaire 1969: *Posters from the Revolution: Paris, May 1968.* London: Dobson Books.

Avril, Pierre 1987: *La Ve République. Histoire politique et constitutionnelle.* Paris: Presses Universitaires de France.

Axford, Barrie 1995: *The Global System, Economic, Politics and Culture.* Cambridge: Polity.

Azéma, Jean-Pierre, Rioux, Jean-Pierre and Rousso, Henri 1985: *Les Guerres franco-françaises.* Special issue of *Vingtième siècle – revue d'histoire*, 5, (Jan.–Mar.).

Azéma, Jean-Pierre and Winock, Michel 1976: *La Troisième République.* Paris: Calmann-Lévy.

Barnavi, Elie and Friedländer, Saul (eds) 1985: *La Politique étrangère du Général de Gaulle.* Paris: Presses Universitaires de France.

Baudouin, Jean 1990: 'Le Moment "néo-libérale" du RPR: Essai d'interprétation'. *Revue Française de Science Politique*, 40 (6).

Becker, Jean-Jacques 1988: *La France en guerre 1914–1918. La Grande Mutation.* Brussels: Editions Complexe.

Bell, Daniel 1960: *The End of Ideology.* New York: Free Press.

Bell, Daniel 1973: *The Coming of Post-industrial Society.* New York: Basic Books.

Bell, David S. and Criddle, Byron 1988: *The French Socialist Party. The Emergence of a Party of Government.* Oxford: Clarendon Press (2nd edn).

Bell, David S. and Criddle, Byron 1994: *The French Communist Party in the Fifth Republic.* Oxford: Clarendon Press.

Bell, David S. and Shaw, Eric 1994: *Conflict and Cohesion in Western European Social Democratic Parties.* London: Frances Pinter.

Benda, Julien 1927: *La Trahison des clercs.* Paris: Grasset. (Translated as *The Treason of the Intellectuals*, New York: Norton, 1969.)

Bénéton, Philippe, and Touchard, Jean 1970: 'Les Interprétations de la crise de mai–juin 1968'. *Revue Française de Science Politique*, 20 (3: June), 503–44.

Bensaïd, Daniel and Krivine, Alain 1988: *Mai si! 1968–1988: rebelles et repentis.* Paris: La Brèche.

Berger, Suzanne 1985: 'The Socialists and the *Patronat*: The Dilemmas of Coexistence in a Mixed Economy'. In Howard Machin and Vincent Wright, *Economic Policy and Policy-Making under the Mitterrand Presidency 1981–1984.* London: Frances Pinter, 225–43.

Bergounioux, Alain 1996: 'Les Fragilités du Parti Socialiste français'. In Lazar 1996: 237–62.

Bergounioux, Alain and Grunberg, Gérard 1992: *Le Long Remords du pouvoir. Le Parti socialiste français (1905–1992).* Paris: Fayard.

Bergounioux, Alain and Manin, Bernard 1979: *La Social-démocratie ou le compromis.* Paris: Presses Universitaires de France.

Bergounioux, Alain and Manin, Bernard 1989: *Le Régime social-démocrate.* Paris: Presses Universitaires de France.

Berman, Marshall 1983: *All That is Solid Melts into Air.* London: Verso.

Berry, David 1994: 'Dossier: "A gauche de la gauche" – Towards an Alternative Left?' *Modern & Contemporary France*, NS 2 (1), 123–30.

Berstein, Gisèle and Berstein, Serge 1987: *La Troisième République.* Paris: M.A. Editions.

Berstein, Serge 1989: *La France de l'expansion*. I. *La République gaullienne 1958–1969*. Paris: Seuil.

Berstein, Serge 1991: 'Political Consensus in 20th Century France'. In Serge Berstein and Peter Morris, *Political Consensus in France and Britain*, Studies in European Culture and Society, 5. European Research Centre, Loughborough University of Technology.

Berstein, Serge 1992: 'La Politique sociale des Républicains'. In Berstein and Rudelle 1992.

Berstein, Serge and Rudelle, Odile (eds) 1992: *Le Modèle républicain*. Paris: Presses Universitaires de France.

Best, Geoffrey (ed.) 1988: *The Permanent Revolution: The French Revolution and its Legacy 1789–1989*. London: Fontana.

Biffaud, Olivier 1988: 'Le Parti communiste. Piège et déclin'. In *Bilan du septennat. L'Alternance dans l'alternance*, in *Le Monde* 1995: 71–2.

Birnbaum, Pierre 1977: *Les Sommets de l'Etat: essai sur l'élite au pouvoir*. Paris: Seuil.

Birnbaum, Pierre 1982: *The Heights of Power: An Essay on the Power Elite in France*. Chicago and London: University of Chicago Press. (Translation by Arthur Goldhammer of *Les Sommets de l'Etat: Essai sur l'élite au pouvoir*. Paris: Seuil, 1977.)

Blondel, Jean 1974: *The Government of France*. London: Methuen.

Bonefield, Werner 1993: 'Crisis of Theory: Bob Jessop's Theory of Capitalist Reproduction'. *Capital and Class*, 50, 22–47.

Bonté, Louis-Michel and Duchadeuil, Pascal 1988: *Eloge de la volonté à l'usage d'une France incertaine*. Paris: Editions Universitaires.

Bornstein, Stephen, Held, David and Krieger, Joel 1984: *The State in Capitalist Europe*. London: Allen and Unwin.

Bottomore, Tom 1983: 'Social Democracy'. In Tom Bottomore, Laurence Harris, V. G. Kiernan and Ralph Miliband, *A Dictionary of Marxist Thought*. Oxford: Basil Blackwell, 441–4.

Bourdieu, Pierre 1988: *Homo Academicus*. Cambridge: Polity.

Bourlanges, Jean-Louis 1988: *Droite année zéro*. Paris: Flammarion.

Bousquet, Gilles 1992: 'Où en est-on de mai 68?' *Contemporary French Civilization*, 16 (1: Winter/Spring), 68–89.

Bowd, Gavin 1994: 'C'est la lutte initiale': Steps in the Realignment of the French Left'. *New Left Review*, 206 (July/Aug.), 71–85.

Boyer, Robert 1986: *La Flexibilité du travail en Europe*. Paris: Presses Universitaires de France.

Boyer, Robert and Durand, Jean-Pierre 1993: *L'Après-fordisme*. Paris: Syros.

Braudel, Fernand and Labrousse, Ernest 1982: *Histoire économique et sociale de la France,* vol. 3. *Années 1950 à nos jours*. Paris: Presses Universitaires de France.

Braun, Christina von (producer) (1990), *De Gaulle and France*, Part III. *Challenging the World (1962–1970)*. Documentary shown on BBC Television (BBC2) on 27 Jan. 1991.

Bridgford, Jeff 1982: 'The Integration of Trade Union Confederations into the Social and Political System'. In Philip Cerny (ed.), *Social Movements and Protest in France*. London: Frances Pinter.

Brohm, Jean-Marie, Touvais, Jean-Yves, Frank, Pierre (eds) 1974: *Le Gaullisme, et après? Etat fort et fascisation*. Paris: Maspéro.

Bunel, Jean and Saglio, Jean 1979: *L'Action patronale, du CNPF au petit patron*. Paris: Presses Universitaires de France.

Butler, Anthony 1993: 'The End of the Post-War Consensus: Reflections on the Scholarly uses of Political Rhetoric', *Political Quarterly*, 6 (4: Oct.–Dec.), 435–46.

Callinicos, Alex 1989: *Against Postmodernism*. Cambridge: Polity.

Callinicos, Alex 1990: 'Reactionary Postmodernism?' In Roy Boyne and Ali Rattansi (eds), *Postmodernism and Society*. Basingstoke: Macmillan.

Capdevielle, Jacques and Mouriaux, René 1988: *Mai 68: l'entre-deux de la modernité. Histoire de trente ans*. Paris: Presses de la Fondation Nationale des Sciences Politiques.

Carrillo, Santiago 1977: *Eurocommunism and the State*. London: Lawrence and Wishart.

Castles, Francis 1975: 'Swedish Social Democracy: The Conditions of Success'. *Political Quarterly*, 46 (2).

Castoriadis, Cornelius 1988: 'Les Mouvenments des années soixante'. In Morin, Lefort and Castoriadis 1988.

Cayrol, Roland and Perrineau, Pascal 1988: 'La Défaite du politique'. In Roland Cayrol and Pascal Perrineau (eds), *Le Guide du pouvoir*. Paris: Editions Jean-François Doumic.

Cerny, Philip 1980: *The Politics of Grandeur: Ideological Aspects of de Gaulle's Foreign Policy*. Cambridge: Cambridge University Press.

Cerny, Philip 1982: 'Gaullism, Advanced Capitalism and the Fifth Republic'. In David. S. Bell (ed.), *Contemporary French Political Parties*. London: Croom Helm.

Cerny, Philip 1988: 'Modernisation and the Fifth Republic'. In John Gaffney, *France and Modernisation*. Aldershot: Gower.

CEVIPOV (Centre d'étude de la vie politique française) 1995 (Sept.): *Les Electorats sous la Vème République. Données d'enquêtes 1958–1995*. Paris: FNSP/CNRS.

Charlot, Jean 1971: *The Gaullist Phenomenon: The Gaullist Movement in the Fifth Republic*. London: Allen and Unwin. (Translated from *Le Phénomène gaulliste* Paris: Fayard, 1970.)

Choisel, Francis 1987: *Bonapartisme et gaullisme*. Paris: Albatros.

Christiansen, Niels Finn 1994: 'Denmark: End of an Idyll?' In Anderson and Camiller 1994: 77–101.

Clapham, John H. 1923: *The Economic Development of France and Germany, 1815–1914*. Cambridge: Cambridge University Press (2nd edn).

Clarke, Simon 1988: 'Overaccumulation, Class Struggle and the Regulation Approach'. *Capital and Class*, 36, 59–92.

Coates, David 1983: 'Reformism'. In Tom Bottomore, Laurence Harris, V. G. Kiernan and Ralph Miliband, *A Dictionary of Marxist Thought*, Oxford: Basil Blackwell, 409–11.

Cohen, Samy 1991: 'Entretien: François le Gaullien et Mitterrand l'Européen'. *L'Histoire*, 143, 30–7.

Cohen-Tanugi, Laurent 1989: *La Métamorphose de la démocratie*. Paris: Odile Jacob.

Cole, Alistair (ed.) 1990: *French Political Parties in Transition*. Aldershot: Dartmouth.

Cole, Alistair and Campbell, Peter 1989: *French Electoral Systems and Elections since 1789*. Aldershot: Gower.

Coleman, James S. 1968: 'Modernization: Politicial Aspects'. In David L. Sills, *International Encyclopedia of the Social Sciences*, Basingstoke and New York: Macmillan and Free Press, vol. 10, 395–401.

Colombani, Jean-Marie and Portelli, Hugues 1995: *Le Double Septennat de François Mitterrand*. Paris: Grasset.

Coriat, Benjamin 1979: *L'Atelier et le chronomètre*. Paris: Christian Bourgois.

Crewe, Ivor 1991: 'Labor Force Changes, Working Class Decline, and the Labor Vote: Social and Electoral Change in Contemporary Britain'. In Frances Fox Piven (ed.), *Labour Parties in Postindustrial Societies*. Cambridge: Polity, 20–46.

Crosland, Anthony 1963: *The Future of Socialism*. New York: Schocken. (1st edn 1956).

Crouch, Colin and Pizzorno, Alessandro (eds) 1978: *The Re-emergence of Class Conflict in Western Europe since 1968*, 2 vols. Basingstoke: Macmillan.

Crozier, Michel 1970: *La Société bloquée*. Paris: Seuil.

Dagnaud, Monique and Mehl, Dominique 1990: *L'Elite rose*. Paris: Ramsay.

Dahl, Robert A. 1966: *Political Oppositions in Western Democracies*. New Haven: Yale University Press.

Dahrendorf, Ralf 1987: 'Das Elend der Sozialdemokratie'. *Merkur*, Dec.

Daley, Anthony (ed.) 1996: *The Mitterrand Era: Policy Alternatives and Political Mobilization in France*. Basingstoke: Macmillan.

Dalton, Russell J. 1989 'The German Voter'. In Gordon Smith, William E. Paterson and Peter H. Merkl (eds) 1989: *Developments in West German Politics*. Basingstoke: Macmillan, 99–121.

Debray, Régis 1978: *Modeste contribution aux discours et cérémonies officielles du dixième anniversaire*. Paris: François Maspéro. (Extracts from pp. 1–45 and 87–90 translated by John Howe as 'A Modest Contribution to the Rites and Ceremonies of the Tenth Anniversary'. *New Left Review*, 115 (May/June 1979), 45–65.)

Debray, Régis 1979: *Le Pouvoir intellectuel en France*. Paris: Editions Ramsay. (Translated as *Teachers, Writers, Celebrities. The Intellectuals of Modern France*. London: New Left Books/Verso, 1981.)

Debray, Régis 1989: *Que vive la République*. Paris: Emile Jacob.

Debray, Régis 1990: *A demain de Gaulle!* Paris: Gallimard. (Translated by J. Howe as *Charles de Gaulle: Futurist of the Nation*. London: Verso, 1994.)

De Gaulle, Charles 1954: *Mémoires de Guerre. L'Appel (1940–1942)*. Paris: Plon.

De Gaulle, Charles 1970a: 'Discours de Bayeux prononcé par le général de Gaulle à Bayeux, le 16 juin 1946'. In *Discours et Messages*, vol. 2. *Dans l'attente (février 1946–avril 1958)*, Paris: Plon.

De Gaulle, Charles 1970b: *Discours et Messages*, vol. 4. *Pour l'effort, août 1962–décembre 1965*. Paris: Plon.

De Gaulle, Charles 1970c: *Discours et Messages*, vol. 5. *Vers le terme (janvier 1966–avril 1969)*. Paris: Plon.

Delale, Alain and Ragache, Gilles 1978: *La France de 68*. Paris: Seuil.

Demichel, Francine 1982: *La Lutte idéologique dans la France contemporaine*. Paris: LGDJ.

De Vroey, Michel 1984: 'A Regulation Approach Interpretation of Contemporary Crisis'. *Capital and Class*, 23, 45–66.

Dreyfus, François-G. 1982: *De Gaulle et le Gaullisme*. Paris: Presses Universitaires de France.

Dreyfus, Michel 1995: *Histoire de la C.G.T.* Brussels: Editions Complexe.

Duhamel, Alain 1983: 'Un consensus hexagonal éclatant', *Le Monde*, 8–9 May.

Duhamel, Alain 1989: *Les Habits neufs de la politique*. Paris: Flammarion.

Dutton, David 1991: *British Politics since 1945*. Oxford: Basil Blackwell.

Duverger, Maurice 1965: *Institutions politiques et droit constitutionnel*. Paris: Presses Universitaires de France; 8th edn 1968.

Duverger, Maurice 1988: *La Nostalgie de l'impuissance*. Paris: Albin Michel.

Eck, Jean-François 1990: *Histoire de l'économie française depuis 1945*. Paris: Armand Colin (2nd edn).

Ehrmann, Henry W. 1968: *Politics in France*. Boston: Little, Brown.

Elam, Mark 1994: 'Puzzling out the Post-Fordist Debate: Technology, Markets and Institutions'. In A. Amin 1994: 43–70.

Elliot, Gregory 1994: 'Contentious Commitments: French Intellectuals and Politics'. *New Left Review* 206, 110–24.

Eveno, Patrick and Planchais, Jean 1989: *La Guerre d'Algérie*. Paris: Le Monde/La Découverte.

Fauvet, Jacques 1960: *The Cockpit of France*. London: Harvill Press. (Tr. Nancy Pearson from *La France déchirée*. Paris: Fayard, 1957.)

Favier, Pierre and Martin-Roland, Michel 1990: *La Décennie Mitterrand. 1. Les Ruptures (1981–1984)*. Paris: Seuil.

Ferner, Anthony and Hyman, Richard (eds) 1992: *Industrial Relations in the New Europe*. Oxford: Basil Blackwell.

Ferry, Jean-Marc 1985: 'Modernisation et consensus'. *Esprit*, May, 13–28. Extracts translated by Franklin Philip as 'Modernization and consensus', in Lilla 1994: 201–8.

Ferry, Luc and Renaut, Alain 1985: *La Pensée 68. Essai sur l'anti-humanisme contemporain*. Paris: Gallimard.

Ferry, Luc and Renaut, Alain 1987: *68–86. Itinéraires de l'individu*. Paris: Gallimard.

Finkielkraut, Alain 1987: *La Défaite de la pensée*. Paris: Gallimard.

Finkielkraut, Alain 1991: 'L'Abandon des principes révolutionnaires'. *L'Histoire*, 143, 63.

Finkielkraut, Alain, Nora, Pierre, Ory, Pascal, Revel, Jacques and Winock, Michel 1987: 'Changement intellectuel ou changement des intellectuels?' *Le Débat*, May–Sept., 40–58.

Flockton, Christopher and Kofman, Eleonore 1989: *France*. London: Paul Chapman Publishing.

Fohlen, Claude 1976. 'France 1920–1970'. In Carlo Cipolla (ed.), *The Fontana Economic History of Europe*. vol. 6, *Contemporary Economies. Part One*. London: Fontana, 128–79.

Forbes, Jill and Hewlett, Nick, with Nectoux, François and Reymond, Anne 1994: *Contemporary France: Essays and Texts on Politics, Economics and Society*. London: Longman.

Foucault, Michel 1986: 'What is Enlightenment?' In Paul Rabinow (ed.), *The Foucault Reader*. Harmondsworth: Penguin, 32–50.

Fourastié, Jean 1979: *Les Trente Glorieuses, ou la Révolution invisible de 1946 à 1975*. Paris: Fayard.

Frank, André Gunder 1978: *Dependent Accumulation and Underdevelopment*. Basingstoke: Macmillan.

Frears, John R. 1972: 'Conflict in France: The Decline and Fall of a Stereotype'. *Political Studies*, 20 (1), 31–41.

Frears, John R. 1981: *France in the Giscard Presidency*. London: Allen and Unwin.

Frears, John R. 1991: *Parties and Voters in France*. London: Hurst.

Fukuyama, Francis 1989: 'The End of History'. *The National Interest*, 16, 3–18.

Fukuyama, Francis 1992: *The End of History and the Last Man*. New York and London: Free Press and Hamish Hamilton.

Fulbrook, Mary 1992: *The Two Germanies, 1945–1990. Problems of Interpretation*. Basingstoke: Macmillan.

Furet, François 1978: *Penser la Révolution française*. Paris: Gallimard. (Translated by Elborg Foster as *Interpreting the French Revolution*. Cambridge and Paris: Cambridge University Press, 1981.)

Furet, François 1988: 'La France unie . . .'. In Furet, Julliard and Rosanvallon 1988: 13–66.

Furet, François, Julliard, Jacques and Rosanvallon, Pierre 1988: *La République du centre*. Paris: Calmann-Levy.

Galbraith, John K. 1977: *The Affluent Society*. London: Deutsch.

Gallo, Max 1983. 'Les Intellectuels, la politique et la modernité'. *Le Monde*, 26 July, 7. (Part of series entitled 'Le Silence des intellectuels'.)

Gauchet, Marcel 1985: *Le Désenchantement du monde*. Paris: Gallimard.

Gauchet, Marcel, 1993: 'La droite et la gauche'. In Pierre Nora, *Les Lieux de mémoire*, vol. 3. *Les France. Conflits et partages*. Paris: Gallimard.

Gauron, André 1983: *Histoire économique et sociale de la cinquième république*, vol. 1. *Le Temps des modernistes*. Paris: La Découverte/Maspéro.

Gaveau, André 1978: *De l'autre côté de barricades*, Paris, Jean-Claude Simoën.

Gélédan, Alain 1993: *Le Bilan économique des années Mitterrand, 1981–1994*. Paris: Le Monde-Editions.

Le Genre humain 1990: *Le Consensus, nouvel opium?* Special issue, no. 22.

Giddens, Anthony 1991: *The Consequences of Modernity*. Cambridge: Polity.

Giddens, Anthony 1994: *Beyond Left and Right. The Future of Radical Politics*. Cambridge: Polity.

Gildea, Robert 1994: *The Past in French History*. New Haven: Yale University Press.

Giscard d'Estaing, Valéry 1976: *La Démocratie française*. Paris: Fayard.

Godin, Emmanuel 1996: 'Le Néo-libéralisme à la française: une exception?' *Modern and Contemporary France*, NS 4 (1), 61–70.

Gorz, André 1980: *Adieux au prolétariat*. Paris: Editions Galilée. (Translated by Mike Sonenscher as *Farewell to the Working Class*, London: Pluto Press, 1982.)

Gramsci, Antonio 1971: *Selections from Prison Notebooks*. London: Lawrence and Wishart.

Grant, William and Marsh, David 1977: *The CBI*. London: Hodder and Stoughton.

Gras, Christian and Gras, Solange 1991: *Histoire de la Première République mitterrandienne*. Paris: Robert Laffont.

Grimaud, Maurice 1977: *En mai, fais ce qu'il te plaît*. Paris: Stock.

Groux, Guy and Mouriaux, René 1989: *La CFDT*. Paris: Economica.

Grunberg, Gérard 1996: 'Existe-t-il un socialisme de l'Europe du sud?' In Lazar 1996: 477–511.

Hall, Peter 1986: *Governing the Economy: The Politics of State Intervention in Britain and France*. Cambridge: Polity.

Hall, Stuart 1988: 'Brave New World'. *Marxism Today*, Oct., 24–9.

Hamon, Hervé and Rotman, Patrick 1981: *Les Intellocrates. Expédition en haute intelligensia*. Paris: Jean-Pierre Ramsay.

Hamon, Hervé and Rotman, Patrick 1984: *La Deuxième Gauche. Histoire intellectuelle et politique de la CFDT*. Paris: Seuil.

Hamon, Hervé and Rotman, Patrick 1987: *Génération*, vol. 1. *Les Années de rêve*. Paris: Seuil.

Hamon, Hervé and Rotman, Patrick 1988: *Génération*, vol. 2. *Les Années de poudre*. Paris: Seuil.

Hancock, M. Donald, Logue, John and Schiller, Bernt (eds) 1991: *Managing Modern Capitalism: Industrial Renewal and Workplace Democracy in the United States and Western Europe*. Westport, Conn.: Greenwood Press.

Hancock, M. Donald, Conradt, Donald, Peters, B. Guy, Safran, William and Zariski, Raphael 1993: *Politics in Western Europe*. Basingstoke: Macmillan.

Hanley, David 1993: 'Socialism Routed? The French Legislative Elections of 1993'. *Modern and Contemporary France*, NS 1 (4), 417–27.

Harvey, David 1989: *The Condition of Postmodernity*. Oxford: Basil Blackwell. (First published 1980.)

Hauss, Charles 1978: *The New Left in France. The Unified Socialist Party*. Westport, Conn.: Greenwood Press.

Hayward, Jack 1983: Governing France: The One and Indivisible Republic. London: Weidenfeld and Nicolson (2nd edn).

Hayward, Jack 1986: *The State and the Market Economy: Industrial Patriotism and Economic Intervention in France*. Brighton: Wheatsheaf.

Hayward, Jack 1994: 'Ideological Change: The Exhaustion of the Revolutionary Impetus'. In Peter Hall, Jack Hayward and Howard Machin (eds), *Developments in French Politics*. Basingstoke: Macmillan, 15–32 (revised edn).

Hazareesingh, Sudhir 1991: *Intellectuals and the French Communist Party: Disillusion and Decline*. Oxford: Oxford University Press.

Hazareesingh, Sudhir 1994: *Political Traditions in Modern France*. Oxford: Oxford University Press.

Held, David (ed.) 1992: 'Democracy: From City-states to a Cosmopolitan Order? In David Held, *Prospects for Democracy*. Oxford: Basil Blackwell. (Special issue of Political Studies, 40.)

Helliwell, John F. 1994: 'Empirical Linkages between Democracy and Economic Growth'. *British Journal of Political Science*, 24 (2), 225–48.

Herberg, Mikkal 1981: 'Politics, Planning and Capitalism: National Economic Planning in France and Britain', *Political Studies*, 29 (4), 497–516.

Hewlett, Nick 1988: 'Repression and Revolt in France: May 1968 and December 1986'. South Bank Polytechnic, December 1988 (unpublished).

Hewlett, Nick 1993: 'Consensus, Socialism and Social Democracy in France', Studies in European Culture and Society, 10, European Research Centre, Loughborough University, 1993.

Hewlett, Nick 1996: 'Moderation and Dissent: The French Presidential Elections of 1995'. *Politics*, 16 (1), 31–8.

Hirst, Paul and Thompson, Grahame 1996: *Globalization in Question: The International Economy and the Possibilities of Governance*. Cambridge: Polity.

Hobsbawm, Eric 1990: *Echoes of the Marseillaise*. London: Verso.

Hobsbawm, Eric 1994: *The Age of Extremes*: The Short Twentieth Century, 1914–1991. London: Michael Joseph.

Hoffmann, Stanley 1966: 'Paradoxes of the French Political Community'. In Stanley Hoffmann (ed.), *In Search of France*, Cambridge, Mass.: Harvard University Press, 1–117.

Hoffmann, Stanley 1974: 'The Ruled: Protest as a National Way of Life'. In Stanley Hoffmann, *Decline or Renewal? France since the 1930s*. New York: Viking Press.

Hoffmann, Stanley, Ross, George and Malzacher, Sylvia (eds) 1987: *The Mitterrand Experiment: Continuity and Change in Contemporary France*. Cambridge: Polity.

Hollifield, James and Ross, George (eds) 1991: *Searching for the New France*. London: Routledge.

Holloway, John 1988: 'The Great Bear, Post-Fordism and Class Struggle: A Comment on Bonefield and Jessop'. *Capital and Class*, 36, 93–104.

Howell, Chris 1992a: 'The Dilemmas of Post-Fordism: Socialists, Flexibility, and Labour Market Deregulation in France'. *Politics and Society*, 20 (1), 71–99.

Howell, Chris 1992b: *Regulating Labor: The State and Industrial Relations Reform in France*. Princeton: Princeton University Press.

Howorth, Jolyon 1987: 'Image and Political Culture in Contemporary France'. In Jeff Bridgford (ed.), *France: Image and Identity*. Newcastle: Newcastle upon Tyne Products.

Huard, Raymond 1992: 'L'Organisation du suffrage universel sous la Seconde République'. In Berstein and Rudelle 1992.

Huard, Raymond 1996: *La Naissance du parti politique en France*. Paris: Presses de la Fondation National des Sciences Politiques.

Huard, Raymond, Lequin, Yves-Claude, Margairaz, Michel, Mazauric, Claude, Mesliand, Claude, Scot, Jean-Paul and Vovelle, Michel 1982: *La France contemporaine. Identité et mutations de 1789 à nos jours*. Paris: Editions Sociales.

Huyghe, François-Bernard and Barbès, Pierre 1987: *La soft-idéologie*. Paris: Robert Laffont.

Institut Charles de Gaulle (ed.) 1992: *De Gaulle en son siècle*, vol. 3. *Moderniser la France*. Paris: La Docmentation Française/Plon.

Jaffré, Jérome 1989: 'Trente Années de changement électoral'. *Pouvoirs*, 49, 15–26.

Jameson, Frederic 1991: *Postmodernism, or the Cultural Logic of Late Capitalism*. London: Verso.

Jaquier, Jean-Paul 1986: *Les Cow-boys ne meurent jamais: l'aventure syndicale continue*. Paris: Syros.

Jeanneney, Jean-Marcel 1992: 'L'Economie française pendant la présidence du général de Gaulle'. In Institut Charles de Gaulle 1992.

Jenkins, Brian 1990: *Nationalism in France: Class and Nation since 1789*. London: Routledge.

Jennings, Jeremy 1993: Introduction: 'Mandarins and Samurais: The Intellectual in Modern France'. In Jeremy Jennings (ed.), *Intellectuals in Twentieth-Century France*. Basingstoke: Macmillan.

Jenson, Jane 1989: ' "Different" but not "Exceptional" ': Canada's Permeable Fordism'. *Canadian Review of Sociology and Anthropology*, 26 (1), 69–94.

Jenson, Jane 1991: 'The French Left: A Tale of Three Beginnings'. In Hollifield and Ross 1991: 85–112.

Jenson, Jane, and Ross, George 1988: 'The Tragedy of the French Left'. *New Left Review*, 171, 5–44.

Jessop, Bob 1992: 'Fordism and post-Fordism: critique and reformulation'. In M. Storper and A. Scott (eds), *Pathways to Industrialization and Regional Development*. London: Routledge.

Jessop, Bob 1994: 'Post-Fordism and the State'. In A. Amin 1994: 251–79.

Jessop, Bob, Bonnett, Kevin, Bromley, Simon and Ling, Tom 1988: *Thatcherism*. Cambridge: Polity.

Joffrin, Laurent 1988: *Mai 68. Histoire des Evénements*. Paris: Seuil.

Johnson, Douglas 1987: 'French Identity: The Historian's View'. In Jeff Bridgford (ed.), France. Image and Identity. Newcastle: Newcastle upon Tyne Products, 11–26.

Journal des élections, *Dépolitisation des Français ou retour au local?* Synthèse des actes du colloque du 11 octobre 1989 (suppl.).

Kamenka, Eugene 1988: 'Revolutionary Ideology and "The Great French Revolution of 1789–?" '. In Best 1988: 75–100.

Katznelson, Ira and Zolberg, Aristide (eds) 1986: *Working-Class Formation: Nineteenth-Century Patterns in Western Europe and the United States*. Princeton: Princeton University Press.

Kavanagh, Dennis and Morris, Peter 1989: *Consensus Politics from Attlee to Thatcher*. Oxford: Basil Blackwell.

Keating, Michael and Hainsworth, Paul 1986: *Decentralization and Change in Contemporary France*. Aldershot: Gower.

Kemp, Tom 1971: *Economic Forces in French History*. London: Dennis Dobson.

Kergoat, Jacques 1983: *Le Parti socialiste*. Paris: Le Sycamore.

Kesler, Jean-François 1990: *De la Gauche dissidente au nouveau Parti socialiste. Ces minorités qui ont rénové le P.S.* Toulouse: Editions Privat.

Khilnani, Sunil 1993: *Arguing Revolution: The Intellectual Left in Postwar France*. New Haven: Yale University Press.

Kirchheimer, Otto 1966: 'Germany: The Vanishing Opposition'. In Dahl 1966.

Knapp, Andrew 1990: '*Un parti comme les autres: Jacques Chirac and the Rally for the Republic*'. In Cole 1990.

Knapp, Andrew 1994: *Gaullism since de Gaulle*. Aldershot: Dartmouth.

Kolodziej, Edward A. 1974: *French International Policy under de Gaulle and Pompidou*. Ithaca, NY: Cornell University Press.

Kriegel, Annie 1968: *Les Communistes*. Paris: Seuil.

Kuisel, Richard 1987: 'French Post-war Economic Growth: A Historical Perspective on the *Trente glorieuses*'. In George Ross, Stanley Hoffmann and Sylvia Malzacher (eds), *The Mitterrand Experiment*. Cambridge: Polity, 18–32.

Laclau, Ernesto 1993: 'Politics and the Limits of Modernity'. In Thomas Docherty (ed.), *Postmodernism*, London: Harvester Wheatsheaf.

Lacouture, Jean 1984: *De Gaulle*, vol. 1. *Le Rebelle*. Paris: Seuil.

Lacouture, Jean 1985: *De Gaulle*, vol. 2. *Le Politique*. Paris: Seuil.

Lacouture, Jean 1986: *De Gaulle*, vol. 3. *Le Souverain*. Paris: Seuil.

Lacouture, Jean 1991: *De Gaulle: The Ruler.* London: Harvill. (Abridged version of Lacouture 1984, 1985 and 1986 published in one vol., translated by Alan Sheridan.)

Lash, Scott and Urry, John 1987: *The End of Organized Capitalism.* Cambridge: Polity.

Lazar, Marc 1992: *Maisons rouges: les partis communistes français et italiens de la Libération à nos jours.* Paris: Aubier.

Lazar, Marc (ed.) 1996: *La Gauche en Europe depuis 1945.* Paris: Presses Universitaires de France.

Lelong, Pierre 1992: 'Le Général de Gaulle et la recherche en France'. In Institut Charles de Gaulle 1992.

Lequin, Yves 1984: *Histoire des Français. XIXe–XXe siècles. Les Citoyens et la démocratie.* Paris: Armand Colin.

Lerner, Daniel 1958: *The Passing of Traditional Society.* Glencoe, Ill.: Free Press.

Lerner, Daniel 1968: 'Modernization: Social Aspects'. In David L. Sills, *International Encyclopedia of the Social Sciences.* Basingstoke and New York: Macmillan and Free Press, 387–95.

Levy, David A. L. 1987, 'Foreign Policy: Business as Usual?' In Mazey and Newman 1987: 166–91.

Lilla, Mark (ed.) 1994: *New French Thought: Political Philosophy.* Princeton: Princeton University Press.

Lipietz, Alain 1984: *L'Audace ou l'enlisement. Sur les politiques économiques de la gauche.* Paris: Editions de la Découverte.

Lipietz, Alain 1985: *The Enchanted World: Inflation, Credit and the World Crisis.* London: Verso.

Lipietz, Alain 1987: *Mirages and Miracles: The Crises of Global Fordism.* London: Verso.

Lipietz, Alain 1989: Choisir l'audace. Paris: Editions de la Découverte. (Translated by Malcolm Slater as *Towards a New Economic Order. Postfordism, Ecology and Democracy.* Cambridge: Polity, 1992.)

Lipietz, Alain 1991: 'Governing the Economy in the Face of International Challenge: From National Developmentalism to National Crisis'. In Hollifield and Ross 1991: 17–42.

Lipietz, Alain 1994: 'Post-Fordism and Democracy'. In A. Amin 1994: 338–57.

Lipovetsky, Gilles 1983: *L'Ere du vide. Essais sur l'individualisme contemporain.* Paris: Gallimard.

Lipovetsky, Gilles 1986: ' "Changer la vie" ou l'irruption de l'individualisme transpolitique'. In *Pouvoirs*, 39, 91–100. (Translated by Lisa Maguire as 'May '68, or the Rise of Transpolitical Individualism', in Lilla 1994: 212–19.

Lipset, Seymour Martin 1959 [1960]: *Political Man.* London: Heineman.

Lorwin, Val R. 1966: *The French Labour Movement.* Cambridge, Mass.: Harvard University Press.

Loubet del Bayle, Jean-Louis 1985: 'La Police dans le système politique', *Revue Française de Science Politique*, 4, 509–34.

Löwy, Michael 1981: *The Politics of Combined and Uneven Development.* London: Verso.

Lyotard, Jean-François 1984: *The Postmodern Condition: A Report on Knowledge.* Manchester: Manchester University Press. (Translation by

Geoff Bennington and Brian Massumi of *La Condition postmoderne: rapport sur le savoir*, Paris: Minuit, 1979.)

Machin, Howard and Wright, Vincent, 1985: 'Economic Policy under the Mitterrand Presidency, 1981–1984: An Introduction'. In Howard Machin and Vincent Wright, *Economic Policy and Policy-Making under the Mitterrand Presidency 1981–1984*. London: Frances Pinter, 1–43.

McLellan, David 1977: *Karl Marx: Selected Writings*. Oxford: Oxford University Press.

Macpherson, C. B. 1966: *The Real World of Democracy*. Oxford: Oxford University Press.

Maddison, Angus 1964: *Economic Growth in the West: Comparative Experience in Europe and North America*. London and New York: Allen and Unwin and Twentieth Century Fund.

Magraw, Roger 1992: *A History of the French Working Class*, vol. 2. *Workers and the Bourgeois Republic 1871–1939*. Oxford: Basil Blackwell Ltd.

Maire, Edmond 1980: *Reconstruire l'espoir*. Paris: Seuil.

Maire, Edmond and Piaget, Charles 1973: *lip 73*. Paris: Seuil.

Mandel, Ernest 1978: *Late Capitalism*. London: Verso.

Mandel, Ernest 1995: *Long Waves of Capitalist Development*. London: Verso.

Manent, Pierre (ed.) 1986: *Les Libéraux*. Paris: Hachette.

Maravall, J. 1992: 'What is Left? Social Democratic Parties in Southern Europe'. Instituto Juan March des Estudios e Investigaciones.

Marcellin, Raymond 1978: *L'Importune Vérité*. Paris: Plon.

Marx, Karl 1946: *Capital. Volume I*. London: Allen and Unwin. (First published in German in 1867.)

Marx, Karl and Engels, Friedrich 1968: *Manifesto of the Communist Party*. In Friedrich Engels and Karl Marx, *Selected Works*. London: Lawrence and Wishart, 35–63. (First published in German in 1848.)

Mauriac, François 1971: *Le Dernier Bloc-Notes, 1968–70*. Paris: Flammarion.

Mayer, Margit 1994: 'Post-Fordist City Politics'. In A. Amin 1994: 316–37.

Mayer, Nonna and Perrineau, Pascal 1989: *Le Front National à découvert*. Paris: Presses de la Fondation Nationale des Sciences Politiques.

Mayer, Nonna and Perrineau, Pascal 1992: *Les Comportements politiques*. Paris: Armand Colin.

Mazey, Sonia and Newman, Michael 1987: *Mitterrand's France*. London: Croom Helm.

Melchior, Eric 1993: *Le PS, du projet au pouvoir. L'Impossible concordance*. Paris: Editions de l'Atelier/Editions Ouvrières.

Mendras, Henri 1988: *La Seconde Révolution française*. Paris: Gallimard.

Merkel, Wolfgang 1993: *Ende der Sozialdemokratie? Machtressourcen und Regierungspolitik im westeuropäischen Vergleich*. Frankfurt: Campus.

Miliband, Ralph 1989: *Divided Societies: Class Struggle in Contemporary Capitalism*. Oxford: Oxford University Press.

Millot, Michèle and Roulleau, Jean-Pol 1984: *L'Entreprise face aux Lois Auroux*. Paris: Editions d'Organisation.

Mitterrand, François 1964: *Le Coup d'état permanent*. Paris: Plon.

Mitterrand, François 1988: *Lettre à tous les Français*. Paris: Parti socialiste.

Mjøset, Lars, Cappelen, Adne, Fargerberg, Jan and Tranoy, Bent Sofus 1994: 'Norway: Changing the Model'. In Anderson and Camiller 1994: 55–76.

Le Monde 1995: *L'Election présidentielle. 23 avril–7 mai 1995*. Numéro spécial des dossiers et documents du Monde.

Le Monde 1997: Législatives 1997. *Le président désavoué* 25 mars–1 juin 1997. Numéro spécial des dossiers et documents du Monde.

Moore, Barrington Jr 1966: *Social Origins of Dictatorship and Democracy*. Harmondsworth: Penguin, 1979.

Morin, Edgar, Lefort, Claude and Castoriadis, Cornelius 1988: *Mai 68: la brèche suivi de Vingt ans après*. Brussels: Editions Complexe.

Moschonas, Gerassimos 1994: *La Social-démocratie de 1945 à nos jours*. Paris: Montchrestien.

Mossuz-Lavau, Janine 1994: *Les Français et la politique. Enquête sur une crise*. Paris: Editions Odile Jacob.

Mulhern, Francis 1981: 'Preliminaries and Two Contrasts'. Introduction to Régis Debray, *Teachers, Writers, Celebrities. The Intellectuals of Modern France*. London: New Left Books/Verso.

Nielson, K. 1991: 'Towards a Flexible Future – Theories and Politics'. In Bob Jessop, K. Kastendiek, K. Nielson and O. Pederson (eds), *The Politics of Flexibility: Restructuring State and Industry in Britain, Germany and Scandinavia*, Aldershot: Edward Elgar.

Niethammer, Lutz 1992: *Posthistoire: Has History come to an end?* London: Verso.

Noblecourt, Michel 1990: *Les Syndicats en questions*. Paris: Editions Ouvrières.

Nora, Pierre 1980: 'Que peuvent les intellectuels?' *Débat*, 1, 1–19. (A shorter version in English and translated by Eugene Weber is published as 'About Intellectuals', in Jeremy Jennings (ed.), *Intellectuals in Twentieth-Century France*, Basingstoke: Macmillan, 1993, 187–98.)

OECD (Organisation for Economic Cooperation and Development) 1991 (July): *OECD Employment Outlook*. Paris.

Organski, A. F. 1965: *The Stages of Political Development*. New York: Knopf.

Ory, Pascal 1983: *L'Entre-deux Mai. Histoire culturelle de la France, mai 1968–mai 1981*. Paris: Seuil.

Osbourne, Peter 1992: 'Modernity is a Qualitative, Not a Chronological Category'. *New Left Review*, 192 (Mar./Apr.), 65–84.

Padgett, Stephen 1989: 'The Party System'. In Gordon Smith, William E. Paterson and Peter H. Merkl (eds), *Developments in West German Politics*. Basingstoke: Macmillan, 122–47.

Padgett, Stephen 1993: 'Social Democracy in Power'. *Parliamentary Affairs*, 46 (1), 101–20.

Padgett, Stephen and Paterson, William 1991: *A History of Social Democracy in Postwar Europe*. London: Longman.

Padgett, Stephen and Paterson, William 1994: 'Germany: Stagnation of the Left'. In Anderson and Camiller 1994: 102–29.

Parti communiste français and Parti socialiste 1972: *Programme commun de gouvernement du Parti communiste français et du Parti socialiste*. Paris: Editions Sociales.

Parti socialiste 1980: *Projet socialiste pour la France des années 1980*. Paris: Club Socialiste du Livre.

Parti socialiste 1981: *110 Propositions pour la France*. Paris: *Parti socialiste*. (Reproduced in *Modern and Contemporary France*, 51 (Oct. 1992), 51–64.)

Peck, Jamie and Tickell, Adam 1994: 'Searching for a New Institutional Fix: The *After*-Fordist Crisis and the Global-Local Disorder'. In A. Amin 1994: 280–325.

Pelinka, Anton 1983: *Social Democratic Parties in Europe*. New York: Praeger.

Perrineau, Pascal (ed.) 1994: *L'Engagement politique. Déclin ou mutation?* Paris: Presses de la Fondation Nationale des Sciences Politiques.

Perrineau, Pascal and Ysmal, Colette 1995a (eds): *Le Vote de crise: l'élection présidentielle de 1995*. Paris: Département d'Etudes politiques du Figaro/Presses de la Fondation Nationale des Sciences Politiques.

Perrineau, Pascal and Ysmal, Colette (eds) 1995b: Le Vote des douze. Paris: Presses de la Fondation Nationale des Sciences Politiques/Le Figaro.

Perrot, Michelle 1986: 'On the Formation of the French Working Class'. In Katznelson, Ira and Zolberg, Aristide R. (eds), *Working-Class Formation: Nineteenth-Century Patterns in Western Europe and the United States*, Princeton: Princeton University Press, 71–110.

Photo 1978: 128 (May–June).

Pimlot, Ben 1988: 'The Myth of Consensus'. In Lesley M. Smith (ed.), *The Making of Britain: Echoes of Greatness*, Basingstoke: Macmillan, 129–42.

Pisier, Evelyne 1986: 'Paradoxes du gauchisme'. *Pouvoirs*, 39, 15–23.

Pontusson, Jonas 1994: 'Sweden: After the Golden Age'. In Anderson and Camiller 1994: 23–54.

Portelli, Hugues 1987: *La Politique en France sous la Ve République*. Paris: Grasset.

Portelli, Hugues 1988: *Le Socialisme français tel qu'il est*. Paris: Presses Universitaires de France.

Portelli, Hugues 1992: *Le parti Socialiste. Paris*: Montchrestien.

Poulantzas, Nicos 1979: *Fascism and Dictatorship*. London: Verso.

Prost, Antoine 1992: *Education, société et politique*. Paris: Seuil.

Przeworski, Adam 1985: *Capitalism and Social Democracy*. Cambridge: Cambridge University Press.

Przeworski, Adam and Sprague, John 1986: *Paper Stones: A History of Electoral Socialism*. Chicago: University of Chicago Press.

Psychopedis, Kosmas 1991: 'Crisis of Theory in Contemporary Social Sciences'. In Werner Bonefield and John Holloway (eds), *Post-Fordism and Social Form*, Basingstoke: Macmillan.

Quid 1983: Paris: Robert Laffont.

Rancière, Jacques 1995: *On the Shores of Politics*. London: Verso. (Translation by Liz Heron of *Aux bords du politique*: Paris: Editions Osiris, 1992.)

Rémond, René 1965 and 1969: *La Vie politique en France depuis 1789* (2 vols). Paris: Armand Colin.

Rémond, René 1982: *Les Droites en France*. Paris: Aubier Montaigne (4th edn).

Rémond, René 1991: *Notre Siècle (1918–1991)*. Paris: Fayard.

Rémond, René 1993: *La Politique n'est plus ce qu'elle était*. Paris: Calmann-Lévy.

Rioux, Jean-Pierre 1971: *La Révolution industrielle 1780–1880*. Paris: Seuil.

Rioux, Jean-Pierre 1987: *The Fourth Republic, 1944–1958*. Cambridge: Cambridge University Press. (Translation by Godfrey Rogers of Pierre Rioux, *La France de la Quatrième République*. Two vols; Paris: Seuil, 1980 and 1983.)

Rosanvallon, Pierre 1991: 'Le Déclin des passions'. In Abélès 1991.

Ross, George 1982: *Workers and Communists in France: From Popular Front to Eurocommunism*. Berkeley: University of California Press.

Ross, George 1990: 'Intellectuals against the Left: The Case of France'. In Ralph Miliband and Leo Panitch (eds), *Socialist Register 1990*. London: Merlin, 201–27.

Ross, George 1991a: 'The Changing Face of Popular Power in France'. In Frances Fox Piven (ed.), *Labour Parties in Postindustrial Societies*. Cambridge: Polity, 71–100.

Ross, George 1991b: 'Where Have all the Sartres Gone? The French Intelligensia Born Again'. In Hollifield and Ross 1991: 221–50.

Ross, John 1982: 'Introduction Générale. La Trajectoire historique de la Social-démocratie'. In John Ross (ed.), *Profils de la social-démocratie européenne*. Paris: La Brèche. 5–68.

Rostow, Walt Witman 1965: *The Stages of Economic Growth: A Noncommunist Manifesto*. Cambridge: Cambridge University Press (2nd edn. 1971).

Rueschemeyer, Dietrich, Stephens, Evelyne and Stephens, John: 1992. *Capitalist Development and Democracy*. Cambridge: Polity.

Rush, Michael 1992: *Politics and Society: An Introduction to Political Sociology*. Hemel Hempstead: Harvester Wheatsheaf.

Sabel, Charles 1994: 'Flexible Specialization and the Re-emergence of Regional Economies'. In A. Amin 1994.

Saïd, Edward 1993: *Representations of the Intellectual: The 1993 Reith Lectures*. London: Vintage.

Salini, Laurent 1987: *Enquête sur le Parti socialiste*. Paris: Messidor/Editions Sociales.

Sartre, Jean-Paul 1948: *Qu'est-ce que la littérature?*. Paris: Gallimard.

Schweisguth, Etienne 1994: *Droite–gauche: un clivage dépassé?* Paris: La Documentation Française, Jan.

Seidman, Steven and Wagner, David G. (eds) 1992: *Postmodernism and Social Theory*. Oxford: Basil Blackwell.

Shain, Martin A. 1980: 'Corporatism and Industrial Relations in France'. In Philip Cerny and Martin Shain, *French Politics and Public Policy*, London: Frances Pinter.

Shain, Martin A. 1991: 'Towards a Centrist Democracy? The Fate of the French Right'. In Hollifield and Ross 1991: 57–85.

Shils, Edward 1955: 'The End of Ideology?' *Encounter*, 5, 52–8.

Shorter, Edward and Tilly, Charles 1974: *Strikes in France 1830–1968*. Cambridge: Cambridge University Press.

Sirinelli, Jean-François 1990: 'La Fin des intellectuels français?' In Martyn Cornick (ed.), *Beliefs and Identity in Modern France*. Loughborough: Loughborough University European Research Centre.

Sirinelli, Jean-François (ed.) 1992: *Histoire des droites en France*. Paris: Gallimard.

Sked, Alan and Cook, Chris 1979: *Post-war Britain. A Political History*. Harmondsworth: Penguin.

Skocpol, Theda 1973: 'A Critical Review of Barrington Moore's Social Origins of Dictatorship and Democracy'. *Politics and Society*, Fall, 1–34.

Skocpol, Theda 1979: *States and Social Revolutions*. Cambridge: Cambridge University Press.

Slama, Alain-Gérard 1995: *Les Chasseurs d'absolu. Genèse de la gauche et de la droite*. Paris: Pluriel (2nd edn).

Small, Melvin and Singer, J. David 1982: *Resort to Arms: International and Civil Wars, 1816–1980*. London: Sage.

Soltau, Roger 1931: *French Political Thought in the Nineteenth Century*. New York: Russell and Russell.

Stevens, Anne 1992: *The Government and Politics of France*. Basingstoke: Macmillan.

Thomson, David 1989: *Democracy in France since 1870*. London: Cassell (5th edn).

Tilly, Charles and Shorter, Edward 1974: *Strikes in France, 1830–1968*. Cambridge: Cambridge University Press.

Tilly, Charles, Tilly, Louise and Tilly, Richard 1975: *The Rebellious Century 1830–1930*. London: Dent and Sons.

Tocqueville, Alexis de 1966: *Democracy in America*. London: Fontana, 2 vols. (First published 1835.)

Touchard, Jean 1977: *La Gauche en France depuis 1900*. Paris: Seuil.

Touraine, Alain 1969: *La Société postindustrielle*. Paris: Gonthier.

Touraine, Alain 1987: 'Limite de la politique. Les intellectuels doivent la remettre à sa place'. *Le Monde*, 8 Oct.

Trebilcock, Clive 1981: *The Industrialization of the Continental Powers 1780–1914*. London: Longman.

Trotsky, Leon 1962: *The Permanent Revolution and Results and Prospects*. London: New Park.

Vedel, Georges 1962: *La Dépolitisation: mythe ou réalité?*. Paris: Cahiers de la Fondation Nationale des Sciences Politiques, 120.

Vionsson-Ponté, Pierre 1976: *Histoire de la République gaullienne*, vol. 2, *Le Temps des orphelins (été 1962–avril 1969)*. Paris: Fayard.

Wallerstein, Immanuel 1979: *The Capitalist World Economy*. Cambridge: Cambridge University Press.

Webb, Paul 1994: 'The Evolution of the Parti Socialiste in Comparative Perspective'. Unpublished paper, Oxford Brookes University.

Weber, Eugen 1977: *Peasants into Frenchmen: The Modernization of Rural France*. London: Chatto and Windus.

Weber, Eugen 1988: 'The Nineteenth-century Fallout'. In Best 1988: 155–82.

Weber, Henri 1978: 'Mai 68: une répétition générale?'. *Critique Communiste*, 23 (May).

Weber, Henri 1986: *Le Parti des patrons. Le CNPF (1946–1986)*. Paris: Seuil.

Weber, Henri 1988: *Vingt Ans après. Que reste-t-il de 68?* Paris: Seuil.

Wilkinson, James D. 1981: *The Intellectual Resistance in Europe*. Cambridge, Mass.: Harvard University Press.

Williams, Raymond 1976: *Keywords*. London: Fontana.

Wilson, Frank L. 1985: 'Trade Unions and Economic Policy'. In Howard Machin and Vincent Wright, *Economic Policy and Policy-Making Under the Mitterrand Presidency 1981–1984*. London: Frances Pinter.

Winock, Michel 1978: *La République se meurt*. Paris: Seuil.

Winock, Michel 1986: *La Fièvre hexagonale*. Paris: Calmann-Lévy.

Wylie, Laurence, Chu, Franklin and Terral, Mary 1973: *France: The Events of May–June 1968. A Critical Bibliography*. Pittsburgh: Centre for West European Studies, paper IV.

Ysmal, Colette 1989: *Les Partis politiques sous la Ve République*. Paris: Montchrestien.

Ysmal, Colette 1991: 'Communistes et Lepénistes: le chassé-croisé'. *L'Histoire*, 143 (Apr.).

Zeldin, Theodore 1979: *France 1848–1945. Politics and Anger*. Oxford: Oxford University Press.

Zolberg, Aristide 1986: 'How Many Exceptionalisms?' In Ira Katznelson and Aristide Zolberg (eds), *Working-Class Formation: Nineteenth Century Patterns in Western Europe and the United States*, Princeton: Princeton University Press.

Index

Action Française 24, 31
affaires d'Etat 209
Aglietta, M. 201
agriculture 16, 17
Alain 31, 188
Algeria 51, 52, 93, 108, 109;
  Gaullist policy 55, 120, 121,
  122, 128, 129, 132, 133, 144;
  intellectuals and 24, 176,
  177–8, 181, 182; threatened
  coup d'état over (1958) *see*
  coups d'état
Alsatian autonomism 31
alternance 69, 131
Althusser, Louis 80, 180, 181,
  186
America *see* United States of
  America
Amin, A. 201, 204
Amnesty International 22
anarchists 191
anarcho-syndicalism *see*
  syndicalism
Anderson, P. 97, 110, 112, 127,
  197, 198
anti-communism 51, 177, 186,
  188, 189, 190; *see also* Force
  Ouvrière
anti-nuclear movement 163

anti-semitism 81
anti-totalitarianism 188, 189
Appollonia, A. C. d' 174, 181
Aragon, Louis 174
Arendt, Hannah 189
Aron, Raymond 172, 175, 188, 189
Auroux laws 64, 86, 88–9
Austria 34, 38, 187; socialism,
  social democracy in 93, 94, 96,
  97, 103, 109, 110
authority, authoritarianism
  19–20, 21, 22, 34; de Gaulle's
  rule 23, 111, 121–8
autogestion 54, 86, 161, 162, 184
Avril, P. 122
Azéma, J.-P. 36

Balibar, Etienne 181
Balladur, Edouard 67, 74, 76, 78
Barnavi, E. 132
Barthes, R. 186
Beauvoir, Simone de 174, 177,
  181, 186
Bell, D. S. 70, 72, 115
Bell, Daniel 3, 62, 200, 205
Benda, Julian 172, 173, 175
Benelux countries 18, 38, 96, 97,
  110, 142, 187
Bensaïd, D. 147, 183

Bérégovoy, Pierre 66
Berger, S. 88
Bergounioux, A. 109, 110
Berstein, G. 30, 31
Berstein, S. 30, 31, 32, 61, 136,
   137, 140
Biffaud, O. 103
Birnbaum, P. 135, 137, 141
Blondel, Jean 195
Bolshevism 31, 94, 189
Bonaparte, Napoleon *see*
   Napoleon I
bonapartism of de Gaulle 9, 121,
   128, 129
Bonefield, W. 204
Bottomore, T. 95
Boulangists 13
Bourlanges, J.-L. 77
Boyer, R. 201
Brasillach, 24
Braudel, F. 134
Breton, André 177
Bridgford, J. 54
Brohm, J.-M. 128
Bunel, J. 27
business people *see* employers

Camus, Albert 24, 175
Capdevielle, J. 124, 141, 155, 160,
   161
capitalism 4, 5, 6, 7, 13, 14, 15, 17,
   35; intellectuals and 177, 183;
   left and 1; *see also* neo-liberal
   economic policy; May 1968
   and consolidation of 150–1,
   155–6, 159, 161, 166–7;
   theorizing change in capitalist
   societies 193, 196–208
Carrillo, S. 70
Cartel des Gauches government
   31, 32

Casanova, Jean-Claude 189
Castles, F. 45
Castoriadis, C. 157
Cause du peuple, La 175
Cayrol, Roland 61, 63, 75
Céline, Louis-Ferdinand 24
110 propositions pour la France
   65
centralization 19, 21–2; *see also*
   decentralization
cercles 19
Cerny, P. 122, 133
Ceyrac, François 55, 88, 161
CFDT *see* Confédération
   Française Démocratique du
   Travail
CFTC *see* Confédération
   Française des Travailleurs
   Chrétiens
CGT *see* Confédération
   Générale du Travail
Chaban-Delmas, Jacques 54,
   164, 165
chambrées 19
chambres syndicales ouvrières 26
Charlot, J. 120, 130
Cheminade, Jacques 83
Chevènement, J.-P. 162
China 35
Chirac, Jacques 67, 68, 74, 76, 78,
   89, 116, 165
Choisel, F. 128
Christian democrats 48, 50, 51,
   95, 176; German 42–4; *see also*
   Mouvement Républicain
   Populaire
Christiansen, N. F. 98
Churchill, Winston 39, 40
civil society 17–19
civil war 34, 36; threatened in
   1958 52, 121

Cixous, Hélène 178
Clapham, J. H. 15
Clarke, S. 204
class 189
class conflict, decline of 78–80,
    156, 163, 200
Clemenceau, Georges 32
clubs 19
CNPF *see* Conseil National du
    Patronat Français
cohabitation 65, 67, 68, 69, 70, 74,
    75, 78, 171
Cohen, S. 69
Cold War 47, 50, 96, 112, 174, 181
Coleman, J. S. 193
Collaboration in Second World
    War 13, 23, 24, 25, 36, 50, 51,
    173, 181
collective action 12, 168; May
    1968 as 156–9, 163
Colombani, J.-M. 67, 209
colonies 33, 192; *see also* Algeria;
    imperialism; New Caledonia
Commentaire 189
communism 5, 32, 35, 212;
    collapse of 6, 61, 90, 91, 117,
    158; intellectuals and 176, 181;
    replaced by liberal democracy
    in end of history thesis 196,
    198; and social democracy
    94–5, 110, 111, 117
Communists, Communist Party
    1, 3, 13, 23, 31, 32; 1945
    onwards 46–56 *passim,* 189;
    1980s and **1990s** 8, 65, 66, 68,
    70–3, 82–91 *passim,* 105, 106,
    109; British 42; Gaullist
    government and 52, 112, 124,
    125, 126, 127, 139; German 43;
    intellectuals and 170, 174, 175,
    181–3, 184, 185, 191;

legislative elections in Fourth
    and Fifth Republics 216–17;
    and May 1968 71, 160, 162,
    167; *Programme commun de
    gouvernement* (1972) 55, 63,
    71, 100, 162, 167; and social
    democracy 50, 93, 95, 99–102,
    105, 106, 109, 112
Confédération Française
    Démocratique du Travail
    (CFDT) 54, 62, 84, 86–7, 89,
    103, 160, 161, 162, 166, 183–4
Confédération Française des
    Travailleurs Chrétiens 103
Confédération Générale du
    Travail (CGT) 27, 47, 48, 49,
    54, 62, 79, 84, 86, 87, 88, 89, 99,
    100, 103, 139, 160, 161, 181,
    184, 191
Conference for Socialist
    Economists 204
conflict 1, 5–7, 192; **1789–1945** 8,
    11–35; **1945–1981** 36, 46–59,
    92; **1980s** and **1990s**, decline in
    1–3, 8, 63–81, 209, 211; limits
    to 81–4; end of history thesis
    196–7, 200
Congrès d'Epinay (1971) 55, 67,
    103, 162
Conseil National du Patronat
    Français (CNPF) 53, 54–5, 165
consensus 30–3, 92, 185, 194,
    195; end of exceptionalism
    1–4, 6, 8–9, 60–91, 194; in
    Europe since 1945 6–7, 37–46,
    70; intellectuals and 177, 188,
    191–2; May 1968 and 146,
    148, 168–9; nature of 208–14
Constant, Benjamin 188
constitutions 11, 20, 23, 34; Fifth
    Republic 70, 131, 154, 176

consumption, consumer society 57, 137–8, 143, 163, 166, 180
Coriat, B. 201
coups d'état 11, 12–13, 32; **1958**, threatened over Algeria 12, 13, 21, 25, 36, 52, 73, 119, 121; **1961**, attempted in Algiers 122, 129
Couve de Murville, Maurice 137
Cresson, Edith 66
Crewe, I. 98
Criddle, B. 70, 72
Crosland, Anthony 5, 95, 96–7
Crossman, Richard 40
Crouch, C. 155
Crozier, Michel 144, 165
Czechoslovakian uprising (1968) 158

Dagnaud, M. 87
Dalton, R. J. 43
De Vroey, M. 202
Débat, Le 171, 189
Debray, Régis 9, 148, 150–1, 152, 153–6, 161, 164, 166, 168–9, 183, 184–5, 186
Debré, Michel 124, 135, 137, 145
decentralization 64, 167, 168
Declaration of the Rights of Man 29, 33
decolonization 119, 132, 138, 178
defence 5; Gaullist policy 56, 57, 75, 132; Socialist government 69
Defferre, G. 69
Delale, A. 141, 147
Delegation for Territorial Planning and Regional Action (DATAR) 137
Delors, Jacques 116
democracy 17, 20, 209–11;

decline of conflict and 3–4; popular 1, 28–30, 122, 129–30; *see also* liberal democracy
democratic corporatism (Hancock) 45
Denmark 18, 38, 187; social democracy 96, 97, 98
dense civil society (Gramsci) 17–18
Depression, the 96
deregulation, economic 74, 97; *see also* privatization
deuxième gauche 183–4
dirigisme 73, 88, 136
Dreyfus, F.-G. 32, 134, 140
Dreyfus, M. 79
Dreyfus Affair 13, 24–5, 30, 32, 173, 192
Duhamel, Alain 61, 127
Duras, Marguerite 177
Dutton, D. 39, 40
Duverger, Maurice 23

Eastern Europe, break-up of 6, 72, 90, 117, 158, 211–12
Eck, J.-F. 134
Ecole Nationale d'Administration (ENA) 137
ecology movements 117, 158, 163
ecology parties 82, 83, 84, 105, 106, 107; *see also* Greens
economic modernization *see* modernization
economic prosperity 5–6
education 29, 30, 32, 149, 154, 175, 179–80; *see also* student protest
Ehrmann, H. W. 20
Elam, M. 201
Ellenstein, Jean 181
Emmanuelli, Henri 116

employers 1, 8, 27–8, 50, 54–5, 65, 87–90, 99, 124, 139; *see also* industrial relations
employment, unemployment 1, 6, 46, 68, 81–2, 84, 114, 167
end of exceptionalism 1–4, 6, 8–9, 60–91, 194; consensus beyond tripartism 90–1; decline of overt conflict 63–84; tripartite harmony of 1980s 85–90
end of history thesis 10, 196–200, 205
end of ideology thesis 3, 62
Engels, F. 14, 183
Entreprise et Progrès 55
equality 15, 95, 188, 199, 211; *see also* justice
Eurocommunism 70, 95, 100, 182
Europe: change in nineteenth century 13–14; *see also* Eastern Europe; Southern Europe; Western Europe
European Community, Union 52, 68–9, 75, 132, 138, 180, 194
Eveno, P. 178
Evian Agreements (1962) 55
exceptionalism 4, 33–5, 36–59; end of 1–4, 6, 8–9, 60–91, 194; persistence of radicalism and absence of Fordist compromise 56–9
exclusion 78, 194, 209
Express, L' 178, 209

Fabius, Laurent 65, 69, 167
Fanon, Franz 175
fascism 32, 35, 94–5, 173, 191, 196
Favier, P. 65
Federal Republic of Germany *see* Germany
Fédération de la Gauche

Démocratique et Socialiste (FGDS) 69, 126
feminism 178–9, 212
Ferry, L. 152, 188
FGDS *see* Fédération de la Gauche Démocratique et Socialiste
Fifth Republic 1, 12, 28, 52–6, 70, 122, 131, 137, 154, 179, 188; elections 217–18
Finkielkraut, Alain 61, 62, 178, 187
First Republic 12, 29
First World War 32, 94, 188; Great Britain and 39
FN *see* National Front
Fohlen, Claude 140
Forbes, J. 65
Force de frappe nuclear deterrent 56, 69, 132
Force Ouvrière (FO) 49, 79, 89, 103
Fordism 10, 57–8, 97, 112, 177, 180, 200–7, 212
Foucault, Michel 178, 181, 186
Fourastié, J. 179
Fourth Republic 12, 33, 46–52, 56, 70, 108, 109, 111, 188; comparison with Gaullist regime 121–2, 129–30, 134, 135, 137, 154, 176–7; legislative elections 216; Third Force period 49
France Observateur 178
Franco–Prussian War 21, 26
Frears, J. R. 76
Friedländer, S. 132
Front National *see* National Front
Fukuyama, Francis 10, 196–20, 205, 208, 211

Fulbrook, Mary 38, 43–4
Furet, François 60–1, 189–90, 200

Gattaz, Yvon 88
Gauche Prolétarienne 183, 184
Gauchet, Marcel 188, 189
Gaulle, Charles de 9, 20, 33, 51,
    52, 53, 73, 92, 112, 117,
    119–45, 210–11; authoritarian
    aspects of rule 111, 121–8,
    177; economic modernization
    134–9, 154–5; foreign policy
    and uses of *grandeur* 55–6,
    74–5, 132–3; and May 1968
    145, 149, 150, 154, 159, 164;
    progress of political stability
    and democracy 128–31;
    unevenness of socio-economic
    change under 139–45
Gaullism 8, 23, 47, 48, 49, 51–2,
    56, 67, 112, 216, 217; decline
    since 1980s 73–8, 165;
    intellectuals and 176, 177, 178,
    180; *see also* Rassemblement
    du Peuple Français
Gauron, A. 120
Gaveau, A. 148, 157
gay rights movement 163
Gélédan, A. 67
Germany 14, 15, 17, 18, 19, 33,
    34, 35, 138, 142, 154; consensus
    politics since 1945 8, 38, 42–4,
    50, 51, 58, 91; de Gaulle and
    56; intellectuals 177, 187;
    social democracy 93, 94, 96,
    98, 103, 108, 109, 110; Socialist
    government and 68
Gildea, Robert 191
Giscard d'Estaing, Valéry 53–4,
    56, 61, 76, 165, 166, 188
Glucksmann, André 189

Gorz, André 107
Gramsci, Antonio 17, 127, 133,
    172–3, 182
grand theories 207–8
grandes écoles 137, 179
Grant, W. 41
Gras, C. and S. 88
Great Britain 14, 15, 16, 17, 18,
    19, 22, 29, 33, 34, 35, 138, 142,
    154; consensus politics since
    1945 8, 38, 39–42, 50, 51, 58,
    91; intellectual activity 172,
    177, 179, 186, 187, 189;
    relations with 75; socialism,
    social democracy 93, 96, 97–8,
    103, 108, 109, 110, 116, 118
Greece 9, 34, 94, 110, 111, 112,
    114
Greens 3, 68, 83, 212, 217;
    German 43, 44; Swedish 45;
    see also ecology parties
Grenelle Agreements 149, 159,
    160
Grimaud, M. 148
Grunberg, G. 113, 115
Guesde, Jules 31
Guizot, François 188
Gulf War 69

Hainsworth, P. 64
Hall, P. 49, 135, 136, 141
Hall, S. 205
Hamon, H. 147, 166, 183, 184
Hancock, M. D. 44, 45
Hanley, D. 77
Hauss, C. 183
Hayek, Friedrich von 189
Hayward, J. 23, 61
Hazareesingh, S. 29, 181
Heath, Edward 41
Hegel, Hegelianism 188, 197–8

Herberg, M. 50
Hewlett, N. 22, 65
historiography 189–90, 200
Hobbes, T. 29
Hoffmann, Stanley 17, 19–20, 65
Howell, C. 88–9, 135, 140, 143
Howorth, J. 22
Huard, R. 17, 19, 29
Hue, Robert 72, 83, 101
human rights 171, 185–6, 191
Huvelin, Paul 54

idealism 24
ideology 6, 22–6, 173, 176, 192;
    end of ideology thesis 3, 62
immigration 81–2, 134, 138
imperialism 177, 178
individual rights, liberty 1, 15, 29,
    30–1, 188
individualism, May 1968 and
    151–2, 156–9, 163–4, 167,
    168–9
Indo-China 52, 121, 177
industrial relations; **1789–1945**
    16–17; **1945–1981** 38, 46–8, 50,
    53, 54, 139–44, 164, 165, 166;
    1981 onwards 62, 64, 78–80,
    89–90, 153–4; British 40–1;
    Fordism and 57–8; German
    43–4; Swedish 45–6; *see also*
    employers; labour movement;
    strikes; trade unions
industrialization, industry 15, 16,
    111, 112; under de Gaulle
    134–9, 144
intellectuals 9–10, 24–5, 60–1,
    80, 82, 108, 170–92, 213;
    decline of left intellectual
    181–7; in post-war politics
    172–80; re-emergence of
    liberal political thought 187–92

international pressures,
    influences; economic crises
    64–5, 104, 113, 165, 194;
    regulation theory 203, 205–6
international relations 20–2, 51,
    52, 57; Gaullist 55–6, 73, 74–5,
    119, 132–3; under Mitterand
    68–9
Irigaray, Luce 179
Israel, relations with 68
Italy 9, 18, 33, 34, 50, 51, 83, 94,
    110, 113–14, 142, 177;
    Communist Party 70, 100

Jacobinism 29, 189
Jaffré, J. 76–7
Jambet, Christian 189
Japan 35, 137, 138, 142, 199
Jaquier, Jean-Paul 89
Jeanneney, J.-M. 134, 135
Jeanson, André 160
Jenson, Jane 112
Jessop, B. 204, 205, 206
Jeunesse Communiste
    Révolutionnaire 183; *see also*
    Ligue Communiste
    Révolutionnaire
Jews 13, 25; *see also* anti-semitism
job creation *see* employment,
    unemployment
Joffrin, L. 148
Jospin, Lionel 67, 69, 78, 83, 107,
    109, 184, 218
Julliard, Jacques 60–1
July, Serge 184
Juppé, Alain 67
justice, political and social 1, 7,
    12, 30, 191, 197, 199, 200; *see
    also* equality

Kamenka, E. 29

Kanak autonomists 191
Kaspar, Jean 89
Kavanagh, D. 39, 40, 41
Keating, M. 64
Kergoat, Jacques 103
Kesler, J.-F. 162, 184
Keynesianism 6, 38, 40, 46, 96, 104, 212
Kirchheimer, Otto 43
Knapp, A. 76, 78
Kolodziej, E. A. 132
Kristéva, Julia 178
Krivine, Alain 109, 147
Kuisel, R. 16

labour movement 26–8, 50, 98–9; **1980s** and **1990s** 85–7, 90, 97, 115, 212; British 39; and May 1968 151, 154–5, 156, 159–61; *see also* industrial relations; strikes; trade unions
Labrousse, E. 134
Lacan, Jacques 178, 181, 186
Lacouture, Jean 127
Laguiller, Arlette 83, 162
Lajoinie, André 72
Lardreau, Guy 189
Lazar, Marc 117–18
Le Chapelier law 26
Le Pen, Jean-Marie 82, 83, 107, 218
Lefebvre, Henri 177
left 8, 9, 12, 13, 92–118, 191, 194, 209, 212, 218; intellectuals and 170, 174, 176, 177, 181–7, 191; and May 1968 161–2, 166–8; nature of 98–103; revolts of 1930s 24, 32; under de Gaulle 52–3, 124–7; *see also* radicalism
legislative elections; Fourth

Republic 216; Fifth Republic 217: 1997 3, 62, 67–8, 72, 78, 84, 94, 107, 109, 117
Leiris, Michel 177
Lelong, P. 136
Lenin, Leninism 95, 183
Lerner, D. 4, 193
Lettre à tous les Français: La France unie 65
Lévi-Strauss, C. 178, 181
Lévy, Bernard-Henri 186, 189
Levy, D. A. L. 69
liberal democracy 5, 6, 7, 26, 28–33, 34, 35, 62, 95, 146, 209, 211–12; constitutions and 23, 30; Fukuyama's end of history thesis 10, 196–200, 211; Gaullism and 53, 112, 121–30, 144; intellectuals and 180, 192
liberalism, intellectuals and 172, 177, 187–92
Libération 184
Liberation (1944) 12, 13
liberty *see* individual rights, liberty
Ligue Communiste Révolutionnaire 109, 162, 183, 184, 191
Lilla, M. 187, 188
Lipietz, Alain 112, 201–2, 206–7
Lipovetsky, Gilles 9, 148, 150, 151–3, 156–9, 163, 164, 166, 168–9, 188
Lipset, S. M. 62, 195
Locke, J. 29
Lorwin, V. R. 26
Loubet del Bayle, Jean-Louis 127–8
Louis Napoleon *see* Napoleon III
Lutte Ouvrière (LO) 83, 162, 183
Luxemburg, Rosa 183

Maastricht Treaty 69, 75
Machin, H. 88
MacMahon, Marshal 13, 32
Maire, Edmond 86, 161, 166
Malraux, André 145, 178
Mandel, Ernest 183
Manent, Pierre 188
Manifeste des salopes 163
Manin, B. 109, 110
Mao, Maoism 175, 182, 183
Maravall, J. 115
Marcellin, Raymond 148
Marseillaise 12, 145
Marsh, D. 41
Martin-Roland, M. 65
Marx, Karl 7, 14, 183, 195
Marxism 56, 63, 80, 93, 111, 152;
    intellectuals and 10, 170, 171,
    172, 175, 177, 181, 182, 183,
    186, 188, 189, 191; mass media,
    intellectuals and 170, 186–7;
    see also press
Mauroy, Pierre 65, 167
Maurras, Charles 24, 25
May 1968 9, 12, 13, 22, 53, 128,
    133, 140, 141, 144, 145, 146–69;
    intellectuals and 178, 184, 192;
    results 54, 71, 159–66; spirit of
    May and socialist years 166–8;
    theories of Debray and
    Lipovetsky 150–9
Mayer, N. 82
Mazey, S. 65
Mehl, D. 87
Mendès France, Pierre 180
Mendras, Henri 61
Merleau-Ponty, Maurice 80
Messmer, Pierre 54, 165
metanarratives 207–8
Middle East, relations with 68
Miliband, Ralph 105, 107

Millot, M. 64
minimum income 66
minimum wage 80, 140, 167
Mitterrand, François 1, 52–3, 55,
    60, 63, 65–9, 77, 83, 86, 87, 88,
    90, 103, 121, 127, 162, 168, 185
Mjøset, L. 98
Moch, Jules 50
modernization 4, 111, 195–6, 211;
    1789–1945 8, 13–20, 29, 33,
    34–5; 1945 onwards 9–10, 36,
    56, 91; Gaullist 9, 53, 119–45,
    155; intellectuals and 171,
    179–80, 183, 191; May 1968 and
    9, 146, 148–9, 150–1, 153–5
modernization theory 4, 8, 193,
    199–200, 208
Mollet, Guy 51
Monde, Le 61, 170, 171, 178
Monnet, Jean 179
Moore, Barrington 34–5
Moreau, Jacques 166
morosité 209
Morris, P. 39, 40, 41
Moschonas, G. 109, 111, 114, 117
Mouriaux, R. 124, 141, 155, 160,
    161
Mouvement des Radicaux de
    Gauche (MRG) 69
Mouvement Républicain
    Populaire (MRP) 46, 47, 49,
    51–2, 100, 127, 216
Mulhern, Francis 179

Napoleon I 12, 15, 20, 21
Napoleon III 12, 21, 26, 128
Napoleonic penal code (1810) 26
National Front 8, 78, 81–3, 105,
    106, 107, 191, 209, 217
nationalism 6, 196; Algeria 51;
    right 31, 177

nationalization 1, 46, 55, 64, 86, 88, 95, 104, 134, 167
NATO 5, 57, 69, 75, 132
neo-liberal economic policy 41, 63, 107, 185, 191, 194, 204, 212
neo-liberal right 6, 97; *see also* Thatcherism
neo-Marxism 103, 162, 205
New Caledonia 27, 191
new social movements *see* social movements
Newman, M. 65
Nicaragua 68
Nielson, K. 202–3
Noblecourt, M. 89
Nora, Pierre 171, 178, 189
Northern Ireland 42
Norway 18, 38, 96, 97, 98, 187

Occupation 13, 20, 25, 32, 173, 181, 192
Office de la Radiodiffusion-Télévision Française (ORTF) 178
Organisation de l'Armée Secrète 128, 129
Organski, A. F. 4

Padgett, S. 43, 95, 98, 99
Panama Canal 14
Papon, Maurice 128
Paris Commune (1871) 12, 13, 20, 26–7, 50
parliament 15
parliamentary democracy 35
Parti Communiste Française *see* Communists, Communist Party
Parti Radical *see* Radicals, Radical Party

Parti Socialiste (PS) *see* Socialist Party
Parti Socialiste Unifié (PSU) 161–2, 183, 184
participation 141, 143–4
Paterson, W. 95, 98, 99
patronat see employers
PCF *see* Communists, Communist Party
Pelinka, Anton 96
Perrineau, Pascal 61, 63, 75, 82
Perrot, M. 27
Pétain, Marshal 50, 181
Philosophes 29
Piaget, C. 161
Pinay, Antoine 135
Pisier, Evelyn 147
Pizzorno, A. 155
Planchais, J. 178
Poincaré, Raymond 31
police 21–2, 127–8, 149, 154, 176
political analysis 7, 213
political modernization *see* modernization
political parties 16, 18, 22–6, 80, 161–2, 170
political science 4, 5, 6, 109, 213
political theory 213
Pompidou, Georges 54, 56, 75, 137, 139, 149, 164, 165, 166
Pontusson, J. 98
Popper, Karl 189
Popular Front government (1936) 12, 32, 50, 79, 87, 100
Portelli, H. 54, 67, 107–8, 164, 209
Portugal 9, 34, 94, 110, 112, 114
post-Fordism 10, 57–8, 200–7
postmodernism 4, 193, 198, 200, 207
Poujade, Robert 120

Poujadists 12, 47, 48, 49, 82
Poulantzas, Nicos 52, 186
Praderie, Michel 87
pragmatism 8, 63, 67, 91, 98, 104, 209
Presidential elections in Fifth Republic 218; **1995** 3, 67, 78, 83–4, 107
presidents 219
press, intellectuals and 170–1, 178, 189
prime ministers 219
privatization 67, 74, 77, 79
Programme commun de gouvernement (1972) 55, 63, 71, 100, 162, 167
Projet socialiste manifesto (1980) 63, 68, 104
Prost, A. 149
protest 3, 7, 12, 22, 82–4, 118, 209; British lack of 42; student 24; *see also* May 1968
Proudhon, Pierre-Joseph 24
Przeworski, A. 100, 111
Psychopedis, K. 204

racism 81
radicalism 1, 56–9; decline of 3, 8, 60, 62, 65, 70, 81, 82, 85, 90, 113; intellectuals and 60, 174, 179, 180, 185; May 1968 and 150, 160, 161–2, 166–8; working class and labour movement 16, 17, 27, 50, 124, 160; *see also* Radicals, Radical Party
Radicals, Radical Party 30, 31, 48, 49, 99, 107, 108, 188, 216, 217
Ragache, G. 141, 147
Ramadier, Paul 134

Rancière, J. 210
Rassemblement des Gauches Républicaines (RGR) 216
Rassemblement du Peuple Français (RPF) 47, 51–2, 175, 181
Rassemblement pour la République (RPR) 73–8, 105, 106, 217
Rawls, John 189
reconstruction, post-war 37, 38, 42, 46, 95–6, 179–80
regimes 215
regionalism 6
regulation theory 10, 38, 57–9, 85, 194, 200–7
religious fundamentalism 196, 212
Rémond, R. 32, 61, 77, 128
Renaut, A. 152, 188
repression 21–2, 23, 24, 112; of labour movement 26–7, 32
republicanism 28–33, 34, 188
Resistance 23, 24, 32, 36, 46, 51, 173
Resnais, Alain 177
Restoration 20
Revenu minimum d'insertion (RMI) 66
revolt 8, 11–35
Revolution: **1789** 11, 12, 15, 16, 22, 28, 35, 189–90; **1830** 12; **1848** 12, 26; **1870** 13
revolutionary syndicalism *see* syndicalism
RGR *see* Rassemblement des Gauches Républicaines (RGR)
right, the 31, 50, 51–2; 1981 onwards 1, 65, 66, 67, 73–8, 91, 191: government (1986–8) 65,

right, the – *cont.*
74, 79, 89; neo-liberal 6, 97; *see also* Thatcherism; under de Gaulle 125, 131, 159; intellectuals and 175, 181, 191; *see also* Gaulle, Charles de; Gaullism; Rassemblement du Peuple Français; right, the, extreme
right, the, extreme 3, 6, 81, 84, 191; **1930s** 13, 23, 24, 32, 82; 1945 onwards 47, 48, 49, 82, 181, 191, 194, 218; British 42; German 43, 44; *see also* National Front; Poujadists
rights *see* human rights; individual rights
Rioux, J.-P. 49
Robbe-Grillet, Alain 177
Rocard, Michel 66, 116, 184
Rosanvallon, Pierre 60–1
Ross, G. 161, 165
Ross, J. 98
Rotman, P. 147, 166, 183, 184
Roulleau, J.-P. 64
Rousseau, J.-J. 29, 130
RPF *see* Rassemblement du Peuple Français
RPR *see* Rassemblement pour la République
Rueschemeyer, D. 17, 18
ruling class 21, 92, 97, 127, 133, 169
Russia 27, 34, 35
Russian Revolution (1917) 94, 101, 188, 189, 192

Sabel, C. 206
Saglio, J. 27
Saïd, E. 172
Sartre, J.-P. 80, 174, 175, 181, 186

Scandinavia 33, 93, 96, 97, 110, 154; *see also* Denmark; Norway; Sweden
Schuman, Robert 179
Second Empire 23, 28
Second International 104, 109, 110, 112
Second Republic 29
Second World War 13, 21, 25, 36, 39, 176, 188, 196; *see also* Collaboration; Liberation; Occupation; Resistance
Section Française de l'Internationale Ouvrière (SFIO) 27, 31, 46, 47, 49, 50–1, 69, 93, 99, 100, 107–8, 109, 112, 126, 127, 154, 181, 216
Sembat, Marcel 31
Service d'Action Civique (SAC) 128
SFIO *see* Section Française de l'Internationale Ouvrière
Shain, M. A. 53, 77
Shaw, E. 115
Shils, E. 62
Singer, J. D. 34
Skocpol, Theda 21, 35
Small, M. 34
SMIC *see* minimum wage
social democracy 58–9, 177; crisis and decline of from 1970s 6, 113–18; German 42–3; history of Western European 94–8; and the left 9, 92–118; Swedish 44–6
social divisions 6, 38
social movements 117, 118, 156
social problems 84, 194, 209
social reform 32, 53, 54, 64, 68, 76, 78, 144, 164–6, 191
social sciences 180

socialism 14, 118; French 31, 48, 50, 53, 92–4, 100, 102, 126, 127, 181, 217; *see also* Section Française de l'Internationale Ouvrière; Socialist government; Socialist Party
Socialist government 1981 onwards 1, 8, 60–91; spirit of May 1968 and 166–8
Socialist Party 9, 92–4, 99, 101, 102, 103–13, 115; 1969: foundation and early years 54, 55, 56, 70; in 1980s and 1990s 58, 59, 62, 63–70, 77, 82, 84, 90, 91, 92, 114, 115-17; intellectuals and 180, 184, 185; May 1968 and 162
socio-economic factors 6
socio-economic modernization *see* modernization
Soltau, R. 31
Solzhenitsyn, Alexander 182
Southern Europe, socialism in 9, 98, 99, 100, 110–12, 113–14, 115
Soviet Union: attitudes to 32, 40, 71, 95, 101, 211–12; collapse of 95; intellectuals and 171, 181, 182, 183, 190
Spain 9, 34, 94, 110, 111, 112, 114; Communist Party 70, 100
Sprague, J. 111
Staël, Germaine de 188
state: Gaullist 142; intellectuals and 171, 175–80; relationship with trade unions and employers in 1980s and 1990s 8, 62, 85–90; violence 127–8; *see also* repression
Stevens, A. 33
strikes 32; **1919–1920** 13;

1945–1981 46, 50, 109, 141, 155; **1980s** and **1990s** 78–80, 168, 185; British 38, 41; May 1968 and succeeding years 149–50, 156–7, 160–1, 166
structuralism 188
student protest 24; *see also* May 1968
Suez Canal 14, 51
suppression by state 21–2
Sweden 18, 142, 187; consensus politics since 1945 8, 38, 44–6, 58, 91; social democracy, socialism 93, 96, 97, 98, 103, 109, 110
Switzerland 18, 33, 142
syndicalism 27, 31, 110

Tapie, Bernard 83
Témoignage Chrétien 178
Terror, the (1793–4) 12, 29, 190
Thatcherism 41, 58, 74, 97, 204, 205
Thiers, Louis Adolphe 13, 26, 33
Third International 94, 95
Third Republic 12, 13, 23, 25, 29, 30–3, 107, 122, 188
Third World 4, 5, 7, 68, 197, 200, 212
Thomson, D. 18
Tilly, C. 12, 33
Tocqueville, Alexis de 19, 152, 172, 188, 189, 190
totalism of French politics 23
Touchard, J. 70
Touraine, Alain 171
Tournoux, Raymond 22
trade 134–9
trade unions 16, 18, 27, 28, 30, 109, 209; **1945–1981** 46–8, 49, 56, 154, 155, 160, 163; after

trade unions – *cont.*
  1981 1, 8, 60, 79, 84, 90, 166,
    167, 194: in tripartism 78, 85,
    86–7, 89; British 39, 40–1;
    German 42, 43; intellectuals
    and 181, 185; repression of
    26–7, 32; and social
    democracy, left 93, 97, 99,
    102–3, 111, 112, 117; *see also*
    labour movement; strikes
  tripartism; **1940s** 46–7, 79; **1980s**
    85–90
Trotsky, Trotskyists 3, 109, 162,
    182, 183, 191
Turkey 34

underclass 6
unemployment *see* employment,
    unemployment
Union de la gauche socialiste et
    démocrate (UGSD) 69
Union démocratique et
    socialiste de la résistance
    (UDSR) 216
Union pour la Démocratie
    Française (UDF) 76–8, 105,
    106, 217
United Kingdom *see* Great
    Britain
United States of America:
    attitude of students and
    intellectuals towards 149, 177,
    178, 181, 189; comparison with
    14, 15, 17, 18, 22, 33, 35, 60, 83,
    138, 142, 172, 195; end of
    history thesis and 197;
    intellectuals 179, 186, 187;
    neo-liberal policy 58; relations
    with 47, 68
universal (male) suffrage 15, 29,
    30, 34, 122, 130

Utopian socialism 24

Vichy regime 25, 36, 52, 121, 173,
    176
Vidal-Naquet, Pierre 177
Vietnam War 149, 177, 178
Villiers, Philippe de 83
Voltaire 29
Voynet, Dominique 83

wealth, distribution of 211
wealth tax 74, 88, 167
Webb, Paul 110–11
Weber, E. 15, 29
Weber, H. 22, 27, 28, 48, 55, 147,
    161, 162, 168, 183, 184
welfare state 46, 58, 97, 114, 194;
    British 40, 41; German 42, 44;
    Swedish 44–6
Western Europe 5–7, 8, 167, 195;
    consensus politics since 1945
    37–46; history of social
    democracy 94–8, 112;
    intellectual activity 177
Wigforss, Ernst 99
Wilkinson, James 173
Williams, Raymond 37
Wilson, F. L. 86
Winock, M. 19, 34, 51
women's movement 162–3, 166,
    179
work *see* employment
Workers' International 26
working class 16–17, 47, 57, 78,
    92, 124, 141, 167, 183; British
    16, 17, 39; in May 1968
    149–50, 151, 153–9; social
    democracy 94, 104–8, 111,
    113, 115, 117; *see also*
    industrial relations; labour
    movement; trade unions

Wright, V. 88

Ysmal, C. 71–2, 73, 82

Zeldin, T. 24
Zola, Emile 25, 173
Zolberg, A. 15, 27